Crocheting in Plain English

MAGGIE RIGHETTI

St. Martin's Press / New York

Also by Maggie Righetti

Knitting in Plain English

Universal Yarn Finder™

CROCHETING IN PLAIN ENGLISH

Illustrations by John C. Yates
Photographs by Tom Hill

Library of Congress Cataloging-in-Publication Data

Righetti, Maggie.
  Crocheting in plain English / by Maggie Righetti.
    p. cm.
  ISBN 0–312–01412–0 (pbk.)
  1. Crocheting. I. Title.
  TT820.R535 1988
  746.43′4—dc19   87–27512

10 9 8 7 6 5 4 3 2

CONTENTS

CHAPTER 25. MULTI-COLOR JACQUARD CROCHET
A Bunch of Balloons • Never-Ending Triangles • Plaids • Two-Color Plaid • Three-Color Plaid
175

PART III—AFTER THE LAST STITCH IS FINISHED

CHAPTER 26. PUTTING IT ALL TOGETHER
Things to Think About in Joining • The Kinds of Joinings You May Encounter • Prepare Yourself for the Job With the Right Tools • Use the Yarn the Item Was Made With to Make the Seams • Yarn Wears out as You Make Seams With It • Some of the Most Common Ways of Joining • Invisible Weaving • Single Crochet • Slip Stitch • Whipstitch • Backstitch • Sewing Machine • Getting Rid of the Tail Ends • Working Edgings on Crochet
183

CHAPTER 27. FINISHING TOUCHES
Fringe • Tassels • Pompoms • Twisted Monk's Cord • Crocheted Cords • Yarn Buttons
197

CHAPTER 28. THE CARE AND FEEDING OF CROCHETED ARTICLES
Cleaning • Dry Cleaning • Washing • Hand Washing • Drying Flat • Machine Washing • Machine Drying • Blocking • Never Hang Crocheted Articles
204

PART IV—LEARNING LESSONS

CHAPTER 29. BELL PULL SAMPLER WALL HANGING
217

PREFACE

If you have never touched a crochet hook before, if you have made only simple crochet projects, or even if you are a skilled and swift worker of the craft, you will find in this book a wealth of information, creative ways to solve problems, and new ideas to speed you and your hook on your way. It is a complete guide to unraveling the secrets of fine crochet.

Using common sense, plain English, and a sense of humor, I try to make clear the workings of making lace in the air. Crocheting is an easy, relaxing, and rewarding handcraft that should hold no mysteries. All its ins and outs can be revealed simply and clearly. If there seem to be cloudy mists and confusion about crocheting, it is because no one before has taken apart the pieces and put them back together, step by simple logical step, in language that everyone can understand.

Beginning with how to choose a project and the appropriate threads, yarns, and hooks, all the way through to simple and elaborate stitches, putting the completed parts together, and adding eye-catching details, this book will build the reader's confidence as the information in each chapter is absorbed. As the crocheter works through the basics, I show how to create variations and think through to other applications. When the crocheter understands the "whys" and "wherefores," he/she can become more proficient and creative.

Crocheting is the conjuring of magic with simple supplies, and it can bring endless joy and delight. This book can take the crocheter from "I don't understand" and "Why did I ever start this stupid thing" to "I figured it out all by myself" and "This piece that I'm making will become a family heirloom to be treasured for years."

There are special people whose help and assistance I wish to publicly thank and acknowledge: Betty Moore, my treasured secretary and trusted friend, who keeps me on the narrow path of the business of writing; Debbie Allen, a dear friend who checked the manuscript for continuity and coherence; Mary Lee Maury, a former student and now friend, who made up the samples for photography and modeled the sweater in the Learning Lessons; Michael Denton of Pang Computers in Atlanta for keeping me from going bald by helping my word processing system stay alive; and Jamie Hill, crochet consultant.

I also wish to acknowledge and give special thanks to: the DMC Corporation and its project manager, Mary Ann Blackburn, who so generously supplied the thread used to make up examples; Craft World and its Vice President of Needlework, Shirley Rothschild, for her help and encouragement as well as the yarns used in examples; Mayme Sanders of Coats & Clark Red Heart® for supplying the photo and instructions for the afghan in Learning Lessons; Hillory Tyre of Lee Ward/Craft Bazaar for the baby yarn used in Learning Lessons; and Joe Kensey, (now retired) Hand Knitting Yarn Specialist of DuPont, for contributing Comfort 12 yarn for projects.

INTRODUCTION

A CROCHET TEACHER TELLS ALL

Not everyone is fortunate enough to have a knowledgeable and kindly crochet teacher. And without one, few people will struggle and stumble along by themselves, hanging on and hanging in, to teach themselves all of the twists and turns of this magic skill. As a teacher with many years of experience in answering students' questions and solving their problems, I think I may have seen every possible misunderstanding and misconception concerning crochet. This book is filled with many of the things I have learned, for I truly enjoy helping others avoid needless frustration.

This book is divided into four parts. Part one covers all the things a crocheter needs to be aware of before making a single stitch. Part two covers all those pesky details of working and shaping the newly made fabric into a wondrous creation. Instructions for many different pattern stitches are included here. Part three explains the finishing touches that transform the pieces into a useful article. Part four is composed of "learning lessons" for the beginning crocheter. These projects are fully explained and may be done alone or in a class with an instructor. Every step of the directions is written in three ways so that the student can read, copy, or think it through.

Finally, the glossary defines terms and untangles the meanings of abbreviations. There is also an index for easy reference.

Because of the way this book is organized, it can be used as a beginner's introduction and guide book, a skilled crocheter's handy reference tool and source of finer points and pattern stitches, and as a text for crochet teachers. My purpose in writing this book is to give confidence, courage, and creativity to crocheters everywhere.

I

BEFORE YOU BEGIN TO CROCHET

1
A LIVING HISTORY

I can still remember the first piece of crocheting I ever saw. It was a small yellow doily, surrounded by lavender pansies, in the living room of the parsonage, and my seven- or eight-year-old mind thought that it was the most wonderful creation in the world. "They look just like real pansies!"

"It is only crocheting," sniffed my mother. "Come over here and sit down and be quiet."

Not too long after that, I saw a wondrous white lace table center-piece. It sat like an angel's crown, stiffly starched into curved ruffles, in the center of a polished dining room table where we had gone to sell eggs. "Look at the beautiful lace, Mama!" To a child inured to the grinding poverty of worn-out, mended, and faded artifacts of the Great Depression, it was the loveliest thing I had ever seen.

"Hush, child, and mind your manners. It is not real lace; it is only crochet," scolded my mother. "Belgian lace is the only real lace," said Mama, who also thought that "genuine oil painting" was the only real art.

"Would you like to touch it, little girl?" asked the nameless woman of the house.

"No," interrupted Mother. "She may not touch anything." Which only made me love the lace more.

And then, for my graduation from the eighth grade, my grandmother in Louisiana sent me a white drawstring bag with bands of inset white roses. "Look at the beautiful lace roses," I cried, happy to own something beautiful for myself.

"It is only crochet," sniffed my Aunt Martha. "Venetian rose point lace is the only real lace."

Undaunted, I asked, "Could I learn how to do it?"

"Poor people do crochet," sniffed my older sister. "Fine ladies do needlepoint." But I treasured that white cotton drawstring handbag embellished with roses and vowed that someday I would make lace like that.

That day came sooner than anyone could have imagined. When I was fourteen, I went to work after school and on weekends at the local Woolworth's Five and Dime. I worked in a dark corner of the store in the Art Needlework Department under the tutelage of a stern and proper woman named Margaret Mines. That first day, Mrs. Mines sent me home with a ball of #10 crochet thread, a hank of 4-ply knitting worsted, a hook and a pair of needles, and two instruction books. "Teach yourself to knit and crochet," she said. "You can't work here unless you know how."

I learned—because I needed the job—and was able to go through the routine of performing the various stitches, but by the time that was accomplished, my fondest dreams were on other things than roses and starched lace—a scholarship to college and dates with boys to relieve the tedium. I had all I could do to go to school, help out at home, and work besides. There was no time or energy to indulge myself in lavender pansies or elegant white thread roses. It would be years, decades, before I ventured into crochet again.

In the meantime, I had rediscovered knitting and had become "The Knitting Lady" at a fine Southern California department store. In my capacity there, I was called upon both to teach crochet and to solve crochet problems, and I was taken aback once again at the wondrousness of this lace-making art. I was determined to research and learn all I could about it.

Strangely, there is very little recorded history about crocheting. There are few ancient pieces in museums, no old woodcuts showing men and women sitting around a fire crocheting, and few references to it in the diaries and histories of the time. This lack of references seems strange, because of all the textile arts, crocheting is the easiest, the most versatile, and perhaps the most beautiful.

The first time that researchers have found any mention at all of crochet is in the 1840s, about the time of the Irish potato famine. Oh, there were rudiments of it, learned and lost, in a Southwest Native American culture as an inner structure to coiled and slab pottery, but no real crocheting to make fabric. There is some suggestion that it may have developed in Scotland to make "ruggies," but why so late in the history of women and men when clothing the body has always been a fearsome challenge, and decorating it such a delight?

Why, when all that is required to crochet is a ball of twine and a hooked index finger, was the art so late in appearing in daily life? Surely some ancient shepherd, trying to make the dragging hours pass as he tended his flock, must have taken a broken branch to use as a hook and made loops in a strand of vine. Surely sailors, idling away the hours on the becalmed sea, must have pulled loop through loop of lanyard to make a simple chain stitch. Perhaps they did, perhaps they did not; we have no record of it.

Some say that the origins of crochet must certainly be French, because "crochet" is a Gallic word, but there are no old crocheted pieces from that country. Others say that surely it has a Scandinavian background because the name is similar to a word for "crook." The first we know of the skill comes out of Irish convents where the cloistered nuns made yards and yards of lace to sell to fine English ladies for the benefit of the victims of the potato blight. A church bazaar to raise money for the poor was the birthplace of crochet! I smile when I think of it; how far we have come, what little distance we have traveled. There is a saying, "The more things change, the more they stay the same."

Still, crocheting burst upon the world at a time when the seams of the old world were themselves bursting, and at a time when there was an explosion in the mind of mankind. Books and periodicals were in print and available to almost all who could read. Travel was common, bringing with it an interchange of ideas across borders and continents. Both books and travel fed the expanding minds, and inventions were being devised everywhere for every purpose. Suddenly the long-dormant human mind began to ask, "What if . . . ?" "Suppose we try . . . ?" "I wonder what happens when . . . ?" And think not that this explosion of curiosity and inventiveness took place only in the mind of man. It occurred in the mind of woman as well. While her husband devised new ways of plowing fields, pumping water, and harnessing energy, women explored new possibilities of preparing and preserving food, protecting the bodies of their families from the cold, and of making lace in the air with a simple hook and thread.

Nameless women in the British Isles and Europe and the Americas took this simple idea of pulling loop through loop, expanded upon it, and made it into a fine art. Unbound by tradition and unfettered by restrictive social structure, it was the pioneering women of the United States who did the most with the new textile craft. They cunningly devised spaces and places and made filet cloth with which to drape their windows. They made spirals and pinwheels and popcorn blocks; they put the blocks together and draped their beds in elegance. They worked their stitches loosely and lacily and draped their bodies with wondrous shawls and capelets. They worked their stitches firmly and evenly and clothed their families with caps and hats and slippers and hoods, weskits and waistcoats, scarves and soakers.

Crocheting made sense. It was so much better and faster than weaving and cutting up the cloth. And they made lace: lace to lighten the drudgery of the day, lace for the yokes of shifts and nighties, lace for corset covers and blouses, lace to cover the raw edges of washcloths and towels, lace for the edgings of pillows and sheets, lace for the hope chest of a frontier bride and lace for the clothing of the new baby. All that was necessary was a spool of thread or a hank of yarn, a hook of wood or ivory, imagination, and inventiveness. The skill was portable; the results rapid.

These nameless women sent drawings and instructions of their creations to *New Idea Woman's Magazine*, *Godey's Lady's Book* and *The Ladies' World*, where other women read about this new-fangled art form, adapted, and improved upon it.

I wish I knew who these nameless pioneer women of crochet were, and where and how they lived. But most of all I wish I knew how they got their ideas and how they devised and planned their marvelous new creations. Unfortunately, no one will ever know who they were and how they came to create such a fine textile craft. We can revere and honor them only by carrying on their tradition of creativity and courage.

How then did crocheting get the negative connotation that I heard when I was a child? "It is not real lace; it is only crochet!" Whence came the put-down? Just as a prophet in his own land is without honor, so crochet in its homeland was without appreciation. Perhaps the disparagement began when the Flapper Girls of the '20s bobbed their hair and kicked off all traces of the old with their high-button shoes. (Anybody could crochet, not everybody could do the Charleston.) Maybe the poverty of the 1930s Depression made women wish for fine imported things. (Crocheting was cheap; you didn't need a lot of money to do it.) And then World War II burst upon the scene and everything changed. Men went off to war; women went to work outside the home; and nobody had time for making lace in the air. The art of crocheting almost died. Then, in the late '60s, vests crocheted with yarn began to appear. A little later the granny square blossomed into all sorts of sizes and shapes, and crocheting was reborn to a new generation of handworkers. But these handworkers came from a land of plenty, from a world of strictly following instructions, from a discipline of going by the book and never making do. Though today we have a new appreciation of crochet as an art form, it is hard to let loose our creativity.

This is what this book is about: carrying on a fine tradition of creativity; keeping alive and well the spirit of experimentation; understanding the basics of building upon them.

2

DREAMS ARE THE STUFF THAT REALITY IS MADE OF

Bloody Mary sang it out loud and clear standing on a coral island in *South Pacific*. "You gotta have a dream! If you don't gotta dream, how you gonna have a dream come true?" And before you begin to crochet a new project you must have a dream of what the finished thing will be like. Without it, you will not have the vision and stick-to-itiveness to complete the article.

But there is a difference between honest dreams and sheer fantasy. Fantasy can lead you astray, as it did me long ago when I saw a friend's grandmother crocheting a square for a wonderful bedspread. It was shortly after I began to work at Woolworth's; I knew the basic stitches, but I had never made anything more than the edging on a linen handkerchief and a small shell-stitch handbag. The grandmother's fingers adeptly flew and a square materialized before my dazzled eyes. I thought surely I could do that, too. My fantasy failed to take into account that there would be hundreds of squares to make, and I didn't have time left from school, house cleaning, and work to make even two. Certainly in those days I did not have the money to buy all of the thread at once to ensure having the same dye lot. But most of all my desire for an embellished bedspread to enliven my spartan bedroom failed to acknowledge that I was a person who was easily bored and that I would tire of making the identical square over and over. Thank goodness I didn't have the money to purchase the thread. It would still be sitting in its box these forty years later. I'm not the type to make a bedspread. I need constant change and challenge.

But a thing too challenging may be a turn-off, too. I want some repetition along the way. Having to follow every line on a graph or keep track of each and every row also drives me up the wall. My neighbor, Elizabeth, loves it. She is not happy without a pencil and pad at her side, marking every row.

The difference, then, between honest dreams and fantasy is honesty with ourselves and an understanding of the project. As you continue through this book, you will gain that knowledge of crocheted projects. Honesty with oneself is something that takes a lifetime of self-scrutiny to acquire. Begin now to look at the inner workings of you. Are you, like me, easily bored with making the same pattern over and over? Or are you reassured by repetition, finding relaxation and comfort in letting your fingers do their own thing while your mind peacefully floats? There is no right or wrong answer; there is only honest acknowledgment of what we are.

More than this, we change. And that is okay, for without change there can be no progress. If you decide, halfway through those hundreds of bedspread squares, that you no longer enjoy the repetition and you can't stand to make another square, *stop making them!* It is far more honest to know that you are no longer the same person you were when you started than to force yourself to remain in an old mold and deny growth. Call the thing a baby crib cover or donate the unfinished project to a retirement home or girls' club and go on to something else.

There is another facet of fantasy that can lead us astray, and that is being fooled by photographs. The gorgeous-looking sweater on the magazine cover, slathered with popcorn stitches and stand-out ridges, may be too heavy to wear. There is a saying among handworkers that when they are beginning and in the midst of making a sweater, they wish it were crochet because it is faster, easier, and more fun. But when the thing is finished, they wish it were knit because it would be lighter in weight, more flexible, and easier to wear.

Crocheting uses one-third more yarn than knitting, and anything crocheted will weigh much more than the same article knitted.

This is no reason not to crochet sweaters. They can be wonderful! But do be aware that they can be heavy. If they are made of bulky weight Class D yarn in a firm stitch, they may be unwearable.

Photographs can deceive in other ways, too. I remember a set of heavy cotton yarn table mats. The table setting looked lovely in the picture in the magazine; raised ridges of crochet gave a wonderful texture. I wondered why I had never thought of that idea before. When I finished one mat, I knew. The raised ridges caused tumblers of water to topple over if they were not set down exactly in between them. This project was makeable, and not too heavy for the purpose, but it was unusable. Again, these are the kinds of things you will learn in this book.

The lovely afghan, fluffy and soft in subtle shades of mohair, may seem like just the thing to make your sister-in-law for a birthday present. But it may cost so much for the yarn that the gift may overwhelm the receiver and cause her to dislike you for having done it. Price should color our dreams with reality.

And how long will it take? Is it an easy evening's or week's worth of time? We all know about the newborn's layette that was completed as the baby took its first steps, and the tablecloth that was finished long after the family had moved and sold the dining room table. It doesn't mean that these projects were not worthwhile and worth doing. It does mean that we were fantasizing and not dreaming realistically.

One must dream. You must see the finished project in your head before a single stitch is made, else no stitch will ever be taken. Dreams are the stuff reality is made of, but dream wisely.

In choosing a project you must first know yourself, your temperament and your available time. Regardless of how much or how little money you have, price is always a factor. You must also know enough about crocheting to know whether or not the project will be practical and usable, or just look-at-able. As you honestly dream, these things will come to you. Dream about it, and then "there's nothing to it, but to do it."

3

OF SPIDER WEBS AND HALYARD LINES

THE THREADS AND YARNS WE USE

Whatever our dream, there is a fiber to fulfill it. Gossamer-fine filament silk, glossy and durable cotton cord, fleecy and fluffy mohair or angora, gleaming metallic ribbon, rugged and twisted strands of wool—we crocheters have a vast array of types and qualities of threads and yarns to delve our hooks into. Our dreams can come true, for anything we can dream of can be realized from sources readily available in today's marketplace. Unlike our foremothers who were restricted to a narrow range of ecru or white threads and a few colors of fingering, sport, and worsted-weight yarns, we can crochet with anything.

We need to be aware, however, that

the thread or yarn we choose will most surely determine the kind of crocheted fabric we get, and may determine the type of project we can make of it.

It is still true that we can't make a silk purse out of a sow's ear, and we need to understand what it is that we are pulling loop-through-loop so that we will not be disappointed.

Once upon a time, not so many years ago, *thread* was cotton, and *yarn* was wool. Not so today. The manmade fibers that have appeared in the marketplace since the end of World War II have changed all of that. The blends and combinations that are available are mind-boggling. They have changed crocheting from doily-making to a high-fashion craft. I can remember, in my own crocheting lifetime, when crocheters discovered that they could work with bumpy, nubby, and slubbed novelty yarns instead of smooth strands. Isn't it funny how most of the ruts that we find ourselves in are self-made. Crocheters had just *assumed* that the thread or yarn had to be smooth.

SIZING SYSTEMS FOR THREADS

The weight of the thread we choose will determine the size of the hook we use as well as the size and number of stitches per inch that we get. The finer the thread, the more stitches per inch, and usually the longer the project will take to complete. Consider how many hours you are willing to spend when selecting the size of the thread you are going to work with. If you need to whip up a blouse by tomorrow night for a birthday present, don't select size 10 thread.

Threads are sold according to size number. The higher the number, the finer the thread.

Size 100 is the smallest commonly made commercial thread for handworkers. It is awfully fine and requires a #14 steel hook to work it; few crocheters attempt to work with it. Size 80 is also a very fine, thin thread. Though I have seen some exquisite museum examples crocheted with it, it is too fine for most of us to bother with. Size 50 is the size of common ordinary sewing thread. And the numbers keep marching on down through sizes 8, 5, and 3. Then there is a rather fuzzy area where there are no numbers, but rather brand names such as "Brilliant Crochet Cotton," "Knit-Cro-Sheen," "Speed-Cro-Sheen," and "Bedspread Cotton," in increasing weights of heaviness.

SIZING SYSTEMS FOR YARNS

Yarns are divided into Classes A, B, C, D and E in increasing order of weight.

Class A is *fingering* or light-weight yarn, used to make elegant blouses and scarves and some baby things. Class B is *sport* or medium-weight yarn. It is used for sweaters, dresses, suits, novelty items, Barbie-doll clothes, and loads of baby things. Class C is heavy, commonly called *worsted* weight. Afghans, sweaters, hats, mittens, slippers, toys, gobs of novelty items; jackets and such are made of it. Good old standard 4-ply knitting worsted yarn falls into this category. Class D is *bulky*-weight yarn. It is used for rugs, craft items, heavy jackets, and outerwear. Class E is *extra-bulky*-weight yarn, and, except for rugs, crocheters have little use for it.

Usually your directions will tell you what thread or yarn the designer used to make the original, and sometimes you will want to use the exact same yarn that the designer used. At other times you may want to experiment with other threads or yarns, either because you can't locate what is called for, or because you want to try something else, just to be creative. Great! Life would be boring if there were no inventive souls. Think of the creativity of women a century and a half ago with their hooks. But you may need a little help in substituting, and that is what interchange charts are for. Not all balls and skeins of thread and yarn have the same amount of yardage, and we use threads and yarns by the yard as they run through our fingers, not by ounces or grams as they are sold. My *Universal Yarn Finder* (Prentice Hall Press), sold in needlework and bookstores throughout the country, is an amplified interchange chart that will help you to substitute one material for another and without running out before the project is finished.

From here on, I am going to use only the term "yarn" in this book, because it will be simpler and make easier reading for you than if I were always saying "thread or yarn or whatever." Please understand that I mean all of the above when I say "yarn."

QUALITY

It would be lovely if we could use an endless cone of thread, always perfect, always flowing freely. Unfortunately, neither life nor crocheting is without its bumps and lumps.

There will always be imperfections, such as knots, imperfectly spun places, and drops of oil from the machinery, in any yarn.

Good-quality yarn will have few knots and imperfections to slow down the progress of our project. A few bad spots are just part of the game and we have to live with them. Frequent blemishes, however, are a real problem. No manufacturer wants to put out a bad product; he would not stay in business long if he did. Still, bad balls do slip through the quality control processes. If you should happen to purchase yarn that is full of knots and blemishes, you don't have to

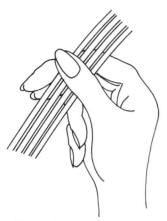

Figure 1
The rub test

work with it any more than you have to eat spoiled food. Return poor-quality yarn to the store and get something else to work with. You shouldn't be slowed down by a spinner's problem. You deserve the best!

Quality also refers to durability. Bad wearing characteristics are not usually a problem with cotton threads, but they are a very real possibility with certain manmade and inexpensive wool fibers. A tendency to "pilling" and "balling" can take all the joy out of a completed article that is afflicted with it. An afghan is not a "one evening watching television" project, and to have it soon sprout ugly globs is not a happy occurrence. Your best protection against "pilling" and "balling" is the "rub test" (see Figure 1). From the skein, before you buy it, place four or five strands between your thumb and first two fingers. Firmly rub back and forth against the strands of yarn. If the yarn looks worn and starts to fuzz up after a few rubs, you can be assured that it will not hold up well in usage. Don't buy it for a time-consuming project that you want to look well over a long period of time.

YARN FINISHES

The finish of a yarn, whether it is glossy or *matte*, which means dull, will determine how the finished article absorbs and reflects light. Long ago thread manufacturers discovered that they could treat cotton with a caustic soda bath that would make it shiny and give it better wearing qualities. Cotton so treated is called *Mercerized*. I like the gloss of it. Go back to your dream and "see" whether or not you want the finished thing to glisten, then decide what purchase you should make to fulfill that dream. If you do want sheen, choose Mercerized cotton thread. If you can't quite "see" it in your head, buy one ball of each and try it out before you dive into the project.

Dull finishes have their own appeal. Raw silk, to which no dye or other treatment has been added, has a matte finish that has a beauty all its own. Sometimes pattern stitches are lovelier and show off better with matte finishes. The only way to tell is to try it.

COLOR AND DYE LOT

Some purists think that crochet thread should be only the time-honored non-colors, white and ecru. Ethnic purity and simplicity have their place; others think that ancient origins are great, but want more variety in their stitches. Modern dyestuffs make this possible. We are fortunate that many yarns come in a spectacular rainbow of colors to satisfy every mood. Color can, however, cause problems in purchasing both yarn and thread. Dyeing is an art, not a pure science. Many factors will affect the way a batch turns out. Humidity, the porosity of the fiber, a few seconds more or less in the dye bath, all can cause slight color variations. Therefore, manufacturers mark each batch with a *dye lot* number. All the skeins or balls with the same number were dyed at the same time and are the identical color.

When you purchase yarn for a project, buy it all at one time, and be sure that each ball or skein is marked with the same dye lot number.

On the ball, yarns of a different dye lot may appear to be the same color. In a made-up piece, they rarely are identical, and you will often have a bold line of change if you don't purchase all of the same batch number.

You need to be aware that color can affect yardage. I became aware of it when the store I was working in was selling five-tone "Ripple" afghan kits. Many crocheters ran out of the darkest color though there was an equal number of ounces of each color. The answer was really simple when we stopped to think about it.

There may be less yardage in an ounce of a dark color than there is in an ounce of the same yarn in a light color.

It takes more dye to make a dark color. Dye weighs something, and it adds weight to the yarn. If you are making an afghan, you may be wise to buy extra of the darker colors to ensure having enough to complete the project.

Color permanence is also a factor in quality. Will fading be a problem with the finished item? Will it be exposed to light? Reds and blues are particularly prone to fading with age. For a Christmas novelty item, colorfastness does not need to be considered; it is used only three weeks out of the year. For a project that is going to take a long time to make and that is going to be used a great deal in well-lighted areas, it is a worry. Sorry to say, there is no "rub test" for colorfastness; however, though it is no guarantee the fiber will not fade in the future, you can see if it has faded in the recent past. Simply slide the paper wrapper (if there is one) to a different spot on the ball or skein. If the yarn has already faded under the simple conditions of storage and display, you will know it and won't buy it. Your best guarantee is to depend on the reputation of the manufacturer and the advice of your local needlework supplier. If something does fade badly, be sure to tell your retailer so that she can warn future customers.

Price is not always a mark of quality. Just because a yarn is expensive does not mean it is good stuff. Some inexpensive yarns are of very good quality.

There are other things to consider in choosing yarn besides size, sheen, and color. How easy is the yarn to work with? Is every stitch a battle, or does it glide through your fingers? If you have made a mistake in your purchase, and find that doing the project is too tough going, exchange the excess yarn for a different one. Crocheting should be pure joy, and you should feel like a queen making lace in the air. If you don't enjoy working with a yarn, don't work with it.

How the owner of this new project will be able to care for it will determine what kind of yarn you will purchase. Don't give a sister-in-law with three babies under five years of age a mohair afghan that will have to be hand washed and laid flat to dry, and then complain that she has insulted you by never using it. Families with small children need machine-washable, machine-dryable articles. (Many other families with casual habits need machine-washable, machine-dryable articles, too!) Today almost all yarn companies give information about cleaning care on their labels. A key to the symbols used is found in the *Universal Yarn Finder*.

Are you making an heirloom, or a soon-to-be-discarded novelty item that will go out of fashion as fast as the Pet Rock did? During the Depression, my grandmother made a lovely pineapple popcorn bedspread of grocery twine, hoping that it would be an heirloom for her granddaughters. It rotted. How long do you want the thing to last?

Always remember that there are just as many stitches and as many hours put into a project made with a cheap, poor-quality yarn that will ball and pill or fade and fray, as there are in a project made with good-quality, fine, and enduring yarn.

Your efforts deserve the best yarn that you can afford. Who knows, some great-granddaughter that you may never meet may want to proudly proclaim, "My great-grandmother made this eighty years ago. Isn't it lovely?"

4
HOOKS CAN HARPOON YOU

All you need to be able to crochet is a stick with a crook on the end of it or a shaped piece of bone. Well, yes, but not exactly; there is more to it than that. Though our foremothers used such things, and used them very well, we have available to us better-made tools that will joyfully speed us on our way.

If you stop and think about it, you will notice that crochet hooks have four necessary parts (see Figure 2).

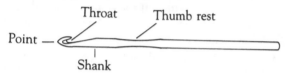

Figure 2
  Parts of hook, throat facing up

The *point* or *tip* is the part of the hook that will be inserted into previously made chains or stitches to make the next row. The point must be sharp enough to allow it to be inserted where it is supposed to go, but it must also be blunt enough so that it goes in between the strands of yarn and does not split or fracture them. A point too sharp may hurt your fingers. A point too blunt will cause delays being inserted and will slow you down. Different manufacturers make differently shaped points. Some look like wedges, others resemble sharp pointed arrowheads. Each shape has advantages.

The *throat* is the cut-open place near the point. The size of the throat necessary for a particular yarn is dictated by the size of the yarn you are using. The throat opening must be large enough to hold the diameter of the yarn so that the previously made loop can slip over it and off the hook. At the same time, the throat opening must be small enough so that it does not swallow that previously formed loop and prevent it from sliding off. Some manufacturers make sharply cut-in throats. Other makers form their throats in more of a "U" shape. Though I personally prefer the cut-in throats for most work, each design has advantages.

The *shank* is the long part of the hook on which the loops will rest while waiting for you to do the next step. The shank will, in part, determine the size of the finished stitches.

The *thumb rest* is the flat spot on the shank where the thumb sits in order to rotate the throat from a position facing you to a position facing down. Early crochet hooks did not have thumb rests. A few modern hooks still do not have them either, and without one it is much more difficult to rotate the throat to the proper position.

OTHER THINGS ABOUT HOOKS

There are other things we need to notice about how a crochet hook is made. The angle or slope of the increase in size from point to shank is very important. If the manufacturer has made an abrupt change in size from the tip to the shank, you will have to fight each and every yarn-over loop to make it move up the shank. If there is a more gradual increase in size, the loops will slide up almost by themselves. When there is no slope at all, the point will be too broad. By studying Figure 3, you'll immediately see what I'm talking about. You need to be aware that the slope from the tip to the shank will affect the size and length of your chain stitches. If the slope is long and narrow, your chains will be tiny. If there is no slope at all or if the hook is fat and wide, your chains will also be fat and wide.

Notice that the crochet hook doesn't end at the thumb rest—it

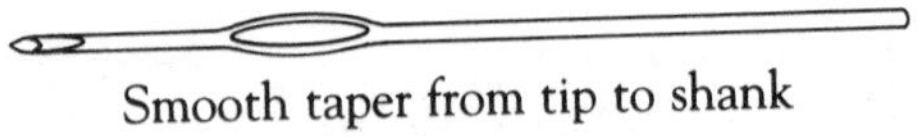

Smooth taper from tip to shank

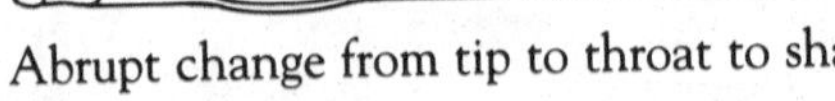

Abrupt change from tip to throat to shank

Figure 3
Parts of hook, throat facing toward you

extends on in length. This is so you can rest your index finger on the area beyond the thumb rest away from the tip, for balance and leverage. And that balancing place is important. It will enable you to manipulate the point of the hook much faster and easier.

Between the point and the other end of the hook there will be a *center of gravity*, the place where there is an equal amount of weight in each direction. Where the center of gravity is on a particular hook will determine how the hook feels in *your* fingers. If the hook is too long there will be too much weight on the non-point end. If the hook is too short, there won't be enough weight on that end.

We need also to be aware of what material the hook is made of. It will determine how heavy the hook is. You need enough weight to feel something in your fingers, and not so much that your fingers are weighted down just holding the hook. The material the hook is made of will also determine its *surface friction*, the "glide and slide" characteristics of the hook. With too much surface friction the threads will "hang up" and refuse to move. With too little, they will slither and slide around. Usually manmade yarns perform better with little surface friction.

HOOK SIZING SYSTEMS

It is only recently that the world has become an international marketplace with patterns, instructions, yarns, and hooks from every country available everywhere else. It used to be the case that American hooks were sold only in America, British hooks in Great Britain, and metric hooks in Europe. The other day I went into a needlework store and there were hundreds of hooks for sale from all over the world. A person needs a guide to wade through a wealth of opportunity like that.

Hooks come in standardized sizes, but what size they are called will de-pend upon what country they came from and what they are made of.

United States steel crochet hook size numbers get larger as the hook gets smaller, from #00, the largest, to #14, the smallest. English steel hook size numbers begin with a decimal size of #2.00 as the largest going to #6.50 as the smallest. Continental steel metric sizes go just the opposite. As the hook size gets smaller, so do the numbers, from 3 mm to 0.6 mm. The following chart gives approximate equivalencies for interchanging.

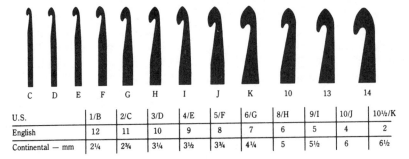

	00	0	1	2	3	4	5	6	7	8	9	10	11	12	13	14
U.S.			1	2	3	4	5	6	7	8	9	10	11	12	13	14
English			3/0	2/0	1/0	1	1½	2	2½	3	4	5	5½	6	6½	7
Continental — mm			3	2.5		2		1.75	1.5	1.25	1	0.75		0.6		

Chart 1

Hooks made of aluminum and plastics follow different numbering systems. With American-made hooks, as the number and/or letter gets higher, the size gets bigger. The British do it the other way: the larger the hook, the smaller the number. The metric system makes common sense: the bigger the number, the larger the hook.

	C	D	E	F	G	H	I	J	K	10	13	14
U.S.				1/B	2/C	3/D	4/E	5/F	6/G	8/H	9/I	10/J	10½/K
English				12	11	10	9	8	7	6	5	4	2
Continental — mm				2¼	2¾	3¼	3½	3¾	4¼	5	5½	6	6½

Chart 2

Of course there are overlaps and discrepancies. And sometimes it is hard to know what sizing system the instructions mean when they call for a #3 hook. We used to be able to know that if the directions came from America they called for an American hook. Not anymore, because those American instructions may be a translation from Italian or German and they may mean a metric size 3. Don't be harpooned on a hook size number just because the typesetter didn't know what country you live in.

Use whatever size hook will get the correct gauge.

And we'll talk more about that in the next chapter.

Beware—and "beware" just means to "be aware"—that Blooper's "Satin-Soft" size C hook may not be exactly the same size as their "Nature-Made" size C. Also the surface tension may be so different that whereas your yarn worked well with a size C "Satin-Soft," it may hang up on "Nature-Made," and you may require a size D in order to fly along.

THE RIGHT HOOK FOR THE PROJECT

From all of the above I hope that you have guessed that

no one kind of crochet hook will fit all situations for all people and all yarns.

What works for you may not work for someone else. Each one of us has a different set of hands. Every set of hands moves in a slightly different way and may require a different kind of hook. Also, what may be great for Blooper's "Stiff Stuff" yarn, may not work at all for their "Gooey-Gooey." If your fingers aren't flying along, it doesn't mean that there is something wrong with you. It can mean that you are trying to use an inappropriate hook.

More than this, crochet hooks are inexpensive; your time to crochet is valuable. Honor yourself and your efforts. If the size G hook you used for the last project doesn't just dance along like a butterfly on a summer's day with the new yarn for the next project, try out other hooks and get yourself one that flutters to a different beat.

TODAY'S HOOKS FOR TODAY'S CROCHETER

Just because your great-grandmother made wonderful things with one flexible whalebone hook without a thumb rest, it doesn't mean that you cannot avail yourself of the wondrous improvements in hooks of our age. She had nothing better to work with; you do!

I smile when I think of hooks. There is a shop here in Atlanta that started out to sell only all-natural products, back to basics and nothing artificial. Originally they sold only hand-carved walnut wood crochet hooks, each one unique and different. And with them their customers got unique and differing results. Now, though they still sell the exquisite natural hand-dyed yarns, they have dropped the hand-carved hooks and sell a complete range of modern, commercially made crochet hooks, and their customers get predictable results. What more can I say?

5

DON'T BE GOUGED BY GAUGE

When I began to crochet, I thought that the funny sentence at the beginning of the instructions that said "Gauge: 7 dc = 2"," was talking about the amount of gas in the car or the needle on the top of the pressure cooker. They were the only gauges I knew about. I didn't have a crochet teacher, only a beginner's direction leaflet to guide me, and I just happily crocheted away, oblivious of gauge. Sometimes things were the right size; sometimes they were not; and I didn't know why. When they were the wrong size, I was disappointed and angry, but I didn't understand whom to be disappointed with or angry at. I had followed the directions exactly and used the materials specified, so I misdirected my hurt feelings at the printer of the pattern and the manufacturer of the yarn. It wasn't until I got very involved in knitting that I began to understand that gauge is important. It wasn't until I began to design my own crocheted items that I understood what gauge is and why gauge is critical. Then I stumbled on the simple truth:

Gauge, or tension as it is sometimes called in European instructions, means the number of stitches of a particular kind that you get with a particular thread or yarn at a particular time in your life with a certain hook in a certain width and length.

Gauge, or tension, is usually stated in terms of inches or centimeters, as in *3 sc = 1"* or *12 sc = 4 inches* or *35 sc = 10 cm.*

Sometimes the gauge or tension will be stated in terms of patterns: *2 shells = 3"* or *6 popcorns = 4 cm.*

At other times gauge may be stated in terms of completed medallions or motifs: *Square = 4 ½".*

And this is vitally important to us all, because there is no magic to the numbers of crochet.

All crochet instructions are made by multiplying the number of stitches in one inch by the total number of inches of desired width.

The designer didn't just dream up the number 62 stitches to chain to begin the bottom of a sweater. She decided that she wanted the sweater to be 20 inches wide at the bottom. She knew that the gauge was "3 dc = 1″" and that $20 \times 3 = 60$. (The extra stitches are for the turning chain. We'll talk about that later in Chapters 10, 11, 12, and 13.) There was no magic to it; it was just simple arithmetic—gauge times desired width.

If you do not get the correct gauge, you cannot expect to have the finished piece be the correct size!

I used to think, back in the dark ages of my crocheting, that it didn't matter if my gauge was off one quarter of an inch. "It is such a little bit, it won't matter." But it does. If each medallion of a jacket is off by a quarter of an inch, the twenty of them that it takes to go around my hips will make the garment five inches too big! My hips don't need five inches of extra width; they are big enough already.

THINGS THAT AFFECT GAUGE

Many things will affect your gauge, the most obvious being the size of the hook with which you make your stitches. Though God gave us all the same number of muscles, bones, tendons and nerves in our hands, each one of us uses our hands in a slightly different way. Some crocheters slide their hooks casually along, making loose and relaxed stitches. Others work firmly and tightly to make small stitches. It doesn't matter which you do; do what comes naturally and comfortably to you. It does matter that you get the correct gauge for the pattern you are working.

No one cares what size hook you use to get the gauge. Everyone cares that you get the correct gauge. The designer cares, because she wants your article to be the right size. The manufacturer cares, because he wants you to be happy with the yarn or thread. The shopowners care, because they want you to be so pleased that you will be a repeat customer.

If you tend to work loosely, use a smaller hook. If you have a habit of working tightly, use a larger hook. Use any size hook that will get the correct gauge; just make sure that you get the correct gauge.

Other things besides hook size will affect your gauge. Whether the yarn slides quickly and easily through your fingers will make your stitches tighter or looser. The humidity and heat of summer making your hands damp with perspiration can change your gauge. If it does, and you're in the middle of a long project, use a different size hook until the weather cools off.

Never make a gauge swatch using someone else's hook.

The shape of the point and shank of the hook, and the material it is made out of, can affect your stitches. We talked about this in Chapter 3. Just be aware that if you make a swatch in a needlework shop with a different hook than the one you have at home and are intending to use, your swatch may not be accurate.

Just because you got the right gauge when you made a vest of white Blooper's "Glop-Glop" yarn with a J hook, you cannot assume that you will get the correct gauge when you use navy blue Blooper's "Glop-Glop" and the same hook again. The process of dyeing yarn can affect the girth of the yarn, and often dark colors will be thicker than light ones. This can cause you to get a different gauge with the same brand of yarn in different colors. Dye can also affect the softness or stiffness of yarn, which will make a difference in gauge.

And our state of mind affects our fingers. I'll never forget a raglan jacket I made. I began it on vacation in the mountains of Arizona, away from home and the children, with Uncle Fritz pouring Bloody Marys for me on a breeze-caressed deck. My stitches were loose, large, and, reflecting my mood, relaxed. I continued to work on the jacket after I got home; my stitches got firmer, more disciplined and closer together. Then number two son, Chris, decided to sail alone with a young friend to Catalina Island. I was frightened for the two teenage boys, but I didn't say, "No, you can't go." The weekend while they were gone, I crocheted to keep from going insane with worry. My stitches were so tight I could hardly insert the hook in them. No two pieces of the finished jacket were the same size. Moral of the story: Your emotional mood will affect your stitches and that will affect your gauge.

HOW TO MAKE AND MEASURE
A GAUGE SWATCH

And how do you know when you are getting the correct gauge? You make a test swatch(es) and you measure it before you begin the project. (If what you are making is a garment, size will be critical. You will want to treat the swatch as you will treat the finished garment. If you are going to wash it, wash the swatch. If you are going to block and apply steam to it, block your swatch.) Your directions will always state the gauge at the beginning of the instructions. However, usually the number of stitches given in the gauge section of printed directions will not be sufficient to make an accurate and reliable swatch. You will need to make a test swatch that is at least four inches square to honestly be able to tell what is happening. Anything less will be deceiving yourself and distorting the whole purpose of making a swatch. Frequently crocheters have to multiply the number of stitches given in printed instructions to determine how many stitches to use to make their swatch. If it is given in terms of one inch, multiply the number of stitches by four. For instance, if your instructions say "Gauge: 3 dc = 1 inch" multiply 3 × 4 to equal 12 and make your test swatch 12 double crochet wide. If the gauge is given for two inches, multiply the number of stitches by two. For instance, if your instructions say "Gauge: 3 shells of 2 dc, ch 1, 2dc = 2 inches" multiply the 3 (shells) by 2 to equal 6 and make your test swatch 6 shells wide, and it should measure 4 inches wide. If, happily, the gauge is given for four inches or 10 centimeters, you are home free.

You'll need a tape measure, a ruler or one of those handy-dandy windowed gauge-checking devices that you can find in the accessory department of knitting stores. And, of course, you'll need the identical yarn or thread and hook that you intend to use.

In a comfortable place at a quiet time, with the yarn or thread you will be using, and with the suggested hook, make a 4-inch-square piece of the pattern as given in the instructions, or, in the case of medallions, one entire one. Stop. Lay the piece on a flat surface. In the middle, measure across the whole width of the swatch, uncurling the edges if necessary. Check yourself in two ways:

1. The total width of the piece. Lay the washed and blocked swatch on a flat surface, right side down. With a tape measure or ruler, measure across the entire width. Divide the number of stitches in the piece by inches of width. If there are thirty-two double crochet stitches in the swatch, and the swatch is four inches wide, divide 32 by 4. Your gauge is 8 double crochet equals one inch.

and

2. The number of stitches in an inch in the middle of the swatch. Count the stitches in one inch or within the window of the knit-check to be certain. If the piece is larger than the stated gauge, redo the swatch with a smaller hook. If the piece is smaller than the instructions say, redo the swatch with a larger hook. Keep changing hook sizes until your gauge is exactly the same as called for in your pattern.

Any piece less than four inches in width just will not tell the whole story about your crocheting. Edges are always somewhat distorted, and if your swatch is nothing but edges, it will lie to you.

Don't cheat and scrunch or stretch your test piece to *prove* to yourself that you are getting the correct gauge when you really are not. Take the time to change hook sizes if the size is not exactly correct.

Don't place pins in your swatch in order to measure between them; they will distort the stitches.

If you are working with a material that is likely to shrink or stretch, such as a cotton or acrylic, measure the swatch and write down the results. Then wash and block it; treat it as the finished piece will be treated. Wash it in the machine and throw it in the dryer if that is what is in store for the finished item. Measure again and know that that dimension is what the "living and breathing" gauge of the item will be. You will have at your fingertips both a working gauge and a finished gauge. It is better to take time before you start, so you'll know that the cotton yarn for that special Irish lace blouse will shrink each medallion a half an inch in washing, than to finish the whole thing, wash it, and find out that the blouse is four inches too small.

If your gauge isn't right, don't start the project. The results will most certainly disappoint you.

Gauge can gouge you with an article that is the wrong size, because it is always gauge per inch times desired inches that determines the finished dimensions. And, I hate to tell you—but I have to—that just measuring the gauge at the beginning of a project is not enough. Many of us happy crocheters relax as our fingers take over and do the crocheting for us and *our gauge can change and loosen as we work.*

It is necessary to constantly measure as we go. I don't mean to take all the fun and joy out of crocheting. I'm not saying that you must proceed with fear and trembling. Not at all. I love crocheting and I want you to enjoy it, too. Just be aware that you may need to change to a smaller hook in the middle of the work as the pattern is memorized and easily repeated.

I think one of the reasons that so many crocheters choose to make afghans is that gauge is not critical. When you know and understand what you are dealing with, nothing, not even gauge, can ever gouge or hurt you.

6
PATTERNS AND INSTRUCTIONS

Beginning (and even advanced) crocheters often look at printed crochet patterns and instructions with reverence and awe, as if they were some mysterious Sumerian cuneiform writing or unintelligible Egyptian hieroglyphics. There seems to be an aura about directions that frightens many people away. Poppycock and nonsense! Though at first glance they may look like gibberish, crochet instructions are simply coded shorthand for simple, logical, ordinary things to do.

Moses didn't bring crochet instructions down off the mountain with him, and Hammurabi didn't encode them in his laws. In the nineteenth century, our great-great-grandmothers, aunts, and second cousins twice removed wanted to share what they were doing with this wonderful new art of making lace in the air, and sent their notations off to the magazines of the day for publication. The editors thought that printing them was a good way to increase circulation. Alas, it took up so-o-o much space on the pages. Then someone stumbled on the idea of abbreviating the words to take up less room, and all that seeming gobbledygook was invented. A specialized, formalized language of crochet began to emerge after 1840. Words were abbreviated *without periods*. (Periods were used only at the end of a set of instructions.) Symbols such as asterisks, brackets, and parentheses began to take on special meanings.

Some crocheters could understand this new language and happily followed the directions printed in magazines. Others couldn't make head nor tail of it all. Thank goodness photography began to blossom about the same time as crochet, for editors often placed photos beside the instructions. Those who couldn't decipher the gibberish just looked at the picture, followed what they saw, and made up the item. Still other crocheters found it simpler to re-devise the whole thing for themselves without following anything. We all still do the same things today for the same reasons.

WHY PATTERNS ARE ABBREVIATED

Patterns, instructions, and directions are written the way they are for one reason only, and that reason is cost!

Typesetting costs money; paper costs money; printing costs money; shipping costs money; storage costs money; disseminating information is expensive! Few people are willing to pay the $10 it would cost to buy a single pattern completely written out in words. In order for you to have at your disposal that wonderful, extensive reservoir of patterns and instructions that can be purchased today, abbreviations have to be used to conserve cost. But somewhere along the way, the plain English of what the instructions are trying to tell you has been lost. Instruction writing has gotten rigid and inflexible. In today's crochet directions, if there is one single thing different on one row from a previous one, the whole row is written out, which defeats the purpose of all the abbreviating! For instance, if the second row is the same as the first, except that it is made over a base of stitches instead of a foundation chain, it will probably be printed as different and separate instructions. If the final row ends without a turning-chain, often the directions for it will be included as a distinct row.

PATTERNS DO MAKE SENSE

Later in this book, Chapters 21, 22, 23, and 24 will lead you gently to an understanding of abbreviated instructions. Now, in this chapter, I simply want to make some general remarks about tackling the sometimes tricky things.

Say to yourself the whole word; don't just say the abbreviation itself. Without stopping, read all the way through to the period. Don't stop at commas.

To keep from repeating the same thing over and over again, a series of directions may be set off with an asterisk, or enclosed in a pair of asterisks (* *). Without stopping, read the whole thing between the asterisks even *if there is a period. Often following the last asterisk (if there is one), you will be told how many times to repeat the instructions between the asterisks. Sometimes, instead, you will be told to "repeat from * across." That means just keep on doing it over and over again until you come to the end of the row.*

Sets of specific things to do are often enclosed in brackets ([ ]). Without stopping, read everything enclosed in the brackets. Following the last bracket you will be told where to put the stitches created by completing the instructions that are bracketed.

HAVE SOMEONE ELSE READ THE PATTERN ALOUD

My eyes have an inordinate amount of trouble focusing on the printed line of instructions. I keep losing my place in the instructions, as I work along with my fingers. If you share my problem, call a neighbor over for a cup of coffee, invite a friend in to share pot luck supper, bribe members of the family with promises of favors, do whatever you have to do, but get someone to read the instructions to you as your fingers do what they say until you get the gist of what is supposed to happen. We are not isolated islands; help is available.

MAKE YOURSELF A PATTERN BOOKLET

If you are having trouble with a pattern, get yourself a stack of index cards. I prefer the 5″ × 8″ size, but the 3″ × 5″ will do. Punch a couple of holes in the long edge. Tie the cards together loosely with a scrap of yarn. On the first card, write the name of the pattern and where you found it. On the second card, write the kind of yarn, size of hook you are using, and the gauge. On the third card, write out the first row of instructions. On the next card, write out the second row. And so on, until the directions are all written out. (I type them, but I'm used to typing.)

Find some peace and quiet, get yourself comfortable and now try the pattern again. (Just the writing out of it will have helped to clarify it in your mind.) At the end of a row, if it is not included in the pattern, mark on the card what you are supposed to have accomplished. For instance, on a medallion, you may want to put down, "8 chain-4 loops made." When you finish a row, flip to the next card.

The booklet will have done its job when your fingers and mind have memorized the pattern. Then you can write on the last card what you made of it, if you enjoyed doing it, and if you would ever want to bother with it again.

ERRORS CREEP IN

Between the designer and the ultimate user of the pattern is a long and twisted road. Usually the designer makes up a design, winging it as she goes. Next, with pad and pen, she goes back and tries to write down what she did. It may be very difficult to put into the stylized hieroglyphics of crochet what actually went on. So she may then write down a slightly different technique from the one she actually used (error # 1 occurs). Off go the finished item and the scribbled instructions to a publisher. The secretary there will type up the directions. She is a professional secretary and probably doesn't know how to crochet. She can easily misread the instructions (error # 2 creeps in). When the editor, who does know how to crochet, looks at the instructions, she may decide that they will take up too much room on the printed page, and will try to shorten them (error # 3 happens). The typesetter, who also doesn't know how to crochet, can make simple ordinary typos. If one comma or one numeral or one asterisk is incorrect, the whole pattern is wrong (error # 4). Of course, things are proofread, but it is impossible to catch everything. In the make-up of the page, a line can be left out (error #5). By the time the individual user gets the directions, they can be so totally incorrect that it is impossible to make the item.

That errors can creep in is a massive understatement. That they are unintentional goes without saying.

In doing the research for Chapters 21, 22, 23, and 24, I was flabbergasted at the appalling number of errors I encountered. Trying to decide which Irish rose medallion I wanted to include in Chapter 22, I tried out eight patterns. *Every one had errors. In not one of them did the directions say to do what went on in the photo!* If I hadn't known what an Irish rose was supposed to look like, I would have been lost.

LEAPING OVER PROBLEMS

If you are going to crochet, you are going to have to understand what is supposed to be happening so you can easily step over errors.

Just as in the yesterdays of our great-grandmothers, there are three ways to crochet:

1. Read and follow the shorthand instructions.

2. Follow a photo or a stylized diagram.

3. Think it through for yourself.

A fourth option is "all of the above." In any one way you choose to work, you must use your own mind. Your mind belongs to you. No other person can tap into its vast resources. If you refuse to use your mind, its wealth is lost and no one else can use it.

I sincerely pray that there are as few errors as possible in this book. If problems do occur, please understand that neither I nor the publisher wanted them to happen. And I hope that the plain English which I have given you along the way will help you to be able to leap over them.

7
SUPPLY AND DEMAND

Crocheting is a beautiful art form. Not only is the finished product exquisitely lovely, but also there is a hidden beauty in the making of it—it is completely portable and few supplies are necessary. Unlike weaving, which requires a heavy, space-consuming loom, or quilting, which calls for a large, cumbersome frame, crocheting can be done on your lap wherever you are. Unlike bobbin lace makers who have to be careful of their fragile pins and spools, we crocheters can happily make our lace in the air with just our sturdy hook and our ball of yarn, and we can do it anywhere. Our crocheting can wander around the house with us, go in the car as we wait to pick up the kids from practice, keep us company as we wait for appointments, and even attend boring committee meetings with us. And we can talk while we ply our magic. (Our fingers don't have to listen to what is going on!)

If we do all of these things while our fingers do their thing, we need a container in which to carry our work around. Depending on your personal habits, you can choose whatever suits your needs.

CHOOSING A CONTAINER

For crocheting that will stay at home, I have chosen a lovely medium-sized handmade basket, as beautiful as the work I am doing. It follows me from the living room to the garden porch in the summer to the cozy den in the winter, and wherever it is set down, it makes an attractive addition to the location. Are you humbly carrying your work around in a worn-out plastic store bag? Shame on you! Your craft is noble and fine. Carry it proudly. Treat yourself to a pretty basket for it.

For crocheting that will live in my car and go with me on my errands, I have chosen a large, handsome, soft canvas tote bag. It can't snag my hose; it can be slung into the back of the car with no damage; it makes no noise sitting on the floor beside any chair I might light upon. Your own lifestyle will determine what kind of carrying container you choose, but whatever you select make sure that it is as good-looking as your stitches. Don't carry them in an old tired sack that looks as if you are hunting for the nearest trash container to dump it in.

And this is a good place to say that I usually have two projects going at the same time, one at home and one to go traveling. That way I can just reach down and begin doing whatever is beside me without having to remember to put the stuff in the car every time I go out. It also gives me the opportunity to work on whichever project is appropriate for the moment. Setting up the first row of an afghan is an endeavor of concentration, and it would be rude to do it in front of company. Putting together granny squares and finishing in the tail ends is a messy job and I wouldn't want to do it while waiting with the kids in the orthodontist's office. Having two projects going at the same time solves the problem of having nothing to do with my hands.

SUPPLIES TO CARRY IN YOUR BAG

This delightful hobby of crocheting does not require a large investment in tools as does woodworking, gardening, or even painting. Still, if you are well supplied with a few essentials before you begin your project, it will be much less demanding of you. To that handsome carrying container you have selected, you will want to add the following simple things:

Small *scissors* or *thread clippers*. Don't try to break off yarn with your hands. It is hard on the hands, and in many cases the yarn just won't break. You need a way to neatly clip out knots and bad places in the yarn, and, when ending, a way to snip the yarn making sure that you leave a six-inch-long tail end. Some people like the small "Stork" scissors that embroiderers use and that are available in needlework stores. Others prefer the thread clippers that seamstresses are fond of and which are sold in fabric stores.

Varied sizes of *tapestry* and *metal yarn needles*. These needles have *blunt points* and are not sharp on the end. They are necessary to tuck in ends of yarn in the middle of the work, and it is important that they do not split the yarn, but rather slide in beside the stitches. Tapestry needles come in a range of sizes from #26, the smallest, to #13, the largest. Metal yarn needles come in two sizes. You will always want to use the smallest needle that you can get the yarn through.

You will want a *tape measure*, a firm one that will not stretch and give you a false reading. Since the world is becoming so international, it is wise to choose one that gives both centimeters and inches so that you are not restricted to following American patterns, and can try out some of the European ideas. With your tape measure you will measure both your swatch when you begin, and your work in progress to make sure that your gauge is remaining the same.

I like to have with me a *knitters' gauge-check device*. As discussed on page 25, I lay it over my work and count the stitches within the window. You can find them with knitters' accessories.

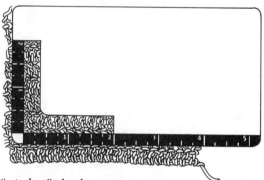

Figure 4
Knitters' "window" check gauge

Crafters' *tiny coilless safety pins* are a must in my crochet bags. They have lots of uses. They help me keep track of increases and decreases, and I'll talk more about that in later chapters. Sometimes they will be used to pin pieces together as I weave seams or attach the parts. At other times I use them to mark a special spot to which I want to rip back. I prefer the coilless pins because they hang down straight and yarns cannot get caught in coils that are not there. If your needlework or sewing store does not carry them, try a craft shop.

From my collection of knitting supplies, I have added to my crochet bags *knitters' slip-on plastic ring markers*. I use them to mark an increase or decrease point within the middle of a piece. In the middle, where they will be moved frequently with each row, these markers are quick and easy to slip in and out. Again, these are available with knitters' accessories.

Figure 5
Knitters' slip-on plastic ring markers

"Idiot tags" are for smart crocheters. When I was the knitting instructor in a large store, one of my patrons taught me to use them. They are little stringed tags on which you can write notes to yourself and then pin to your work. It is so much easier than trying to remember everything in your head. "Make back of sweater 2″ longer = 6 rows," pinned to the spot where you will begin working again. "Make 3 more granny squares this color pattern," pinned to a square. "Resume work on row 36 of pattern" pinned in where you have to abruptly leave off to go and clean up the mess the kids made in the kitchen. Only stupid people are afraid to use "idiot tags." I purchase mine in a stationery store. They are called "inventory tags."

When I was fourteen and went to work at Woolworth's Five and Dime, round plastic *ball holders* for thread were commonly for sale for the art-needlework department. Now they are as scarce as the ten-cent stores are. But people who used balled thread still need them so that the ball can freely unroll and not wander all over the floor. Thank goodness little plastic margarine tubs are so readily available. When working with balled thread, I place the ball in an appropriately sized plastic container in the bottom of my basket or bag. It saves a lot of grief.

People working with yarn need freezer-weight *zip-locking* plastic bags to protect their yarn from dirt and dust, puppies and kittens, children and spills. Don't misunderstand. I dearly love puppies and kittens and little children; they are a regular part of my household. The problem is that they love to play with my yarn. It is easier to protect the yarn than to provide scolding remarks. One bag holds an extra skein safely until I'm ready to use it. Another bag, closed across the top except for an inch for the yarn to run through, holds the skein I'm working with. If the yarn tangles in the bag, I just open it up, straighten it out and re-close the bag. It is that old ounce of prevention that is worth a pound of cure.

If the yarn that you are putting into your plastic bag has a tendency to stick to itself, as man-made fibers often do, try tucking in one of those *fabric softener sheets* that are meant to be used in automatic clothes dryers. Static electricity is often a problem with some yarns just as it is with socks, and the dryer sheets solve it.

Another ounce of prevention is a *plastic page sleeve* for a copy of my instructions. I drink coffee, and smoke (and even sometimes snack, to which my hipline testifies) while I crochet, and my instruction sheet is a handy place to set down my coffee mug. After a couple of spills that obliterated the directions, I now protect them. You can find these page protectors in stationery departments and office supply stores.

While I am talking about instruction sheets, this is a good time to tell you about something that happens to all knitting and crochet instructors. It happens more frequently than you would imagine. A customer will come into the store in tears, sobbing, "Tell me what to do."

The instructor will respond, "What do your instructions say?"

And the crocheter or knitter responds, "I don't know. I lost my instructions!"

"Perhaps we have another copy that you could buy."

And then the tears will flood the floor. "I—I got it out of a ladies' leisure magazine from five years ago. Please tell me how to finish this."

"What did it look like?"

"Like the picture in the magazine!"

And of course the instructor can't tell the customer what to do; she doesn't know what it is supposed to be. She can, and every good instructor will, tell all of her patrons to duplicate their instructions *before they start* a project.

Just as soon as you select a pattern, run, don't walk, to the nearest duplicating machine and make a copy for yourself. Keep the original in the box with the remainder of the yarn at home.

Carry the copy with you, protected by a plastic sleeve.

Having just said to copy your instructions for your own use, I now need to get on my soapbox and preach about when not to copy instructions. Do not copy instructions for your friends and neighbors. Let them buy their own! Publishers print instructions as a business; the more magazines, books, and leaflets they sell, the more they can afford to print and the more there will be available for you in the marketplace. Designers usually earn their living from the small royalties that they receive when you buy their patterns. When you copy and give away instructions you are stealing their living away from these people. If they can't make a living at it, they will stop producing instructions. You will have cheated yourself of the opportunity to have instructions to work with.

Some crocheters like to carry with them a small *note pad and pencil*. Some people like to make hash marks on the pattern to note rows completed. Others like to jot themselves notes while they are relaxing with their hook and thread. Crocheting is a form of meditation and often, when your mind is clear, ideas pop up. "Buy a birthday card for Johnny," or "Don't forget toilet paper and coffee on the way home."

There are a couple of emergency items that should be a part of every crocheter's supplies. An *emery board* and a couple of *Band-Aids* can be lifesavers. If you snag a fingernail on the car door as you charge out to meet the school bus, which will be an hour late returning the kids from a game, you may need the emery board so that you can continue to crochet instead of just sitting and stewing. The Band-Aid may keep you from bleeding all over your work if you have nicked yourself running to catch a plane (which may also be an hour late).

Since you don't want all of the above-mentioned little goodies rattling loose in the bottom of your bag or basket, a little *pouch* to keep them in is a good idea. I know some people who use a tiny zippered cosmetic holder for the stuff. I prefer a see-through students' zip-locking pencil holder that I found among the school supplies at the drugstore.

Do not carry all the yarn for a project with you. There is no reason to carry the extra weight. Take only a little extra. Let the rest stay safe at home. Make a space on a shelf and keep the original container along with the original of the instructions and the *receipt* for the purchase all together in one place. That way, if you have left-overs, you may be able to return them to the store for credit if they were not purchased on sale.

The motto "Be Prepared" shouldn't be restricted to Boy Scouts. Crocheters of both sexes and all ages will have a happier, easier time when they are well equipped with the tools of their trade.

II

DETAILS, DETAILS, DETAILS

8

MAKING MUSIC WITH YOUR HANDS

Your hands are the instruments that make the music of crochet. Your mind is the conductor of the orchestra.

Now you are ready to begin to crochet. You are ready to begin to make lace in the air, to make wonderful shaped fabric from nothing more than a ball of string. You will have three things to work with, the hook, the yarn, and your hands. Of the three, your hands are the most important. Respect and honor them, and they will serve you well as you create magic with crochet. In one sense, crocheting is like playing the piano in that both hands are used to make the music. But really, in another sense, crocheting is more like playing the violin. One hand adjusts the tension of the strings or yarn and holds the thing that you are working on, and the other hand holds the bow or hook. Just as a violinist cannot make music without both hands, you cannot crochet without using two.

At this point, crochet instructors are always asked, "What do you do about left-handers?" The answer is that we first try to teach them right-handed because, unfortunately, this is a right-handed world and all the diagrams and photos and instructions they will encounter in their crocheting life will be aimed at right-handers. Then, if that is not possible, we get them a copy of the Susan Bates booklet *Learn to Crochet* (#17370), which has diagrams for left-handers. (The booklet isn't perfect, but it helps.) We then sit the student directly in front of us, knees to knees, give them a hook and yarn, have a hook and yarn in our own hands, and talk them through the formation of the basic stitches. After that, they will be on their own to interpolate and transpose directions for pattern stitches.

Nonetheless, left-handers should not abandon this book, for here we are talking about much more than the basic stitches. I am going to be discussing things that are way beyond the basics. In Parts II and III and IV, I am going to talk about what kind of an animal this crocheting really is and how to tame it. Read on, interpolate where you must, learn and enjoy.

Experienced right-handers should not skip these "basics" sections either. Even if you have crocheted for years, there are always new tricks that you can pick up that will make your crocheting even more joyful.

SUPPLIES FOR BEGINNERS

Once you know how to crochet, you can crochet with anything, thick or thin, bumpy or smooth, stretchy or firm. I have found, however, that beginners learn faster and easier with a large resilient yarn. They need the large size in order to see what they are doing, and they need the stretchiness to work with in beginning to form their stitches. I insist that my students use a good quality, smooth, classic worsted *wool*, Class C heavy-weight yarn. It is commonly called "4-ply knitting worsted."

An appropriate size hook for this yarn is a size H. I also insist that my beginners use a hook that tapers in a straight line from the point to the shank.

In addition, they have to have a pair of scissors at their side to cut off the yarn as it becomes worn and frazzled.

A REMINDER

Remember, as we go along, that in the interest of simplicity, I will use only the term "yarn" when I'm talking about techniques. This does not mean that I don't believe in using thread. I do. I'm just saying "yarn" in order to make these directions clearer.

THE SLIP LOOP

We have to start somewhere, and the starting place of all crocheting (and knitting) is the *slip loop*. In the air we make a sliding loop and slip our hook into it.

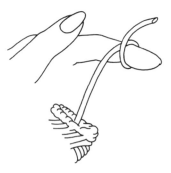

Figure 6

Hold your left hand in front of you with your index finger extended. Hold the yarn in your right hand. With your right hand, wrap the yarn completely around that left finger, from front to back, to the front and back again. (See Figure 6.)

With your left thumb, push/slide the crossover point of the yarn to the end of the extended forefinger. With the hook in your right hand, from back to front, scoop up the shorter end of the yarn, and pull it partway through the circle you have formed. (See Figure 7.)

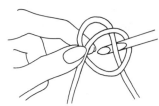

Figure 7

Gently pull down on both ends of the yarn to firm up the loop on the hook. The loop needs to be secure, but still able to slide easily along the hook. (See Figure 8.)

For practice, remove the hook and pull the two strands of yarn apart. Practice making the slip loop over and over *until your hands know how to do it without your mind having to tell them.*

Your mind should just say, "Slip loop," and your fingers should simply obey.

Figure 8

In crocheting the slip loop does not count as a stitch.

(In knitting it does.) You will never go into, or use the slip loop in making other stitches. It just sits there doing nothing, but you have to make it in order to get started.

The abbreviation for the slip loop is *sl lp.* Remember, I said that periods are not used in crocheting abbreviations.

The symbol for the slip loop is a solid-colored oval. (See Figure 9.)

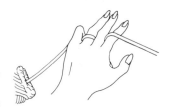

Figure 9

HOW TO HOLD THE LEFT HAND

Usually the left hand holds the yarn and adjusts its tension. From the cut end, the thread runs over the outstretched index finger, under the second finger, over the ring finger and under the little finger which curls around to hold the thread against the palm. The ball of yarn sits on the floor on the left-hand side of the worker. (See Figure 10.)

Figure 10

Usually the thumb and second finger of the left hand pinch together to hold the work in progress, situating it properly for the next stitch, manipulating it when necessary. (See Figure 11.)

The left hand will constantly move and flex to allow more yarn to be pulled up and through the hand as it is used.

Place the yarn in your left hand as shown in Figures 10 and 11, and with your right hand pull on the thread in order to get the feel of how it will be when you begin. Can you make your index finger stand out alone? Can you make your little finger curl around and down to your palm? Can you touch together your thumb and your second finger? Can you make your fingers clamp down so that the

Figure 11

yarn stops flowing through them? Can you expand your fingers so that the yarn will run free? These are the things that your left hand will have to do as you make your stitches. Play with the yarn in your hand and try out these things, and remember to be good and kind to yourself. No one learned to play the violin in a few moments.

HOW TO HOLD THE RIGHT HAND

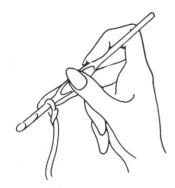

Figure 12

Your crochet hook is not a plow or a hoe for gardening. Your right hand must never rest on top of the hook. The hook is a delicate, well-balanced instrument for making music. Think of it as a delicate silver cocktail fork and think of yourself at an elegant dinner party dabbling with your hook into a luscious lobster cocktail. Respect your hook and it will hum happily along. With your right hand pick up the hook and hold it with the open part of the throat facing you. Place your thumb squarely on the thumb rest. Slide your second finger down the back of the hook and let it rest behind the throat. Move your index finger up the back of the hook, so that the hook rests happily in the first joint of your index finger. (See Figure 12.)

With your right thumb, practice rotating the throat of the hook one quarter turn (90 degrees) so that the open part of the throat is facing down.

Your hand must always be under the hook—never on top of it. (See Figure 13.)

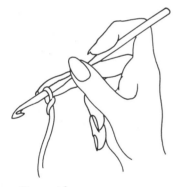

Figure 13

Using your thumb as the midpoint, maneuver and swing the hook around a bit just to get the feel of it. These are the motions that your right hand will make—rotating the throat from facing you to down, and swinging the hook around with your thumb as the fulcrum. See how easy it is? Soon your hook will become an extension of your right hand just as the bow of a violinist is. Your mind will conduct your hands; you will soon be making music.

I am fully aware that not everyone's hands will work in exactly the same way. First try what I have described above. If it does not work for you, try some adjustments. Some crocheters cannot get their left forefinger to sit out in space; they pick the yarn off of that finger with their hook. It is a little hard on the skin of the finger at first, but it soon toughens up. Some crocheters cannot make their left little finger curl tight enough to control the tension; they give the yarn an extra wrap around either the little finger or the extended left forefinger.

If you are an audio-visual type of person rather than a reader, you may wish to take a look at some of the video tapes that I have done. All of the details of holding the hands and making the basic stitches are illustrated in crochet instruction tapes that I have done both for Revere Productions and Jeanette Crews Designs, available from your local yarn supplier.

Now that your hands, hook, and yarn are ready, there is nothing to it, but to do it.

9

THE CHAIN STITCH

The first stitch of crochet is the *chain stitch*. It is just pulling a loop, through a loop, which you could do with your crooked index finger. But let's be fancy and use a hook.

With your hands in position as described in the last chapter, with your left thumb and second finger, hold the tail end of the yarn up close to the slip loop. With the throat facing you, slide the hook toward the air-space between your right hand and your extended left forefinger. That air-space between your right hand and your left forefinger is the working area in which all stitches will be formed. (See Figure 14.)

Swing the hook back slightly so that the yarn falls over the hook. (See Figure 15.)

Rotate the hook so that the throat faces down and pull to the right, bringing the new yarn under the old. (See Figure 16.)

Pull a little bit more to the right and allow the old loop to slip off of the hook. (See Figure 17.)

Move your right forefinger to the new loop just formed to keep it from getting too large or too small. Move the thumb and second finger of the left hand up on the chain you have just made so that they are again near the hook.

Congratulations, you have just made one chain stitch. Now go back to the first asterisk (*) and repeat the three steps all over again to the second asterisk. Be aware of the movement of your hands.

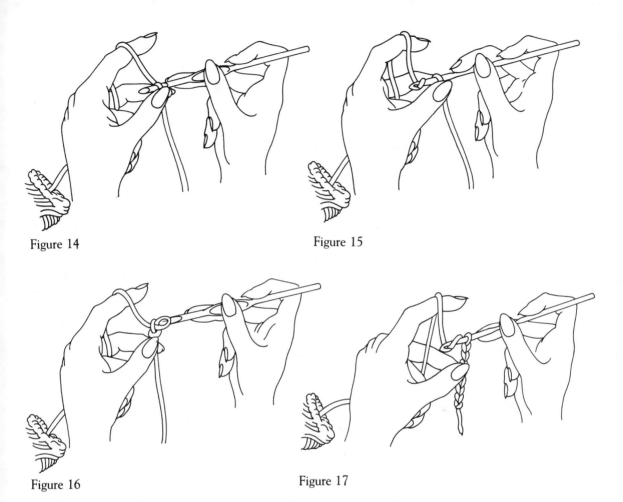

Figure 14

Figure 15

Figure 16

Figure 17

You are after economy of motion and ease of movement. Imagine an eagle swooping down, catching up its prey and soaring upward, never missing a beat of its wings. Your hands must swoop and soar like an eagle does. The less motion you waste on each stitch, the more stitches you can make!

I want you to say the words describing the three steps aloud as you make the chain stitch. Make the words and the movement a part of your memory. I find that if my students understand the complete formal word directions for each thing as we go along, in the future they are able to do new things easier, faster, and better.

Go back and repeat the words over and over again while your hands make the stitch until you get the hang of it, always remembering to rotate the hook down. If the hook faces the sky, nothing can ever slip off it. Keep in mind that, Itzhak Perlman didn't learn to play the violin the first time he touched the instrument. People who have had the opportunity (or the necessity) to use their hands and their minds together in such things as playing the piano or typing, will learn to crochet much faster than people who have never had to make their hands obey their minds. But that does not mean that everybody, with patience and dedication, cannot learn to crochet.

I make (read: *force*) my students to make the chain stitch over and over again *repeating the words* until they can quickly make a smooth and even chain of stitches. Students need to be aware of their *tension*. Tension means both evenness of the stitches, and that they are large enough to insert the hook into for following rows, but not so large as to be sloppy and messy.

When you have made a chain that you can be proud of, take a moment to stop and look at it.

> *It is really an upside-down pyramid with a bumpy ridge along the bottom of it. (See Figure 18.)*

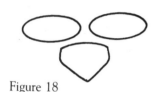

Figure 18

Hold the chain in your right hand and use your left thumb to flatten it. You will see that

> *there are three strands of yarn that make up the width of the chain—the two symmetrical strands on the top and the loop along the bottom side of the upside-down pyramid.*

When you learn to make the next stitch it will be important that you remember the three loops and where they are.

A long series of chain stitches at the beginning of a piece is sometimes called the *starting chain* or the *foundation chain*.

The word "chain" is abbreviated *ch*. The word "stitch" is abbreviated *st*. Combining the two, "chain stitch" would be abbreviated *ch st*. Usually, "yarn over the hook" is abbreviated *yo*. "Hook" is often abbreviated *hk*, and remember from the slip loop that "loop" is *lp*. Later on we'll get into reading abbreviated instructions. For now I want you to be aware that the instructions for the chain stitch can be written, **Yo, pull through lp.** Earlier I wrote it the other way, the long way, because I believe that beginners need all the help they can get.

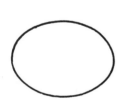

Figure 19

A hollow oval is the international symbol for the chain stitch. (See Figure 19.) Also, later on I'll explain how to look at and follow the symbol directions for pattern stitches.

Sometimes I swear that there is a malicious genie in my house that makes the phone ring, the puppy need to piddle, or the pot on the stove to boil over whenever I am counting a long chain. There used to be nothing to do but to recount or, just as easy, start over. Now I take a simple precaution in the event something urgent happens while I'm getting started. If I need to make a long chain, such as for an afghan or the bottom of a sweater, I mark every twentieth stitch with a safety pin. That way, if I am interrupted, I only have to count the 20s over again, not every single stitch.

Once a foundation chain is completed it can never be added to. You can remove the excess, but you can't make any more. If your instructions call for a long chain for a complicated pattern, make more chain stitches than called for. That way, if you make a mistake either in counting or in setting up the pattern, (or if there is an error in the instructions), you won't be caught short.

Any unnecessary chain stitches left over can be clipped off and removed. Make a cut with your scissors across the chain 5 stitches from the last stitch used. Pick up a tapestry needle and pick out and undo the excess stitches.

We could chain on endlessly until our yarn ran out, but it wouldn't be a very useful thing to do. We need to learn different kinds of stitches.

10
THE FIRST REAL STITCH

Firsts are always difficult. A baby's first step is the most difficult it will ever make. The first day of school isn't easy. The first day on a new job can be terrifying. But a baby is soon off and running. Going back to school in the fall becomes fun instead of frightening, and most jobs soon become easy and routine. The first real stitch of crocheting is no different. The first time you do it is hard and scary. By the time you have made twenty or thirty of them your hands will be flying. Don't let your hands get discouraged; the first row is the most difficult, even for experienced crocheters.

Setting up the first row of crochet is always the hardest.

Even when you are a pro, that first row can be difficult because the chain wants to wiggle around on you, and your fingers haven't much to hold onto and firmly grasp.

Now that your hands are behaving themselves and obeying your mind, now that you can make a smooth and even chain with ease and joy, you are ready to learn the first real stitch of crocheting, the *single crochet* stitch.

(British readers should be aware that in "going across the pond" some differences in terminology arose for the names of crochet stitches. Since I am a US citizen, I have used the American terms.

American	British
single crochet	double crochet
double crochet	treble crochet
half-double crochet	half-treble crochet
treble crochet	double treble crochet

The silly things are made in exactly the same way, they are just called by different names, as what we call a truck, you call a lorry, and what you call a loo we call a john.)

We must begin with a slip loop and a foundation chain.

Place a slip loop on your hook and make yourself a chain of ten stitches.

Abbreviated instructions would say:

Place a sl lp on hk, ch 10.

or simply

Ch 10.

expecting you to know that you have to make a slip loop first.

THE SINGLE CROCHET STITCH

The first row is made in the following way.

*Skip the first chain that is next to the hook (see Figure 20)
and insert the hook into the next chain so that the two symmetrical strands
are on the top of the hook and one strand is under the bottom of the hook.
Slide the hook forward. Swing the hook back slightly and let the yarn fall
over the hook. (See Figure 21.)*

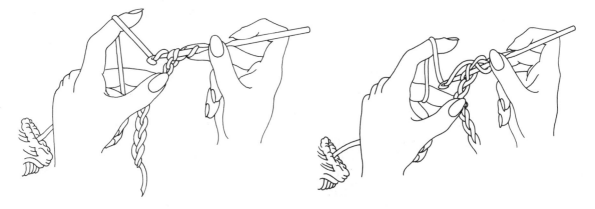

Figure 20

Figure 21

Pull the hook to the right, bringing it through the chain stitch and with it the new loop of yarn. You now have two loops on your hook. (See Figure 22.)

Slide the hook forward again, swing it back and let the yarn fall over it again. Pull the new loop through the two loops on your hook. (See Figure 23.)

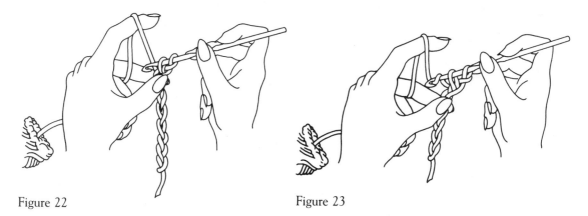

Figure 22   Figure 23

You now have just one loop on the hook and the single crochet stitch is completed. (See Figure 24.)

Figure 24

Remember to move your right index finger to the loop just completed and to reposition your left thumb and second finger in place to hold the piece to make the next stitch.

Congratulations, you have just made a single crochet. Now work across the remaining 8 chain stitches, making a single crochet stitch in every one of them. You must learn the terminology of crochet for future work, so say the following *shortened form of the words* to yourself as you make the stitches so that you develop the mind-hand coordination that is essential to enjoyable crochet.

Insert the hook in the next stitch, yarn over and pull through the stitch (two loops on hook), yarn over and pull through two loops.

When you have made a single crochet stitch in the last loop (not including the slip loop), stop and admire both yourself and your work. You have learned something new and you have made a piece of fabric. At this point, don't worry if your stitches are not even and perfect. That will come later with repetition and increased speed. Your piece will curl up like a spiral; don't be upset about it, that is normal. It will straighten out with the next row.

TURNING CHAINS

You are ready now to make the second row of single crochet. But you have to travel up to be in a position to make that second row.

Make one chain stitch, and then flip the piece over so that you can work back across it.

In shortened terms that would be

chain 1, turn,

or

ch 1, turn.

This chain stitch on the end of the row is called the turning chain *and will count as one stitch.*

Old-fashioned crochet directions used to include the directions for the turning chain at the beginning of the next row. Newer instructions will tell you to make it at the end of the row you are working on. It doesn't make any difference! You simply can't start the next row without some traveling-up and turning room to work in, and that is why we make the extra stitch or stitches at the end or beginning of the row.

ROW TWO

You are ready for row 2.

Unless otherwise instructed never *make a stitch into the base of the turning chain.*

Skip the spot that is the base of the turning chain, and insert your hook under *both top loops* of the next stitch. (See Figure 25.)

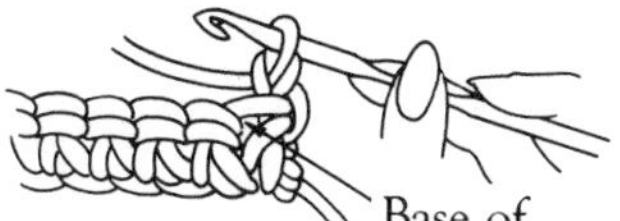

Always, unless otherwise instructed, insert your hook under both of the loops of the stitch of the previous row. (See Figure 26.)

Figure 25

Base of turning chain

Make a single crochet stitch into every stitch of row 1. That would be a total of 8 stitches (plus the turning chain at the beginning of the row which counts as one stitch.) Count them and see.

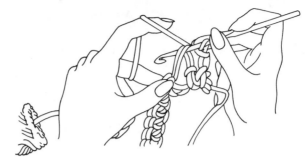

Figure 26

You must always work one final stitch into the top of the turning chain to complete the row.

And where do you put that final stitch? Anywhere you can get your hook in! Hopefully, you will have two loops on the top of the hook as you insert it. When this final stitch is completed, this will make a total of 10 stitches (the 9 single crochet that you made plus the turning chain), and you are ready to start row 3. Row 3 is made just like row 2. Make one chain stitch to turn with, flip the piece over and make 10 more single crochet stitches.

A DEFINITION

As you move along in your crocheting life, you will notice the word *post* appearing frequently, and trying to figure out just what the word means can be as confusing as trying to program a VCR. (I've had mine six months, and I still can't do it right.) A post can mean simply a stitch. If it is an *end post* it can mean the beginning turning chain and/or the final stitch. It can also mean an upright stitch on the previous row.

WHEN YOU WANT TO STOP

When you want to stop for a few moments, pull up on your hook to make a loop about half an inch long. Quickly pin a small safety pin in that loop. It will keep your work from accidentally unraveling until you are ready to go back to it again.

If your hands are tired, stop and rest them. They are learning something very difficult and wonderful. Look at your hands. In all of creation, they are unique and unusual. Touch your thumbs to your fingertips. You have an *opposable* thumb. You can do things with your hands that no other creature can. Be good to your hands and they will be good to you.

When you have completed your piece, *fasten off* the yarn in the following way:

> *Clip the yarn about six inches away from the hook. Pull straight up on the hook and bring the cut end of the yarn through the final loop. (See Figure 27.)*

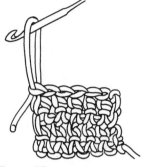

Figure 27

That is all you need to do. Your piece is safe and secure. Please don't tie a knot. It is not necessary and will just make an ugly bump.

For homework after this class, I have my students make a perfect swatch of 20 stitches (including the turning chain) and 20 rows (not including the foundation chain) of single crochet before I will let them go on to the next stitch. No skips, no blobs, all neat and tidy, while their hands have learned to soar and swoop like an eagle. Just understanding what the stitch is supposed to be doesn't carve the turkey. It has to be known in both the mind and the fingers, and making this perfect 20-stitch square will do that; the Thanksgiving bird will be perfectly carved.

When your swatch is completed, stop and look at it. A piece of fabric that is made up of all single crochet stitches is firm and tight and a bit stiff. Unless the yarn is quite fine, it will make a sweater that is bulky and rigid. The edges of your piece will curl up and the piece will have a tendency to roll. It is just the nature of the stitch. Single crochet edges of articles are usually finished off in some decorative way or worked into a seam.

If you work back and forth in rows of single crochet, your swatch will be completely reversible and have no distinguishing front and back sides. All crocheting has a definite top and bottom that can easily be seen. If later you work single crochet in *rounds*, it will have a front side and a back side.

Remember our turning chain that was one chain long? Look at your swatch and see that your individual single crochet stitches are pretty much square. Their height is the same as their width, and their height is one chain tall.

> *The height and width of a single crochet stitch is one chain.*

In shortened instructions, the "single crochet" stitch is almost always abbreviated *sc*. Often the turning chain is abbreviated *t-ch*.

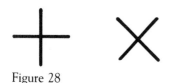

Figure 28

British readers are reminded that what Americans call the single crochet stitch is to you a double crochet.

The international symbol for single crochet is usually a short vertical stick crossed in the middle. Occasionally a single crochet will be represented by a capital letter "X." (See Figure 28.)

The chart of a simple single crochet swatch looks like this:

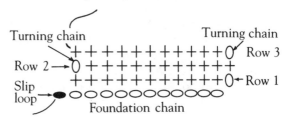

Chart 3

BUTTONHOLES

Figure 29

Before we leave the subject of making these simple stitches I want to talk about a technique that is unique to crocheting. We can stop in the middle of a row and turn around with no harm done, no extra steps necessary. Say, for instance, that you are working on a cardigan jacket. If you wanted a vertical buttonhole you could:

Work the few stitches between the front edge and the location of the buttonhole. Turn around at the appropriate spot, work back and forth over those few stitches until you have a length the diameter of the button you've chosen to use. Fasten off. Re-attach the yarn at the other side of the buttonhole where you left off, and work across. Go back and forth now until that area is as long as the area on the other side of the buttonhole. Fasten off. Re-attach the yarn, and work over the whole piece. (See Figure 29.)

Sometimes you will use the buttonhole just as it is. At other times you may want to work a row of either single crochet or slip stitch around it for extra firmness.

It is even easier to make a horizontal buttonhole. Decide where you want the buttonhole to be.

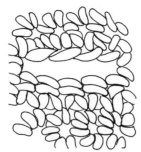

Figure 30

When you get to that spot, chain however many stitches are necessary to equal the diameter of the button. Skip that many stitches on your piece and then start to crochet again. When you come to the buttonhole chain stitches on the next row, work them as usual, making sure that you insert your hook under two loops of the chain. (See Figure 30.)

No other finishing is necessary.

Did you notice how carefully I worded the two italicized paragraphs above? It was done with forethought. They are the general rules for making buttonholes in any pattern stitch. Take time now to make both kinds in single crochet. That way you'll have the technique under your belt and will understand it whenever you come across it in whatever stitch you are doing.

Single crochet is a vital and frequently used stitch. It makes nice place mats and pot holders, but, alas, it is too heavy and firm for most sweaters. We need to go on and learn other stitches. They won't be as hard to do because you have already had a good beginning on the first day at school, and a fine start on the first day on the new job.

11
MAKING IT SOFTER
AND LONGER

THE HALF-DOUBLE CROCHET STITCH

When something "works all right, but not exactly quite," like the syncopated clock in the old song, some people just never even think about it and put up with the inconvenience. Other people, the creative ones, think about it and dream up something better. Our single crochet stitch "works all right, but not exactly quite." It makes fabric, but the fabric is a bit stiff and firm. Long ago one of our foremothers took a look at the single crochet stitch and asked herself, "How can I make it softer and longer?" She stared at a piece of single crochet as she was making it, and then said, "Ah-ha! What if I make a yarn over the hook *before* I insert it into the next stitch?" She tried it and it worked and the *half-double crochet stitch* was born. Try it and see for yourself what happens.

To begin, make a slip loop and a chain 11 stitches long. Or as abbreviated instructions would say:

Ch 11.

The first row is made as follows:

Yarn over the hook, insert the hook into the third *chain from the hook. (See Figure 31.)*
Yarn over and draw up a loop through the chain (three loops are now on the hook). (See Figure 32.)

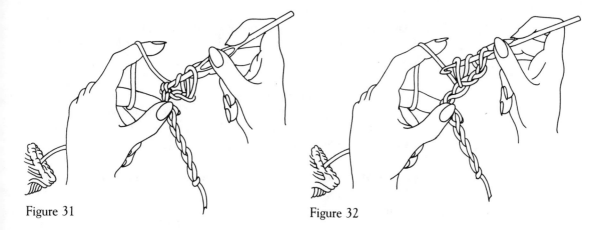

Figure 31

Figure 32

Yarn over and pull the new loop through all three loops on the hook. (One stitch made). (See Figure 33.)

Just keep on and do it over.

Yarn over the hook, insert the hook into the next stitch. Yarn over and draw up a loop, yarn over and pull through three loops.

Figure 33

Remember, as you complete each stitch, to move your fingers to the proper position for the next stitch; the right forefinger moves to the stitch just completed to keep it from getting too tight or too loose, and the thumb and second finger of the left hand move the completed piece into position for the hook to be inserted in the next stitch.

See, since you have a good background of understanding, it wasn't hard at all. Go back to the italicized paragraph above and repeat the words in between the asterisks (*————*) to fill up your foundation with 6 more stitches. This will make a total of 8 actual stitches plus the turning chain of 2 chain stitches.

The turning chain for half-double crochet needs to be 2 stitches long because the stitch is taller than a single crochet stitch. All crochet stitches are considered to be equal to one chain wide.

Remembering not to go into the base of the turning chain, make yourself another row of 9 half-double crochet (including the turning chain) to make sure you have gotten the feel of it, chain 2 and turn again.

Smile at yourself and your piece. Somebody had a new and better idea for a crochet stitch, and it works! You have just learned how to do it.

As you crochet, stop frequently and admire both your work and yourself. If there are imperfections in your work you will see them immediately and can correct them. And you should be proud of yourself for doing such fine work in this exquisite craft.

Half-double crochet stitches are usually abbreviated *hdc* in simplified instructions. To save space, often simple words are shortened in printed instructions. *Ea* is often used as an abbreviation for "each," and "repeat" is sometimes shortened to *rep* or *rpt*. In like manner, "pattern" or "patterns" is often represented by *pat* or *pats*. What you are doing would be written like this:

Ch 11.

Row 1) Hdc in 2nd ch, hdc in ea ch across, ch 2, turn.

Row 2) Hdc in ea st across, ch 2, turn.

Rpt row 2 for pat st.

Make a few more rows of half-double crochet stitches for practice and then stop and look at your piece. Compare it to the swatch of single crochet. See how the individual stitches are taller and how the finished fabric is softer. It tends to curl less than single crochet, but still some finishing of the edges will be needed. Worked back and forth, it is reversible. Wearable sweaters and jackets can be made of half-double crochet stitches, yet it is a bit too firm for many purposes.

British readers need to remember that their instructions will call this stitch a half-treble.

The international symbol for the half-double crochet stitch is like a fat capital letter "T." (See Figure 34.)

Figure 34

A chart of 9 stitches of half-double crochet looks like this:

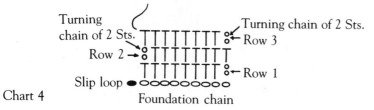

Chart 4

Note that in this chart of nine stitches there are only eight half-double crochet stitch symbols on each line. This is because the turning chain always counts as one stitch.

The next time you are faced with a situation that "works all right, but not exactly quite," remember your crocheting fore-mother. Look carefully at the problem and ask yourself "How can I make it better?" Scratch your head and say, "What if . . . ?" Who knows, you may invent a better way to load a dishwasher, a better kind of clothing, or a kind of shoe that doesn't hurt our feet and still looks good!

12

AND LONGER

THE DOUBLE CROCHET STITCH

Good ideas are like stepping-stones; each one leads to the next. Each step is further along the way to our goal. Crocheting might have stopped with the half-double crochet stitch if some creative person had not said, "That is a good idea; the half-double is better than the single, but I can make it even better. I can yarn over the hook before I start the stitch and then work off the loops only two at a time, as I did with the single crochet stitch, to make it even longer." With the courage of her convictions, she tried it and the *double crochet stitch* came into being.

Try it and see what happens:

Make a chain of 12 stitches. Yarn over the hook, insert the hook in the fourth chain from the hook. (See Figure 35.)

Yarn over again and draw up a loop (three loops on the hook). (See Figure 36.)

Yarn over again and pull through first two loops (two loops remain on the hook). (See Figure 37.)

(By this time I sincerely hope that you know how to hold your hands. In the following figures, as the stitches get more complicated, in order to show the threads more distinctly, I will usually eliminate the hand positions.)

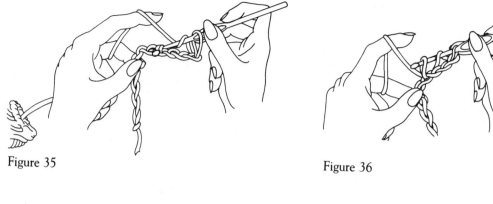

Figure 35

Figure 36

Figure 37

Figure 38

Yarn over again and pull through final two loops on the hook. (See Figure 38.)

A double crochet stitch completed, with the next stitch started, is shown in Figure 39. It is called a double crochet stitch because it takes two steps to work all of the loops off of the hook. It is the most versatile and most used of all the crochet stitches. (British crocheters are reminded that their instructions will call it a treble.)

I could take up pages and pages here writing out separate instructions for the second stitch of the first row and for the second row. Technically, on the first row, to make the second stitch one has to say "next chain" instead of "4th chain." On the second row, one has to say "stitch" instead of "chain." In shortened form the instructions to make the double crochet stitch read:

Figure 39

> *Yo, insert hk in next st and draw up a lp, yo and pull through 2 lps, yo and pull through 2 lps (dc completed).*

It is important that you learn how to read and completely understand this kind of jargon, because in the future you will encounter it in special fancy stitch instructions. Learn it now—let it become a

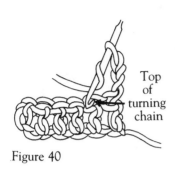

Top
of
turning
chain

Figure 40

part of your muscles, bones, and tendons as well as your mind—and it cannot frighten or intimidate you when you encounter it in the future when an instructor may not be available to talk you through the gibberish.

You *must* remember not to go into the base of the turning chain when you are ready to begin the next row. On double crochet, it is very easy to make a mistake and put your hook into the wrong spot to start off a new row. (See Figure 40 for the correct hook placement.)

To make a piece of double crochet fabric, Standard Simplified Instructions would say

Ch 12. Row 1) Dc in 4th ch and in ea ch across, ch 3, turn. Row 2) Dc in ea st across, ch 3, turn. Rep row 2 for pat st.

The turning chain for double crochet is 3 chains long.

If you haven't already started to do it on your own, it is time to begin to swoop and to hook the yarn in the air-space instead of just pushing back on the hook and letting the yarn fall over it. The difference between amateur ballet and a marvelous professional performance is that the pros swoop from one position to another in one long smooth gliding motion, whereas amateurs tend to stop between positions. If you are going to be a "pro" at crocheting, your hook needs to move in that same kind of long smooth gliding way. Make another row of dc practicing making your hook really dance.

When they begin to make the second row of double crochet stitches, beginners often panic and cry out, "What am I doing wrong? The stitches don't sit straight one on top of another." And they are right, they don't stack up straight. The crocheter is doing nothing wrong, that is just the way they sit. When one turns around and goes back on the third and following rows, things appear to even up. (See Figure 41.)

Go ahead and make a few more rows and see what I'm talking about.

If you mess up a stitch halfway through, don't try to rescue and save it. Gently pull it out and start over.

The making of the stitch was cheap; the finished thing is valuable. The worked-over stitch may show up later when it is difficult to do anything about it. It is better to redo it now.

Now stop and look at your newly made swatch. Like the fabric of single or half-double crochet, if you go back and forth in rows, it is

Figure 41

reversible. If, in the future, you work in rounds, it will not be reversible, and will have a definite front and back. In either case, it does have a top and a bottom. The fabric of double crochet tends not to curl, but to lie flat. It is softer and more pliable than fabric of either single or half-double crochet. Depending upon the size of the yarn and the hook used, the vertical spaces between the stitches may or may not be a "catch place" for fingers and knobs. Double crochet makes a lovely fabric, sturdy and durable, but not heavy. It is ideal for sweaters and scarves.

THE EDGES OF DOUBLE CROCHET

You may also notice that there is an unusually large spot on the ends of the rows between the turning chain and the first stitch of a row. Some crocheters are bothered by this, others take it in stride. Two things are happening here:

1. There is always a gap in width where the base of the turning chain sits, before the spot in which to place the first stitch. Some crocheters like to make one single crochet into the base of the turning chain and then chain 2 stitches before they make the first double crochet, to help fill this gap. Try it and see if you like the effect. Some people don't mind the gap at all and do nothing about it.

2. Not all of us make our chain stitches exactly the same length. I tend to work my chain stitches loosely and either have to make a conscious effort to tighten the chains that I make for the turning chain to keep that large spot from becoming huge, or I make just two extra long chains instead of the three called for in instructions. Some other crocheters chain very tightly and find that their turning chain is too short. Their solution is to make an extra one, that is, four chains long for the turning chain for double crochet.

This is where individuality begins to appear in crochet. And individuality in good crocheting is a *must*.

The object of crocheting is to have fun making lace in the air and to have a good-looking article when you are through. The object is not to follow the instructions precisely and end up unhappy with something ugly. Adjust the directions to serve your purpose. Make any turning chain however many chains long it needs to be to look good.

And how can you tell how long is long enough? You experiment and try, just like the women of the nineteenth century tried different things with their hooks and yarn.

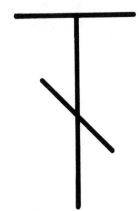

Figure 42

The two letters *dc* are the abbreviation for the "double crochet stitch" in simplified shortened directions.

The symbol for the double crochet stitch is a tall capital letter "T" with a diagonal slash across it to represent the "yarn over" before the hook is inserted. (See Figure 42.)

If you made a piece of fabric of three rows each of single crochet, half-double crochet, and double crochet the chart for it would look like this:

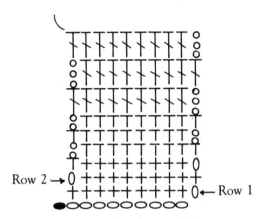

Chart 5

13
AND LONGER STILL

THE TRIPLE CROCHET AND OTHER LONG STITCHES

I have never yet taught a crochet class where the students weren't ahead of me on this next stitch. When I say, "Could you make a stitch that was taller than the double crochet?" there is a resounding "Yes, of course," in the room. When I ask, "How would you do it?" they tell me:

Just yarn over the hook twice before you insert it into the next stitch, and work off the loops two at a time.

It takes three times to get rid of the loops so it is called a *triple crochet.* (British terminology for it is *double treble crochet,* but it is the same thing.)

And I hope that you are off and running ahead of me, too. Still, you do need to know the precise jargon for the triple crochet stitch for future reference in working from printed instructions, so here it is:

Figure 43

Yarn over the hook two times, insert the hook into the next stitch, yarn over and draw up a loop (four loops on the hook), yarn over and pull through two loops (three loops on the hook), yarn over and pull through two loops (two loops on the hook), yarn over and pull through last two loops (triple crochet stitch made.) (See Figures 43 and 44.)

The turning chain for a triple crochet stitch is either four or five chains long, depending on the designer of the instructions. Try four

Figure 44

first and see what happens. Make a chain of 13 and begin the first triple crochet stitch in the fifth chain from the hook.

Work three rows of it so that you get the hang of it. Notice that, like its previous stepping stone the double crochet, the stitches of triple crochet do not sit exactly on top of each other, but that after a couple of rows the fabric looks okay. Notice also that the stitches look like daddy-longlegs spider legs. They are wiggly and offer places for fingers and knobs to catch on. Rarely is triple crochet used alone to make sweaters and scarves or afghans, just for that reason. The fabric is squiggly. But it is often used in other places as we will see in later chapters.

The abbreviation for the "triple crochet stitch" or "treble crochet" is *tr*.

About this time at least one student will say, "You could make a stitch that was even longer, couldn't you? You would just yarn over three times before you inserted the hook and work off the loops two at a time." And of course the student is right. It is variously called the *double triple*, (*dtr*) stitch in American books or the *treble-treble* in English books. The abbreviated instructions for it are:

Figure 45

Yo 3 times, yo and draw up a lp, [yo and pull thru 2 lps] 4 times (dtr made.) (See Figure 45.)

(See, you are reading and understanding abbreviated crochet instructions already, and they aren't difficult at all!) The abbreviation for the "double triple" stitch is *dtr*. *The symbol is a tall capital letter "T" with three slashes across it.*

I'm not fond of it, but make a few rows of it and try it out for yourself. I find it a laborious and time-consuming way to make a very unstable fabric. It does have its uses, however, and can come in handy, but you won't be using it often. You just need to know it can be done.

And, of course, my students ask me, "Could you make the stitch even taller?" Sure you can, and occasionally it is done, but why do it? It wouldn't be of value for a plain fabric because even doorknobs would catch in it. It can be done, and it even has a symbol and an abbreviation, *tr tr*. Still, I don't know of anybody who uses it other than in very special circumstances.

My students are also ahead of me on recognizing the symbols for triple and double triple crochet stitches. "It is a tall skinny capital letter "T." The triple has two diagonal slashes on it because you yarn over twice before you insert the hook. The double triple has three diagonal slashes on it because you yarn over three times," they inform me, and they are correct. (See Figure 46.)

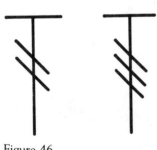

Figure 46

If you made a swatch 10 stitches wide of two rows each of triple crochet and double-triple crochet stitches it would look like this:

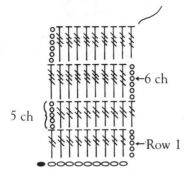

5 ch

←6 ch

←Row 1

Chart 6

Conclusion: If the teacher has taught well, thoroughly, and comprehensively, the students will take off and surpass the teacher. And that is what a good teacher wants. If the students do not turn out to be as good as or better than the teacher, one of two things is true. Either the teacher did not teach well, or she chose only fools and dullards for students.

14

THE SLIP STITCH

Sometimes there are vital pieces of information that we need to function easily. These data may serve no purpose on their own, but without them other things just don't work right. I'm thinking of the bank teller machines in grocery stores and all around town. You may have money in your bank account and you may have your bank card in your hand, but those silly machines just won't work without your secret code number.

The *slip stitch* in crochet is like your secret bank code number. You would never use the slip stitch by itself to make anything, but without it many other pattern stitches just won't work. It is really very simple to make:

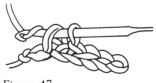

Figure 47

Insert the hook into the appropriate spot, yarn over, and draw through both loops on the hook. (See Figure 47 and Figure 48, which show a slip stitch on top of single crochet.)

USES OF THE SLIP STITCH

The slip stitch is used for attaching, joining, traveling, and fastening, and for these things only. It is an ideal way to join two parts of a pattern together, to travel along on the top of a different stitch to get to the place where you want to be, and to attach things together.

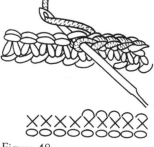

Figure 48

The slip stitch has almost *no height* and becomes nearly invisible when completed. Moreover, the little flat thing is almost impossible to get your hook back into to make another stitch on top of it.

Never make a slip stitch where you will have to go back into it again for you will pay the devil trying to force an opening in it.

Printed American directions abbreviate the "slip stitch" as *sl st*. Please don't get this confused with the slip loop (sl lp) which we talked about earlier. They are two entirely different things. The slip loop is how we get started and it is made with our fingers; the slip stitch is how we join things and it is made with the hook. (British directions often use *ss* as an abbreviation for the slip stitch.)

The international symbol of the slip stitch is a simple arch. (See Figure 49.)

Figure 49

When we get into the chapters on pattern stitches and medallions you'll notice that the slip stitch is used a lot, and you'll know that the simple arch is its symbol.

From here on in crocheting, there are no more new stitches to learn. Eveything else that you will ever do is simply combining and recombining the things you already know. Isn't it nice to be assured that the basics are embedded in your being and you will never be caught at the teller machine without your secret code?

15

ADDING NEW YARN

The well-stocked pantry was a great idea of our great-grandmothers. Having extra supplies on hand and being prepared for an emergency can take much of the pressure of running a smooth operation off of a hard-working person. It is unfortunate that today's small homes and apartments simply don't have room for storage of much more than an extra light bulb or an extra roll of paper towels. Ideas are about all we can store for emergency use.

And there is an idea that you need to store in your mind for frequent pulling out and use. You may have already had need for it, but up to now there wasn't really a good place in this book to tell you about it. Now that you know the basic stitches, I need to tell you about it.

WHEN TO ADD NEW YARN

As we discussed in Chapter 3, all yarns and threads contain imperfections. The blemishes may be huge knots in the entire piece, or a knot in just one strand of the plied yarn. An imperfection can be a length of the yarn that is not properly spun, or a blob of foreign material in the yarn. It can also be a spot that is either not colored at all or that is discolored. Whatever the reason, imperfections *must* be cut out, and the yarn joined in again into your work as if it were a new ball of thread.

Never work bad spots in the yarn into your crocheting.

At the moment, you may resent the time and effort it takes to clip the yarn, cut out the bad spot, and join in the new yarn. But you will resent it even more if ugly imperfections raise their unsightly heads in your otherwise lovely finished piece like flies swimming in the soup.

How we join in the fresh yarn will depend upon where the joining occurs: 1) in the middle of a row, or 2) at the end of a row. (Jacquard color work is a whole different story and we'll discuss that in a later chapter.)

However and whenever you join new yarn, make sure that you leave tail ends that are at least six inches long.

Thrift is to be admired. Saving and making do with what we already have can enrich our lives by allowing us to have more. But thrift can be overdone. If you leave tail ends of your yarn that are less than six inches long, it will be difficult to safely, securely, and invisibly fasten in those ends.

I have a lovely, richly embossed and elegantly interworked fine cotton sweater that was crocheted for me by a dear sweet little old woman. To make sure that she had enough of the thread to finish the thing, she didn't waste a quarter of an inch when she joined in the new pieces. She didn't cut out the bad spots in the thread for fear of not being thrifty. As a result, the first time the sweater was washed in an attempt to rid it of discolored spots, it sprouted short fuzzy tag ends all over. The discolored spots didn't disappear, and there is no way to hide or work in these quarter-inch ends. If I were to cut them off, the whole sweater might disintegrate. It is sad that an otherwise beautiful work of art has been disfigured by unwise thrift.

JOINING YARN IN THE MIDDLE OF A PIECE

Unlike knitting where we don't want to join new yarn in the middle of a row unless we simply have to, adding new yarn in the middle of a row or a pattern stitch is no problem in crocheting.

Between whole stitches, never in the middle of the stitch, clasp the six-inch-long ends of yarn in back of the first three fingers of your right hand and between the third and little finger. (See Figure 50.)

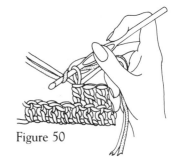

Figure 50

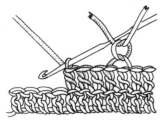

Figure 51

Make the next three stitches in the ordinary way. Stop. Turn the work over to the back. Tie the first half of a square knot just as you would begin to tie your shoe, that is, right over left around and through. Turn the piece back to the front side. Inspect the spot. Is the top of the stitch in question the same size as its neighbors? If not, adjust the tension of the knot. (See Figure 51.)

When the stitches and spacing are properly adjusted, turn the piece to the back again and complete the square knot, left over right around and through. Leave the tail ends dangling.

JOINING YARN AT THE END OF A ROW

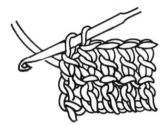

Figure 52

Often the reason that we join new yarn at the end of a row is because we want to change to a new color. There are two very different ways of doing this with good-looking results. If we just started the turning chain with the new color of yarn, we would get an ugly effect because the final loop of the old color would appear on our turning chain. Instead, we can 1) complete the final stitch of the row of the old color with the new color or 2) begin the new color of the new row in the air.

The first method is the one often called for in conventional instructions. It goes like this:

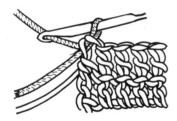

Figure 53

Begin the last stitch of the row with the old color, and work it in the ordinary way until two loops remain on the hook. (See Figure 52.)

Leaving a six-inch-long tail end, complete the final step of the stitch with the new yarn. (See Figure 53.)

Most conventional instructions don't tell you, but sooner or later after you have worked a few stitches of the new row, you will have to stop and tie a knot. I have never been entirely happy with these results. I prefer to use the second method:

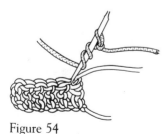

Figure 54

Complete the final stitch of the row with the old color. Leaving a six-inch tail end, clip the yarn and fasten off by pulling straight up on the hook. Turn the work around. With the new yarn, place a slip loop on the hook. From up in the air, make the first stitch of the next row into the final stitch of the previous row.

In this case, there is no turning chain, so there cannot be a color change appearing on it. It does require that either conventional instructions be rewritten without the turning chain and with one additional stitch in its place, or that the crocheter understands what is happening and adjusts his or her counting to make up for the loss of the turning chain. My students have been taught that the turning chain counts as one stitch of the new row and aren't bothered by the change at all. Make your own choice of which way to add a new color of yarn.

PLAN AHEAD

A little earlier, I said that you must always leave a six-inch-long tail end when adding new yarn in order to have enough to hide in the ends securely. Now I am going to tell you that you need not limit yourself to only a six-inch-long tail end.

If the edge you are working on is later going to become part of a seam, plan ahead and leave a piece long enough to make that seam, or at least part of it. Wrap the excess yarn around your little finger and secure it to the work with a small safety pin until you need it to make the seam.

Let's get down to for-instances: When I start the back of a sweater, I know that I will have to make a seam to join it to the front pieces. I make my beginning slip loop 20 inches from the end of the yarn. After the first row is completed, I make a tidy bundle of the saved-for-the-seam yarn and secure it to the piece. When I am ready to make the seam, the yarn is already there to do it with.

When I fasten off the final stitch of a hexagonal medallion, I clip the yarn long enough to make the necessary seam before I pull it through the last stitch.

Finishing work is not my favorite thing to do. Leaving the long tail ends for seams makes it easier. When I am ready to make the seam, the yarn is already there. Moreover, I am saved the bother of hiding in both the tail end of the piece *and* the starting tail end of the seam yarn.

HIDING IN THE ENDS SECURELY

"What am I supposed to do with all of these long tail ends? I can't just leave them dangling forever!"

Of course you can't. At some point you must invisibly hide them in so that they will never come undone. Some crocheters like to keep their work tidy as they go along. Others prefer to do all the tidying up when the article is completed. In either event, you should work a few rows beyond the joining before you finish in the ends.

When you are ready to finish in the ends, from the supply pouch in your crocheting bag,

select the smallest size tapestry needle that can be threaded with the yarn you are using.

How do you know that it is the smallest size needle you can use? You try to thread it and see. No licking the thread and pushing, please; there is an easy way to thread a tapestry needle with yarn.

Hold the eye of the needle in your right hand. Fold the yarn over the tip end of the needle. Pull very firmly down on the folded yarn with the thumb and forefinger of your left hand. (See Figure 55.)

Slide the tip of the needle out of the fold, turn the needle around, and place the eye of the needle over the fold. From the front to the back, roll the eye over the tightly held fold of yarn. The folded spot should just slide into the eye of the needle. (See Figure 56.)

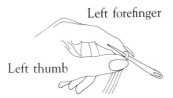

Left forefinger

Left thumb

Figure 55

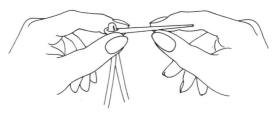

Figure 56

Practice it a few times and soon the yarn will just slide into the eye. With a threaded needle,

going in between the two loops at the top of the parent stitch, slide the threaded needle down the stitch, making sure that you are going between the strands and not splitting them.

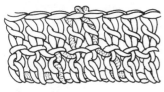

Figure 57

Pull the needle up, select another stitch to follow, and trace its path downward. Repeat this until you have followed the paths of about four stitches. Clip the yarn about ¼ inch from the fabric. Pull gently but firmly on the fabric to seat the hidden yarn.

The tail end will absolutely disappear and your work can never come unraveled or get messy-looking.

I wish great-grandmother's pantry existed in my house, filled with supplies for supper at a moment's notice. I'd like to be able to keep on with my crocheting until the last moment and then simply open the pantry door and find dinner there all prepared. A ham to slice, green beans with tomatoes to open up and heat, pickled beets to dish up for color, even home-canned peaches and cookies for dessert. Instead I will hop in the car and run to the market, losing time from my beloved handwork. Still, I have in my head a pantry full of ideas to make my crocheting the very best possible. That's what heads were invented for, the storage of ideas. Hands were invented to implement those ideas.

16
YOUR CUP RUNNETH OVER

INCREASING

One of the reasons crochet took off and blossomed in the latter half of the nineteenth century was that the fabric could be shaped as one went along. The crocheter can see it widen or narrow, flare or taper as it is worked.

In this respect crocheting is unlike any other fabric art form. The weaver must make the whole nine yards of her woven goods all the same width and then, if clothing is desired, cut up and sew the finished fabric. The knitter can widen and narrow, taper or flare as the article grows under her needles, but she can't see and measure what she is doing until long afterward. A crocheter knows if the circle lies flat immediately, if the ruffle ruffles gracefully instantly, if the cap curves to fit a head in a jiffy. This capability of *increasing* or *decreasing* the number of stitches on a row allowed our foremothers to make a centerpiece just the right size and shape for the table, a shawl that flared in perfect elegance around the wearer's shoulders, and a cap that fit baby's head precisely. Later on, at the end of Chapter 22, we'll get into the formulas for making circles, ruffles, and curves, but first you need to learn the techniques for making increases.

There was also another reason that crocheting flourished in this country before the War Between the States: Fancy and elaborate pattern stitches were easy for individuals to create by making multiple increases and multiple decreases at regular intervals.

So long as the crocheter is consistent, making the same increases and decreases over and over forms a pattern.

These increases and decreases, which are easy to count and to duplicate, form exquisite patterns.

TO INCREASE IS TO MAKE MORE

All this time I've had you students making straight rows, forcing you to make the same number of stitches on each and every row because it was important for you to learn how to keep even rows and straight edges, always maintaining the same number of stitches. The word *even* in crocheting means just that, without increasing or decreasing. Here and now it is time to learn to make pieces wider and add more stitches to the rows.

It is also time to tell you something about the way in which I look at life, for it affects the way in which I keep track of the increasing and decreasing of my crocheting. I sincerely detest the tediousness of ordinary life; I thrill to the creativity and abundance of living. Alas, many times my creativity involves the correct proportioning of minutiae, or to say it in crocheting terms, you often have to count the spaces between increases (or decreases) in order to achieve the lovely undulating effects. Besides enjoying creativity, I am also a lazy person. I don't mind counting something once, but I abhor counting the same thing over and over, so I use lots and lots of markers to avoid repeated counting.

Let markers keep track of increases and decreases for you.

My favorite markers are tiny coilless safety pins and knitters' slip-on plastic ring markers, which I have already told you to add to your crocheting supplies. Now it is time to tell you how to use them.

If I am making a sleeve that flares from a narrow wrist to a greater width at the underarm, and if my instructions tell me to increase one stitch on each side every fifth row twelve times, I make a chain of twelve safety pins. At the beginning of each increase row, I remove one pin from the chain and fasten it into the first increased stitch. I can easily see and count the rows before the next required increase. When all my safety pins in the chain are used up, my increasing will be complete, and I will know that I have the width that I need. For me it is easier than keeping track on paper of the rows and the increases, for someone is always stealing my pencil. Certainly it is much quicker than continually checking my piece and trying to find how many increases I have already made—and where.

If I am making a large lacy shawl that has an increase at the center back, I place a knitter's slip-on ring marker in that center back stitch so that without counting, my fingers and eyes will alert me to the need to increase at that point. I remove the marker, make the increase, and replace the marker in the center stitch for the next row.

As a crochet instructor, I did not at first force my students to use the safety pins or the slip-on markers; however, after numerous occasions of students bringing me pieces in progress, saying they had lost count, and asking me to tell them how many increases (or decreases) they had already made and how many more they needed to do, I enforced the safety-pin chain technique. After watching the complete frustration of a dear sweet lady trying to set up a ripple afghan and getting the increases off center, I enforced the slip-on marker technique until the patterns were well enough established to see what was happening.

Don't get me wrong, counting and making hash marks on paper serves a real purpose for some people. They seem to require the intense concentration on their crocheting that will shut out all the interferences of living in order to relax and enjoy. If you need that concentration and soleness of purpose to find peace and quiet, forget the markers. If you choose to let your mind float free while your fingers do their thing, use the little goodies.

Please, never let your crocheting become an avenue of rudeness. To say, "Shut up! I'm counting," when a child wants to tell you what happened at school, or "Go away! You're bothering me," when a question is being asked of you, is to defeat one of the prime purposes of crocheting—the attainment of a peaceful frame of mind and a relaxed attitude toward time.

TWO WAYS TO INCREASE

There are two ways in which you can increase the number of stitches on a row: 1) you can make more than one stitch in any stitch of a previous row, or 2) you can add extra stitches at the ends of rows. And it doesn't matter what kind of stitch you are making; these same rules hold true for single, half-double, double and treble crochet stitches.

MAKING MORE THAN ONE STITCH IN AN OLD ONE

There is no rule that says you must make only one stitch in each and every stitch of a previous row. You can make as many stitches in one stitch as you like, or, more properly, as the stitch will hold. In fact, making many stitches in a previous one is the basis of many lovely fancy pattern stitches as you will see in Chapters 21, 22, and 23.

Two stitches made in one in the middle of a row will simply and subtly broaden the piece.

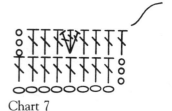

Chart 7

This is the basis of making a circle lie flat, which we will discuss in a later chapter. Adding a few stitches now and then can make a tightly fitted bodice enlarge enough to contain the bosoms without having definite dart lines.

In chart language more than one stitch is rooted in the appropriate stitch in the row at right (see Chart 7).

If repeated over and over in the same spot on subsequent rows, 3 sc, or 5 dc, or 7 tr in the middle of a row will make a right angle, as shown at right (see Chart 8).

Now are you beginning to see the magic of inventive crochet?

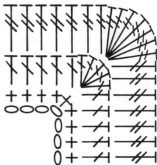

Chart 8

ADDING SINGLE STITCHES AT THE ENDS OF ROWS

Remember, way back when we were talking about the single crochet stitch, I told you the rule, "never, unless otherwise directed, insert your hook into the base of the turning chain"? Well, now I'm directing you otherwise.

To add one stitch at the beginning of a row, make an extra stitch into the base of the turning chain. (See Figure 58.)

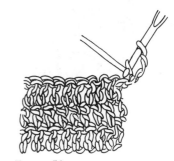

Figure 58

This kind of an increase will leave a smooth, tapered edge. To make a matching increase at the end of a row, simply

make one extra stitch into the top of the turning chain of the previous row. (See Figure 59.)

Again you have a smooth tapered edge.

But sometimes we don't want an invisible increased edge. There are times when we want the increases to show. To make an increase stand out next to the edge stitch:

Add one extra chain to the turning chain at the beginning of a row, and make a chain-one space before you make the last stitch into the top of the

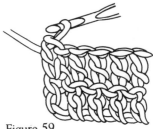

Figure 59

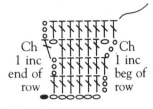

Ch 1 inc end of row | Ch 1 inc beg of row

Chart 9

turning chain of the previous row. On the following row, make an extra stitch into each of the chain-one spaces. (See Chart 9 at left.)

This kind of an increase will leave a small hole or wide space beside the outside stitch. If we wish that hole to become a truly decorative element of our design, we can move it in from the edge two or three spaces as follows:

Row 1) Work 2 sts, ch 1, work across row until one st and top of t-ch remain, ch 1, work st in last st and one stitch in the top of t-ch.

Row 2) Work one st in each st including the ch-1 sps across. (See Chart 10.)

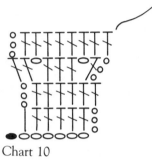

Chart 10

ADDING MANY STITCHES AT THE ENDS OF ROWS

Both of the following methods are done at the *ends* of rows. When beginners use these ways in making a symmetrical piece, that is, one in which both sides are the same, they are often terrified at the results. "But, Mrs. Righetti," they cry, "the two sides are not identical. One side is one row higher than the other." And, yes, it is true that they will be. For most articles, however, that one row will not matter, and no one will ever notice it.

The first method is to:

Work extra stitches in the bottom-most outermost loop of the last stitch of a row. (See Figure 60.)

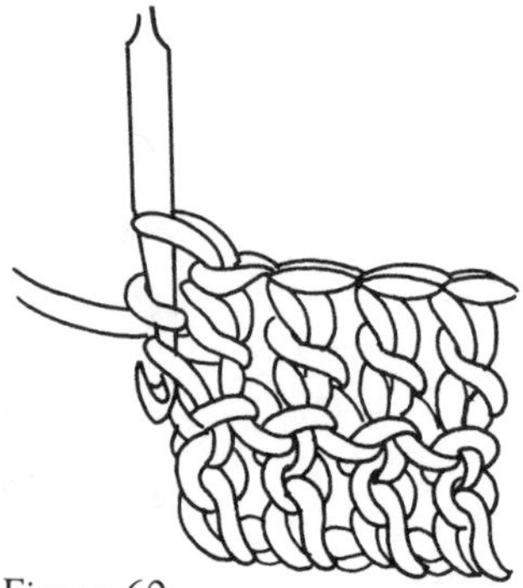

The second method is to:

Figure 60

In addition to the regular turning chain, make one additional chain for each additional desired stitch. On the following row, fill up each of those additional chain stitches with an ordinary stitch, whatever it is you happen to be doing. (See Chart 11.)

I sincerely hope that you will become as creative and inventive as the women of a hundred and fifty years ago who devised centerpieces for the size and shape of their (your) table, shawls that fit perfectly around the wearer's (your) shoulders, and caps that fit the head of that special baby. You are gaining the knowledge and confidence to be able to do it on your own.

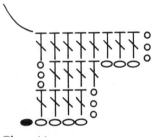

Chart 11

17

GATHERING IN
THE FLOCK

DECREASING

I recently went through my closet, giving it an end of season sort-ing-out, and got rid of a lot of excess baggage that will never be used again. Shoes that hurt my feet, summer tops that were too tired and sad to see the light of another June, and threadbare slacks that were an embarrassment, all got sent away so that I could more fully and easily utilize the things that remained.

So too in crocheting we periodically need to get rid of excess stitches and gather in the flock of remaining stitches that we intend to keep on using. Just as I rid the closet of the excess baggage and got it out of the house, we need to eliminate stitches in a safe and secure way. Simply passing by those unwanted stitches, leaving them sitting there unused, will not solve our problem. Jumping over unneeded stitches on the next row will leave a hole in our work. And that hole may be well and good if it is part of a design element of spaces and places. If, however, we simply want to nar-row our piece, the skipped-over hole may be unsightly.

Long ago, some other crocheter was faced with the problem of getting rid of stitches without leaving a hole and devised the all encompassing answer to the problem:

To decrease however many of whatever type of stitch, count and allow one more stitch than the number to be decreased. Begin to make the first stitch, but do not complete the final step of it, leaving the remaining loops on the hook. For as many stitches as you wish to decrease, begin the next stitch(es), but do not complete it (them) either. When you have gathered in as many stitches as you wish, yarn over and go through all the loops remaining on your hook at once.

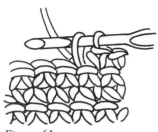

Figure 61

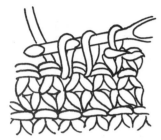

Figure 62

Figure 63

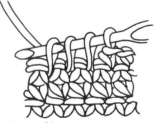

Figure 64

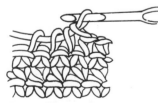

Figure 65

If all of that italicized paragraph above seems a bit much to grasp at once, let's slowly go through some of the possibilities.

SINGLE CROCHET DECREASES

Say, for instance, you are working in single crochet and want to get rid of one stitch. That would be a *single single crochet decrease.*

On the stitch before the one you want to decrease, after you have inserted the hook, make a yarn over and draw up a loop (see Figure 61), stop before you yarn over again and pull through the two loops on the hook to complete the stitch. Instead, insert the hook for the next stitch, yarn over and draw up a loop. (See Figure 62.) Now yarn over and pull through all three loops on your hook, and two stitches have been made into one, forming the decrease. (See Figure 63.)

In abbreviated crochet directions this would appear on the printed page as:

Insert hk in next st, yo and draw up a lp, insert hk in next st, yo and draw up a lp, yo and pull through 3 lps (dec made).

Try it and see for yourself how it looks. Make three of them across a row of ten stitches. The result is smooth, flat, and almost imperceptible, and you will have only seven stitches left.

Single single crochet decreases can be casually scattered throughout a piece to make it narrow in an almost invisible way.

But there is no rule that says that you can get rid of only one stitch at a time. You can also make a *double single crochet decrease,* getting rid of two stitches at one time; as follows.

Start to make the stitch before the decrease point, but leave the stitch unfinished. Begin to make each of the next two stitches and also leave them unfinished. (See Figure 64.)

Yarn over and pull through all four loops on your hook at once. (See Figure 65.)

If you should encounter a double single crochet decrease in the shorthand of standard directions it would look like this:

Insert hk for next st, yo and draw up a lp, rep bet *'s twice, yo & go through 4 lps.*

There will be lots of times when you will come across a *triple single crochet decrease*, for this little maneuver will form an inside right-angle corner. In it you are decreasing four stitches into one and thereby getting rid of three stitches. The general technique is the same, you just do more of it.

Insert hk for next st, yo and draw up a lp, rep bet *'s 3 times, yo & go thru 5 lps.*

The raised ripple afghan pattern stitch calls for this type of decrease for, if repeated every row at the same place, it makes the fabric move up at an angle.

You could of course go on infinitely decreasing as many stitches as you could fit loops onto your hook, but at some point it would make a lump and a bump in your work. Unless you particularly wanted this sort of distortion in your piece, it would never be called for.

DOUBLE CROCHET DECREASES

Double crochet is so frequently used as a fabric stitch to make articles of clothing, sweaters, vests, and such, that decreases in it are often encountered. Often we want our piece to narrow, as from the armhole to the shoulder, or for the cap of a sleeve, and we want to work on fewer stitches, but we don't want any holes in our crocheted cloth, so *single double crochet decreases* are called for. They can be made at the end of a row so that the piece remains smooth-looking and simply narrows, or they can be made a few stitches in from the edge where they become more of a decoration. In any event, my students are always ahead of me on this one, as you probably are. "Leave the last two loops on the hook, and simply don't finish the last step of the first stitch, then complete it as one with the second stitch." (See Figure 66.)

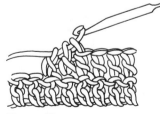
Figure 66

Figure 67

Figure 68

Leave the first double crochet unfinished with two loops remaining on the hook (see Figure 67); Now work the second double crochet until there are three loops only on the hook (see Figure 68); and complete both stitches as one, by making a yarn over and pulling through all loops on the hook at once.

This is the way it will look in printed abbreviated instructions:

*Yo, insert hk in next st, yo and pull thru 2 lps *, rep bet *s, yo and pull thru 3 lps (dec made).

(I hope now you understand why I was so insistent that you learn the proper terminology for making the various stitches! And I repeat once again that you will never be at a loss to understand simplified abbreviated instructions if you will read them aloud using the whole words.)

Single double crochet decreases at or near the edges of a piece make it narrow at a smooth angle. Decreases made in the middle, directly above one another, will form a dart. Those same decreases casually scattered across the piece will make a slightly curved piece.

Many afghan instructions require you to make a *double double crochet decrease* as part of the fancy pattern stitch in which you are getting rid of two stitches and working three into one. The idea is the same, you just do it one more time.

[Yo, insert hk in next st, yo and pull thru 2 lps] 2 times, yo and pull thru 3 lps (dbl dec made).

I used brackets ([————]) in the directions above to get you acquainted with them. Brackets are often used instead of asterisks (*————*) to enclose a group of instructions that are to be repeated. Often the brackets are used within a set of asterisks. Sometimes the brackets enclose a set of things that is done in one place. As for instance "[dc, ch 1, dc] in next st."

As with the series of single crochet decreases, you could go on adding stitches to your double crochet decrease, decreasing four or five or six stitches into one. It might make a very messy-looking place, but you could do it following the same basic idea of starting a stitch and not finishing it until you finally complete all of the stitches in one. Multiple double crochet decreases are the basis of the second row of My Lady's Fan pattern stitch on page 135. In that case, there are nine stitches decreased into one.

In chart language, decreases are represented by pulling the tops of the stitches together and making them wear one hat. See Chart 12 for an example of a double double decrease.

Chart 12

THE PUFF STITCH

An interesting variation using both increases and decreases in the same spot is the *puff stitch*. It is made by decreasing four or five double crochet stitches into one in one stitch of the previous row. It makes a lovely little bobble and adds an interesting raised texture. Often standard directions will write a puff stitch of three double crochet this way:

In next st [yo, insert hk, yo and draw up a lp, yo and pull thru 2 lps] 3 times (4 lps on hk), yo and pull thru all lps (puff st made). (See Figures 69 and 70.)

Figure 69

TRIPLE CROCHET DECREASES

Though less frequently used than the double crochet, triple crochet stitch is a favorite for many things and of course *single triple crochet decreases* will be used. Because there are more steps to the triple crochet stitch itself, there are more steps to the decrease. It isn't harder, it just takes longer to do it.

Figure 70

* Yo twice, insert hk into next st, yo and draw up a lp, [yo and pull thru 2 lps] twice *, rep bet *s, yo and pull thru 3 lps.*

(I threw both asterisks and brackets into that one on purpose and it didn't even bother you. Whoever said that abbrev cro insts were frightening and mystifying?)

In this same manner *double triple crochet decreases* can be made as well as *triple triple crochet decreases.*) You have the idea and there is no point in clobbering you with the details. They are worth knowing about, though, because I once ran across a gorgeous pattern stitch in a Japanese book of crochet charts using a multiple decrease of triple crochet. You may run across one too some day.

DOUBLE TRIPLE CROCHET DECREASES

Those daddy-longlegs spider stitches in which you yarn over three or four times before you insert the hook can also be decreased. *Single double triple crochet decreases* are made in the following way by working two stitches into one:

*Yo 3 times, insert hk in next st, yo and draw up a lp, [yo and pull thru 2 lps] 3 times *, rep bets *s, yo and pull thru 3 lps.

Double double triple crochet decreases simply get rid of two double triple crochet stitches by working three into one. It is done in the same way as above except that you repeat between the asterisks two times and finally pull through all loops.

When you understand the principle behind it, decreasing crochet stitches can be just as joyful and rewarding as cleaning out your closet. There is never any excuse in life for carrying excess baggage around, whether it be accumulated junk, old emotional wounds, or excess crochet stitches. Just be sure that, when you dispose of old possessions, you do it in a neat and tidy way.

18

FISHING WITH
YOUR HOOK
IN OTHER WATERS

Some people are opinionated and think that creativity means only that some individual can make a lovely original oil painting or write a symphony. Though paintings and music are fine expressions of creativity, they are hardly the only examples. Creativity is much more than that. It is finding new solutions to old problems; the new backless computer chair that I sit on to write this book is a fine example of solving an ancient problem in a fresh new way. Using the unexpected for the obvious; putting kitchen utensils that are needed by the stove in a crock beside the range instead of in a drawer is the result of a creative mind at work. Just seeing a definite pattern in what at first glance appears to be a random scattering is creativity also.

And creativity is not the property of youth alone. It belongs to the not-so-young as well. One, many, of our crocheting fore-mothers said, "I don't have to just put my hook in the next stitch; I could skip one or several." Another said, "I could put my hook in another row instead of the one I'm working on." Yet another said, "I could put my hook into the end of the chain I'm making and form a circle." And some very original soul said, "I can take my hook out of the stitch I'm working on and put it in somewhere else in order to pull the stitches together." And all of this was creativity at work.

Over time, with the writing and rewriting of instructions, we have lost sight of the creativity of these women at work. Our directions are put down in stylized shorthand and we forget that some-one found variation and diversity in a small handful of basic stitches. If, once they are beyond the basics, I use the understanding of creativity to teach my students more advanced techniques, I find that they learn quicker, more thoroughly, and in a more joyful way. So let us examine some of the next steps from a perspective of creativity.

YOU DON'T HAVE TO WORK THROUGH BOTH LOOPS

When you were a beginner, I told you to "always, unless otherwise instructed, work through both loops of the chain and of the stitches of the previous row." You were told to do so because that is what is expected unless the designer is after a special effect. And lovely effects can be achieved by working in a single loop only.

You can make the next row by working through the *back loop* only of the stitches of the previous row. (See Figure 71.) You will want to use the thumb and second finger of the left hand to tilt the fabric to the front so that your hook can easily find the single back loop. At first it seems awkward and slow, but you and your fingers will soon get the hang of it and fly along.

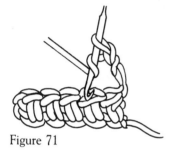

Figure 71

Working into the back loop only creates a ridge on the front side of the work.

Instructions often abbreviate directions to work in the "back loop" as *bk lp* or simply *bl.*

If you are making a flat, back-and-forth piece, always working into the back loop only will result in ridges on both sides of the fabric and fabric that resembles knitted ribbing. There is a favorite striped ripple afghan pattern that uses this technique to enhance the light and shadow patterns and to add trapped air space for extra warmth.

You can also work into the *front loop* only of the stitches of the previous row. Though not many instructions call for it, it can easily be done. Use your left thumb and second finger to tilt the fabric to the back and simply slide the hook, from front to back, into the forward loop. (See Figure 72.)

Figure 72

Working into the front loop only creates a ridge on the back of the work.

In crocheting edgings on garments, I often work into the front loop only, on the first row, because it makes the transition between the fabric of the garment and the edging smoother and almost imperceptible.

The abbreviation for "front loop" is *ft lp* or sometimes simply *fl.*

In either event, whether you work in the back loop only or in the front loop only you will get a fabric that is much more elastic vertically than ordinary. Fabric made by working in the back loop is often used for ribbing on crocheted sweaters for just that reason.

YOU DON'T HAVE TO PUT YOUR HOOK IN THE NEXT STITCH

Just because, for the sake of learning, I have always told you to "insert the hook into the *next* stitch . . ." doesn't mean that you will have to do it that way forever and ever. We talked about it very briefly in the chapter on decreases, and I want to talk about it more thoroughly here.

Skipping a stitch will leave a hole in the work.

This is fine when you want a hole, and spaces and places are the basis of many elegant and lovely fancy crochet pattern stitches. And you may skip as many stitches as you choose or as your instructions direct you to. If you simply skip over a stitch without doing any other compensating thing, you will have decreased a stitch and made a triangular hole. If, however, you make a corresponding chain stitch over the skipped stitch, you will have retained the same total number of stitches and made a square hole. Obviously, if you skip several stitches and make several chain stitches to bridge over them, you will keep the same number of stitches and have a rectangular hole.

Remember that single, double, triple, and double triple crochet stitches are all considered to be one chain wide.

The word "skip" is often abbreviated *sk* or *skp*.

To make a hole without a decrease, simply chain as many stitches as you skip over and you will have the same number of stitches that you started with. If you make more chains than stitches skipped over, you will have an increase.

YOU CAN PUT YOUR HOOK INTO A SPACE INSTEAD OF A PLACE

If you have made spaces and holes on the previous row, on this next row you can either make a stitch into the chain over the hole-space or you can *insert your hook into the empty space.* Simply insert the hook into the hole, pretending that the entire chain above it is the two loops of a stitch, yarn over, draw up your loop.

This is a good time to tell you about the abbreviation you will encounter in printed directions in this situation. The abbreviation for the chain stitch (ch) is followed by a hyphen and a number, such as "*ch-1 space* or *ch-6 sp.*" Your directions may tell you to "Sc in ch-1 sp," or "6 dc, ch 1, 6 dc in ch-6 sp." I hope that this paragraph makes it obvious that the word "space" is often abbreviated *sp.*

YOU CAN PUT YOUR HOOK
IN ANOTHER ROW

Your hook is a versatile tool and can do all kinds of things. In making a piece of fabric in different colored stripes, a lovely herringbone effect can be achieved by working some of the stitches *in any row below.* You will be glad that you learned that crocheting is a two-handed operation because you will need the leverage given by your right index finger high up on the hook to place it in the right spot, and you will also need the help of that left thumb and second finger to place the previous row in the right location for the hook to find it.

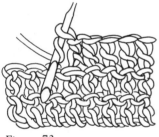

Figure 73

Simply put your hook into the area to the left of a stitch of any previous row, reach your hook way up to grab the working yarn, and yarn over and draw up an extra long loop because this stitch will be longer than its neighbors, and then continue to finish it in the ordinary way.

Printed directions might read:

Row 1) Sc in 2nd ch from hk and in ea ch across, ch 3, turn.

Row 2) Dc in ea st across, ch 3, turn.

Row 3) Dc in first st, *inserting hk in sp between sts of first row of sc, work 1 dc, dc in ea of next 2 dc *, rep bet *s across, ch 3, turn.

Especially if different colors have been used for the different rows, this can make a very pretty effect. The long stitch will appear as a letter "V" against the background of a different color.

Also, you can make a stitch *in the chain-space several rows below.* It is usually easier for your hook to find this spot, but you will again need the help of your left thumb and second finger to move the fabric into working position. Once more, be sure to draw up a healthy long loop so that the fabric doesn't scrunch up and shorten. Instructions might say:

"Dc in ch-1 sp of 3rd row below."

YOU CAN WORK AROUND STITCHES INSTEAD OF INTO THEM

Just because, as beginners, I had you work into the top of the stitch of the previous row doesn't mean that you can't also work around stitches. Working *around the front of a post of the previous row* gives an interesting raised ridge on the front of the fabric. Usually it is done in double crochet where both the row you are working on and the previous row are double crochet stitches. Occasionally it is done in triple crochet. In either event, the stitch directly below is used and it is called a *post*. These are the directions for double crochet. It is easy to do:

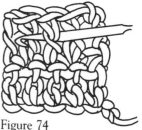

Figure 74

Yarn over and from right to left, from front to back, insert the hook around the post of the stitch directly below in the previous row, yarn over and draw up a loop, yarn over and, ignoring the post, pull through two loops, yarn over and pull through the two final loops. (See Figures 74 and 75.)

In abbreviated instructions, sometimes you'll come across *fp* for "front post." The directions may say,

" Dc, dc fp *, rep bet *s across, end dc."*

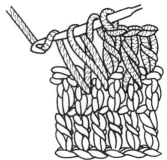

The meaning of that shorthand is, "Make an ordinary double crochet in the next stitch, make a double crochet around the front post of the stitch in the row below, then keep on alternating these two things all across the row, making one final double crochet in the last stitch."

Figure 75

You can go around not only the front of a post, but also *the back of a post.* This will create a raised ridge on the back of the fabric. Again, these instructions are for double crochet:

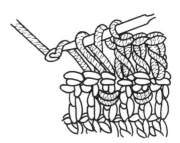

Yarn over and insert the hook from right to left, and from back to front, around the post of the stitch directly below in the previous row, yarn over and draw up a loop, yarn over, and ignoring the post, pull through two loops, yarn over and go through the two final loops. (See Figure 76.)

Figure 76

"Make a stitch around the back of the post of the previous row" is abbreviated simply *bp*.

The only difference in *working around the front or back post in triple crochet* is that you yarn over one more time before you begin and take one more step to work off the remaining loops. The finished effect is the same, only longer. And of course it could be done in double triple or triple triple crochet as well. The principle is the same.

By combining these two techniques on alternate rows on a flat, back-and-forth piece, a strong vertical raised line can be achieved. It is an easy way to add texture and visual interest.

YOU CAN MAKE A CIRCLE

Who made a rule that crocheters must stop at the end of a chain or row, turn around and go back? No one! Crocheting can be made into a circle, and it is easier to crochet in a flat circle than it is to knit in one. Knitters have to use four or five short, double-pointed needles to do it, the needles are always falling out and there is always an open place in the center of the circle. Crocheters have it easier with only the one hook, and there are two types of circles they can make.

Often a *single crochet closed circle* is begun by making a chain of two (remember that a single crochet stitch is one chain long), and then putting a bunch of single crochet stitches into the second chain from the hook. When you have as many single crochet as you need, you will fasten the first and last ones together with a slip stitch, and then travel up with a chain for the next round. Instructions might say,

> "Ch 2, 11 sc into 2nd ch from hk, join with sl st, ch 1 (first ch counts as one st)." (See Figure 77 for chart.)

> The number of stitches made into the center of the circle on the first round is determined by two things. 1) You have to have enough stitches so that the piece will lie flat, and 2) you need enough available stitches to be able to set up the pattern (whatever it may be) on the next row.

So don't be upset if one circle calls for 12 single crochet in order to become a hexagon and another pattern calls for 14 single crochet in order to become a true circle later on. The difference just means that someone was planning ahead.

Working into the second chain from the hook will make a tightly closed center of a circle of single crochet.

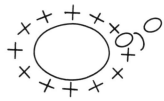

Chart 13

You can also make *a circle of single crochet with an open center.* This gives you more leeway in the number of stitches that will be available for setting up the pattern on the second round. You make a short chain to start with, and then join one end of the chain to the other with a slip stitch to form a ring. (See Figures 77 and 78.)

Next, you work directly into the ring, putting the hook into the open space at the center of the circle instead of into a stitch, making as many single crochet as will lie flat and be appropriate for the second round.

Directions for an open-center single crochet circle might read:

Figure 77

> *"Ch 7. Join with sl st to form a ring, ch 1 (counts as 1 sc). Work 23 sc into ring, join to first st with sl st, ch 1 (24 sts rem)."*

Rem is an abbreviation for the word "remain," and good instructions will tell you how many stitches you are supposed to end up with. It can drive even the very finest crocheters up the wall when the designer or printer makes shortcuts and the instructions don't tell you what you are intended to have accomplished.

The length of the original chain will determine the diameter of the open part of the circle and will vary according to what you or the designer wants.

A *double crochet closed circle* will begin with a chain of four. (Remember that a double crochet is three chains long.) You will then work however many double crochet stitches into the fourth chain from the hook as desired. When you are finished, you will join to the top of the three-chain length with a slip stitch. That original three-chain length will count as one stitch or post.

Figure 78

Of course you can make a *double crochet open circle.* You begin with a chain of however many stitches you need, and then join that circle in exactly the same way as above to form a ring. Next, you will travel up with chain stitches, which will count as one stitch or post to begin the second round. A traditional granny square can begin with a double crochet open circle as follows:

> *"Ch 4, join to form a circle. Rnd 1) Ch 3, 2 dc into circle, ch 2, * 3 dc into circle, ch 2, rep from * twice. Join with a sl st to 3rd ch of first ch-3."*

When making both open and closed center circles, you can crochet over the tail end of the beginning yarn to help to hide it in. If the area is long enough, that may be all the fastening-in you need to do for that tail end.

Thousands of variations are possible: open circles, closed circles, single, double and triple crochet stitches filled in tight or interspersed with lots of spaces. There is no limit to the number of combinations that can be created.

Before we leave the subject of circles, there are two more things I need to tell you. When you get to the point where you are inventing your own circles, for additional rounds, the rule of thumb is that every time you double the diameter of the circle, you must double the number of stitches around the circumference. (There is more about this in later chapters.)

The other thing is that you can also make a hollow tube of your crocheting. Make a loose foundation chain the length of the circumference of the desired tube. Join with a slip stitch, make a turning-chain the appropriate length for the stitch you are using, and then, without turning but going in the same direction, make a stitch into each stitch of the foundation chain. When you get back around to the beginning, you have two choices. You can just keep on going, making a continuous spiral, or you can join with a slip stitch, travel up with a turning-chain, and make a distinct new round.

YOU CAN GO BACKWARDS
FROM LEFT TO RIGHT

CRAB STITCH

You and your hook do not have to move from right to left across your crocheting. You can work *backwards, from left to right,* and form *the crab stitch.*

> *After completing a row of single crochet, do not turn the work around, chain one (for working room), *insert the hook into the next stitch to the right, and yo and draw up a long loop. Yarn over by hooking the yarn down from the back, and pull through both loops on the hook *. Proceed across the row, repeating between the *s.*

It is sometimes called *backwards single crochet,* but there are three things that make it different from ordinary single crochet: 1) Moving from left to right along the row, 2) drawing up a longer than normal loop, and 3) the direction from which you grab the yarnover.

Crab stitch over a base of regular single crochet gives a lovely rope-like braid finishing to many types of articles. I use it often.

CROSSED STITCHES

By working alternately forwards and backwards along a row you can make a series of "X"s on your fabric. They are usually made with either double or triple crochet stitches because you need their extra length to have enough working room. A single crochet just doesn't give you enough breathing room. The instructions might say:

*Sk 2 sts, dc in next st, ch 1, dc in first skipped st. Rpt from * across.*

The trick is that when you make the second double crochet in the first skipped stitch, you insert the hook behind the first double crochet (still from front to back, of course), and then you finish the stitch from behind the work.

PICOTS

Often *picots* are made by going backwards on a series of chain stitches and pulling a bunch of them together to form a lovely design. They are found frequently in Irish crochet, on edgings, and in the final row of a piece.

Simply take your hook backward and join the third chain from the hook with a slip stitch to the working loop on the hook; that is, yarn over and go through both loops on the hook at once.

Once again, the thumb and second finger of the left hand will position the needed chain stitch into place, and you will understand why I was so insistent in the beginning that you make your two hands perform together in concert.

Instructions for a three-chain picot might read:

Ch 7, insert hk into 3rd ch from hk, sl st . . .

Though three is the usual number of chain stitches used to make a picot, there is no rule that says it always has to be three. Picots can be made over any number of chain stitches—four or five or six or seven or more. Loop buttonholes are simply a picot of however many chains it takes to go around the button. (Often the picot-loop will be finished off with single crochet to make it easier for the fingers to grasp.)

YOU CAN REMOVE THE HOOK AND INSERT IT SOMEWHERE ELSE

When they are first told this, some students go into spasms of horror. "Take the hook out of the stitch?" they ask. "Won't the whole thing come apart?" Well, it would if you left the hook out for very long, but if you quickly insert it somewhere else, and draw that stitch and the dangling loop together rapidly with a slip stitch, nothing bad will happen and all kinds of good things can occur.

At any time in between stitches, not in the middle of making one, the hook can be removed and reinserted in another place.

POPCORN STITCH

The easiest way to explain it to you is to describe how you make a simple *popcorn stitch*. A popcorn is a raised group of stitches that adds interest and texture to flat crochet stitches.

Popcorns are easy to make. The only frightening thing about them is that beginners are afraid to remove the hook from the working loop. The trick to not losing your already-made stitches is to pull up a fairly long loop before you remove the hook. Usually the popcorns are made with double crochet stitches.

Over a base of whatever kind of stitches your fabric is made of, make five double crochet into the next stitch. Pull up a loop and slide your hook out of it. Reinsert your hook into the top of the first of the just-made five double crochet stitches. Let your hook catch the loop that you left hanging. Pull the loop through the top of the first double crochet. Though many instructions do not call for it, if you choose, you may make an additional tight slip stitch to firm up the thing and make sure that it stays securely puffed. (See Figures 79 and 80.)

Figure 79

Standard simplified instructions might read:

* Dc in ea of next 2 sts, [5 dc in next st, draw up a lp, remove hk and insert hk in top of first dc of 5-dc group, pull lp thru st (popcorn st made <PS>)], dc in ea of next 2 sts *, rep bet *s 6 times.

Here you are making a series of seven popcorn stitches separated by two double crochet stitches. These instructions do not call for that extra slip stitch that I like to add.

Figure 80

There are as many abbreviations for the simple, unassuming

"popcorn stitch" as there are designers and pattern writers. I have seen *pop*, *pc*, *Pc*, *PC*, and *PS* all used. When the procedure is first mentioned, the directions will usually tell you what the abbreviation is, as is done in the directions above.

But who says that popcorns must be made in only double crochet, or that they must contain five stitches? No one! If you wanted, you could make triple crochet popcorns of six or seven or more stitches. The imagination and the sense of creativity are the only limiting things.

ANOTHER WAY TO MAKE A PICOT

An alternative method of making a *picot* is by removing the hook. Some people find it faster and easier than going backward on the chain. Quickly make a chain of about 5 stitches and try it out.

Pull up a loop on your hook so that you can safely remove the hook. Insert the hook into the third chain from the loop and through the pulled-up loop. Make a firm and tight slip stitch, going through both the original loop and the chain st.

I have had you make a three-stitch picot, but the number three is not a hard and fast rule. You could make a two-stitch or however-many-stitch picot as you wished.

There will be other times and other places where you may be called upon to remove your hook from the working stitch and put it in somewhere else. Lovely interwoven and interlaced patterns can be achieved by doing this.

In this chapter, I've introduced you to a few of the most common places that you can take your hook fishing in other waters. By no means am I saying that these are the only places and fishing holes that exist. Some years ago when knitted Aran fisherman sweaters came into great popularity, hardbound and determined crocheters decided that they could imitate them. And they did, very successfully. In doing so they invented many more intricate maneuvers that can be achieved with your hook. I'm sorry that there isn't room here to show you all of them. There is no limit to the combination of stitches and the number of things that can be done with a hook and yarn. The only limiting factor is a narrow idea of creativity. With the basics given here, you can be as creative as you wish.

19

IMPROVISE AND INVENT

After I have taught my students for a series of weeks, at the final class I like to give them an exam. The purpose of the test is not to qualify them for further classes, but so that students will be assured that they really do know how to crochet, that they can read instructions, and that they can figure things out. Sometimes I give them a pattern for Queen Anne's lace (without a picture), and at other times I give them a problem to solve.

Pretend for a bit that you are at that final class. You were told to bring some Class C smooth classic knitting worsted (standard 4-ply), a hook that is of a size appropriate to the yarn and to your hands, and a tumbler from your kitchen. If you don't have them handy now, go and get them.

Your problem is to make a crocheted coaster to fit over the bottom and part way up the sides of that tumbler. Your foremother of crochet could do it by herself without a pattern, and so can you. The first thing to do, as with any kind of problem solving, is to study the task itself. Look at the tumbler. It is basically a cylinder that is open on one end and closed on the other. The most obvious answer for a coaster-cover is to make a circle the size of the bottom and then shape up the sides depending on the contours of the glass. We are after a tight fit so the coaster won't easily slide off the tumbler by itself. (Few of the students in the class will have brought exactly the same size and shape tumbler, so everyone is on his/her own.)

Make some kind of circle and fill it with some kind of stitches, open or closed, single or double crochet. (This is an "open book" test and you have permission to go back and look things up.) Be sure to put enough stitches into that first round so that the piece lies flat, and not so many that it ruffles and puckers. It doesn't matter what you do, just so you do it.

After joining with a slip stitch, travel up for the next round with an appropriate length of chain. (Do you remember how many chains long each stitch is?) You'll have to have some kind of increases in this second row or the piece will cup up and won't lie flat. How many of what kind is your choice. It will also depend on what kind of a circle you made in the first place. To increase, you can make two stitches in one, or a chain-space between stitches. Do anything you need to do, just make it lie flat.

Keep on making rounds until you have a circle that is the size of the bottom of the tumbler. Now stop and think what you want to do about covering the sides of the glass. You can do anything you want! Would you like the sides to be smooth and tight? Perhaps unincreased rounds of single crochet is your answer. Do you want to make strong vertical ridges by going around the front of the post of the double crochet stitch in the round below? Or would you like to have bumps and blobs of puff stitches or popcorns studding the sides of the coaster? Should those lumps and bumps sit one on top of another, or do you want them staggered, or forming a design, perhaps a square or a circle? *You can do anything you want to do!* So what if it doesn't turn out perfectly the first time, try again. The purpose of this learning lesson/test is to allow you to realize that you are master/mistress of your fate, and that your creativity and pride of accomplishment are things that you can control, just as your foremother of crochet did years ago.

This does not mean that you are never going to follow someone else's directions or plan. Of course you are; there is no point in reinventing the wheel. If someone before you has figured out how many stitches to begin with and how many increases to make to have enough stitches to make a certain design, go ahead and take what they have given you and build on that. But if that plan or design doesn't quite suit you and your needs, modify and change it. If there is an error in the instructions, rewrite them so that they will work out correctly. Your crocheting belongs to you!

As you continue through this book, learning a group of pattern stitches, motifs, and edgings that have already been carefully figured out by others before you, you will become familiar with some of the basic "rules of the road" of crochet techniques. And you will know that to get this or that effect, it is necessary to do thus and so. You will recognize that this shell should fit over that chain-space, or that, of the chain of five, three are for traveling to the next row. And when, in the future, you encounter errors, as you most certainly will, you will know how to handle them. You will know what the designer intended, even if there was a flub somewhere between the concept of the idea, the writing and typesetting of the page, and your reading of it. You will know how to make the patterns work, and you will be unafraid to add what is missing or to subtract what is not necessary to get the effect you are after. Your crocheting belongs to you; do whatever you need to do to get the effect you want. Don't be bound by someone else's mistakes. You have the right and the freedom to make your own mistakes and your own successes. And you cannot have successes without mistakes. I know that out of ten things I design, three of them will be absolute duds. But that doesn't keep me from continuing to design. We must acknowledge our mistakes and go on.

MAKING IT WORK

Years ago, when I was an instructor in a large department store in California, a yarn company came out with a kit and pattern for "hot pants," the short-shorts that were all the rage that season. They were darling! But they didn't fit many people quite right. I knew from my seamstress days that what they needed was a dart at the waist. With a couple of my favorite patrons beside me, I sat at the worktable and began to write out the instructions to put a dart into the shorts. "Row 1) Work across 35 sts, dec in next 2 sts, work across rem 23, ch 1, turn. Row 2) Sc in ea of next . . ." Just then an older woman with a very serene and sweet face happened by and asked the three of us what we were doing. I explained that we were writing instructions to put a dart in a pattern. "Oh," she said and went on about her shopping. A half an hour later, we were still struggling with the row-by-row instructions, "Row 8) Sc in each of next 28 or is it 29 sts . . . will a single decrease every row be enough?" when the same woman passed us again. She leaned over the table and smiled. "You are going to an awful lot of work," she said. "The pants will fit better with a dart," I responded. "Of course they will," she said, "But you don't have to go through all that work to do it.

> "Just take a paper dress pattern for whatever you want, lay your crocheting over it, and shape your piece as you go. Make a decrease wherever there is a dart. See if a single or double decrease makes the piece the same as the pattern. Slip stitch and move in wherever there is an indentation such as an armhole or crotch. Make your piece fit the pinned-together pattern. Do what you have to do to make it work."

I sat back and laughed loud and long. Of course! Why not? Why struggle with writing it out? Do what you have to do to make it work! I have no idea who the woman was. I never saw her again. But she gave me a precious gift and I am passing it on to you. In making crocheted garments, you are not at the mercy of printed shorthand instructions. Find either a completed garment or a dress pattern like the one you want. (If you use a paper pattern, Scotch-tape the darts together and cut off the seam allowances.) Begin at the bottom and simply make your crocheted piece conform to the garment or the pattern.

You must understand that you will never see these kinds of instructions in a magazine or pattern leaflet. Editors do not like to print wishy-washy/make-do/make-it-work directions. They need to have instructions that say: Row 1) Blap, blap, blap; Row 2) Blap, blap, bloop; Row 3) Blap, bloop, blap, giving you each and every row separately and distinctly, *even if they don't fit any human body—yours in particular*. (Another reason that these kinds of directions are not printed is that with any variation at all, there will be a corresponding variation in the amount of yarn used.) But just because you are unlikely to see "make it do" patterns at your local yarn supplier does not mean you cannot crochet wondrous things on your own. (If it doesn't come out quite right, admit your mistake, rip it out, do it over or do something else.)

IF IT ISN'T RIGHT, CHANGE IT!

Once long ago there was a gorgeous pattern in one of the women's magazines for an exquisite Irish rose crochet blouse. The model who wore it was skinny and flat-chested. One of my patrons made it, following the directions exactly. She brought it into the store to show me. In the box it was handsome. But when she put it on, we all just about died laughing. Sitting prominently on each of her bosoms was a huge Irish rose. "I feel like a striptease dancer with pasties," she said. "Is there anything I can do about it?"— meaning the placement of those large roses. Of course there was. After the shoulder joining row was removed, we added more rows of fishnet with lots of picots to the top of the blouse. Doing that lowered the lovely roses to a less striking position.

If it is not working out, work on it in a different way.

A dear friend of mine had a crocheted tablecloth that she had inherited from her grandmother. She never used it because it didn't fit her table, "And though I can crochet, I would never be able to match that thread in size and color. I'd like to use it, but it's hopeless."

"No, it is not," I said. "Your good china has blue flowers on it, doesn't it?"

"Yes, but what has that got to do with it?"

"You could crochet more medallions just like the other ones, only with blue. Add them all around the edges and, presto, the table-cloth is the right size." And so she did.

Triangular shawls are a good example of what can be done with adaptation. Long ago a patron made one from a pattern in a women's magazine. She brought it in to show me and to tell me how disappointed she was with it. "I wore it to a cocktail party the other night. It was a mess. It kept falling off my shoulders. I'm sorry I wasted my time making it."

"Show me what happens," I told her. She draped it over her shoulders, and sure enough it slid right off. "Do you have any more yarn?" I asked.

"Just this little ball," she replied. "What do you want to do with it?"

"Let's make a row or two of single crochet with lots of decreases in it on the front in the area where it is supposed to rest between your shoulders. That should tighten it up and keep it from slipping off. It is such a pretty thing that it would be a shame not to use it." The trick worked. But we had learned a valuable lesson. The next time a patron wanted to make a triangular shawl, we put an increase in the center back so that the thing looked more like a boomerang than a triangle. It lay perfectly and didn't slide off her shoulders.

Just remember, if you can make a simple coaster without a pattern, you can solve most of the problems that you will ever encounter in crochet.

20
OOPS!

Mistakes are going to happen. Nothing in this wonderful wiggly-wobbly world always runs smoothly without error or imperfection. Machines hiccup and cough; computers glitch; genes mutate and change; predatory animals pounce and miss; people stumble and fall; crocheters leave out a stitch, make too many, or do the wrong thing. An error-proof world is not possible; God did not set it up that way.

And there is nothing wrong with making a mistake. In a way, mistakes are the only way we progress and change. Without them nothing would ever change, and if nothing can ever change, nothing can ever get any better. If the same mistake recurs often enough, it becomes a pattern in itself, and that may be okay. It may be all right if we acknowledge it, accept it, and integrate it into the overall scheme of things.

Still, a mismade, incorrect, omitted, or extra stitch *can* cause problems in our crocheting. We need to stop now and talk about them, before we go on to the following chapters of pattern stitches in which errors, when they occur, can cause problems that may disfigure our project. So far, we have been talking about the stitches themselves and the plain flat fabrics they produce. Next, we will be talking about mixing up those stitches and arranging them in special ways. Mistakes can stand out like a red sock in a load of white washing.

If we deny that a mistake is there and just go on and gloss over it, the error may come back to haunt us and ruin the otherwise glorious effect of our work. A missing petal on a rose can scream "imperfect" at us. An increase not made can affect the size of a piece; we may end up with a five-sided piece instead of a six-sided one. Extra, unintended increases can cause our article to ripple and ruffle where we wanted a flat surface. Errors have to be reckoned with, and the sooner we find them, the easier they are to cope with.

Stop frequently and inspect and admire your work. The more you actually stop and look at what you have done, the quicker you will find those inevitable errors.

When a mistake is found, it is time to halt and assess the situation. There is no point in going further until you decide what you want to do about it. And there are lots of different ways of handling errors depending on what they are, how long ago they were made, and, most important, how you feel about them.

You must know your own personality in order to cope with errors, because the kind of person you are will determine what you will choose to do about the mistake.

Some of you are perfectionists and idealists and insist on an absolutely perfect finished product. For you the only way is to correct the mistake in one way or another and make the piece flawless. And that is okay, if that is the kind of person you are.

Some of you are pragmatic realists. "I know that the mistake is there, but unless someone inspected it with a magnifying glass, no one else would ever know about it. I'm not going to do it over. I'll just put this motif at the underarm of the blouse, and no one will ever see it." And that is perfectly all right if you are that kind of person.

Some of you are more relaxed, more interested in the joy of doing the project than in the finished results. To you an error that does not bend the article terribly out of shape is perfectly acceptable. "Who cares about a few stitches more or less? Who cares if one side of the pillow is longer than the other? Making it is the fun of it." And it is okay if you feel that way.

Only when you accept the kind of person that you are, can you look at the things that can be done about the mistake and decide what to do.

LEAVE MISTAKES IN

There are times when mistakes don't matter. In Chapter 24, "Precious Little Jewels To Add," a couple of loop-petals more or less on the daisy or the chrysanthemum won't make any difference in the finished product. (Only a botanist would know how many petals are on a real chrysanthemum.) On the final rows of a doily-turned-pillow cover, a few loops or stitches more or less aren't going to affect the outcome.

If a mistake does not affect the end result, if it does not show, it can be left in.

Even if an error, such as gaining an extra half-shell at the edge of an afghan, which can easily happen, does make the piece one half inch wider, it is not going to matter when the finished thing is cuddled around your knees on a cold winter evening, unless the imperfection bothers you.

MAKE A PATTERN OF YOUR MISTAKES

I once started the next-to-last row of a foundation-chain-edging doing the wrong thing. The edging was miles and miles long, and I didn't notice the mistake for a long while. I looked at it and said, "My pattern of stitches is just as interesting as the designer's." So I made a value judgment and kept it.

Anything done over and over becomes a pattern, even a mistake. If the pattern is acceptable to you, just keep on doing it.

It is mistakes, not necessity, that are the mother of invention. If there was anything our foremothers really needed, it was disposable diapers. It was not the need that produced them. Some woman made a mistake and forgot to take cloth diapers along with her. She used paper instead. Thank goodness she made a mistake!

MAKE A COMPENSATING INCREASE FOR AN OMITTED STITCH

In every crocheter's life there will come the day when she discovers that she forgot to make a stitch. Say, for example, she was supposed to make "4 dc in the ch-2 loop," and made only three instead. She discovers it the next time across when she is supposed to make "1 sc in each of next 4 dc." Often she can then make two stitches in the center stitch of the three double crochet to end up with the required four.

Often a forgotten stitch or two can be inconspicuously added in the middle of the area on the next row or round. Just make two stitches in one.

The crocheter will have made up for the stitch she forgot with an increase. It probably won't show in the finished article, and it is an easy way to solve a simple mistake. On the other hand, if she were to deny the error, and go on, continuing to make only three stitches where there should have been four, she may be in for trouble.

If the crocheter made only two double crochet in the chain-two loop instead of four, simple increases may not be the answer. She may need to open it up as described later in this chapter.

MAKE A CORRESPONDING DECREASE FOR AN EXTRA STITCH

Just as you can make up for a forgotten stitch, you can also get rid of an extra unwanted one. Simply decrease it.

If the crocheter accidentally made five double crochet in the chain-two loop from the example above, and discovers it on the next row when she is to make "1 sc in each of the next 4 dc," she can make a single single crochet decrease in the center stitch and end up with the correct number.

It is usually best not to skip a stitch to get rid of it. In the center of the piece, the skipped stitch will cause a hole. At the edge, it will cause a stair-step.

And don't try to get rid of two extra stitches at the same time by making a double decrease. You may get a bump. It is usually better to decrease one stitch at a time.

OPEN IT UP

I remember the time I was making a soft, shell-pink shawl in the car as we were driving down the California coast from Gaviota Pass to Malibu. Though I knew the highway well, I spent more time watching the crashing surf than I did watching and admiring my crocheting. The shawl was one that started at the back of the neck and every row grew increasingly longer with increases at the center back and the ends of each row. Nearing the end of the shawl, when the rows were very long, I discovered that on the previous row I had forgotten to make the center back increase. It had to be there. I could not go on without it. Something had to be done, and I did not choose to rip out those long, long rows just for a simple little increase. I cut it open.

When you have forgotten an important increase or decrease, cluster or group, on the previous row, you can cut the work open and put in or take out the forgotten or unwanted stitches.

With the scissors from your supply pouch, clip a single thread in the area that needs attention. Using your tapestry needle as a pick, carefully undo the stitches in both directions until the threads are long enough to be fastened in later.

Using new yarn, insert your hook into the last good "saved" stitch and then, going in the direction in which the row was made, do what needs to be done. Make the stitches as they should have been made in the first place. When you reach the spot where you stopped undoing the stitches, join with a slip stitch and fasten off.

Later, you can go back and hide-in the tail ends of yarn.

The decision whether to cut it open or rip it back is a value judgment *you* will have to make. How much time will be spent in ripping back and reworking as opposed to splicing-in may be the deciding factor. But there is something else as well. Sometimes you may opt for the challenge of opening it up, as I did, just for the sake of doing it. Remember that the reason for crocheting is to feel good about ourselves. If opening it up will make you proud of yourself, do it, even if it takes more time.

RIP BACK AND START OVER

Often mistakes are made at the beginning of a piece, where the basic elements of the design are being set up. That mistake is disastrous. If the foundation of a building is made wrong, the walls will come tumbling down. And it is not always our fault. Errors are easy to make when the instructions tell us to repeat a certain set of things "around" or "across," not telling us how many times that will be. If the directions do not tell us that we *must* have eight chain-loops, we can easily end up with only seven and then the design will not work.

At times like this there may be no way to cope with the mistake except to take it out. Then we must grit our teeth and rip it out.

Mark the spot with a safety pin through two adjacent stitches. Rip out all the stitches that follow the mistake, winding up the yarn as you go. Then start again at that place and do it over.

Now take a pen or pencil and mark on the directions that at the end of that row or round there *must* be eight chain-loops. If you ever decide to make the item again, you will be two giant steps ahead.

TRY TO AVOID ERRORS

As you work your way through the following chapters, learning new pattern stitches, try to avoid making errors. Check yourself as you go. It is your project and it is up to *you* to do the best you can.

Stop frequently and count. Do you have enough loops or clusters or groups? (No fairy godmother is going to add the missing ones for you while you sleep.)

Does it look right? Are you understanding what the designer intended to say in the directions? Sometimes I, a professional teacher, have to do a thing half a dozen times before I understand what the designer intended me to do. It isn't fair; bad instructions are not your fault, but the finished effect is your responsibility. It is like the Internal Revenue Service, saying "You must follow our advice, and if our directions are wrong, we'll penalize you."

Stop frequently and measure the piece. Lay it out flat and put a tape measure around it. Don't fall into the trap of making a thing too large or too small. No baby in the world is going to shrink just so that he or she will fit into that darling sacque and cap you are making. Just because the designer called it a "six months" size doesn't mean every six-month-old child can squeeze into it. Measure the child; measure the piece (and guesstimate how long it will take you to finish it).

If an item is too small, you have two options. Don't just finish it as it is. You can start over with a larger hook, or you can use more stitches (or rows), depending on the pattern. The other side of the coin is equally true. If a thing is too large, you can do it over with a smaller hook. Or you can make either fewer stitches or rows according to the design.

Stop frequently and admire your work, and admire yourself for having done it. Pride of accomplishment is the best source of self-correction.

If the piece is not perfect, or if you can't admire it here and now, do something about it. Crochet stitches do not improve with age like fine wine. Mistakes won't mellow out. The stitches can never look better in the future than they do now.

Whether mistakes are the hiccups of machines, glitches of computers, misplaced steps that cause us to fall, or errors in crochet, they are going to occur. The only problem that mistakes can ever cause comes when we fail to admit and acknowledge them, honestly assess what damage (if any) they may cause, and understand how we personally feel about that damage. Only then can we do what is necessary to either live with them, or correct them.

21
FANCY THAT!

A SMALL COLLECTION OF PLAIN AND FANCY PATTERN STITCHES

Making neat and even rows of just the same stitch over and over again is boring, and not much fun for the eye to look at either. Thank goodness we don't always have to do the same thing. The number of different things that we can do, however, is endless. To put them all down would take volumes and volumes of nothing but fancy pattern stitch instructions, and that would defeat the purpose of this book.

Instead, what I have done in this chapter is to simply walk you through, with both plain English and abbreviated instructions, and charts and photos, some of the very simplest and fancy flat-fabric pattern stitches. Along the way, I will suggest simple variations for you to try on your own after you have gotten the basic idea. Whether you are a beginner or an experienced crocheter, you are advised to work through the pattern stitches that follow in the order in which they are presented. I have set them up to follow a logical progression from easy to more intricate. What you learn from one pattern stitch you will carry with you to help you on the next.

SOME TERMS DEFINED

Before we begin, however, we need to define some terms that are used in dealing with fancy pattern stitches:

odd: a number that is not divisible by two. Three, five and seven are all odd numbers.

even: a number that can be divided by two. Four, six, and twenty-four are all even numbers.

repeats [rep(s) or rpt(s)]: the number of stitches or rows that it takes to complete a pattern. Also a completed pattern.

plus: the number of stitches to be added to the required multiple to form the end-of-the-row-stitches, which are sometimes called the *selvage.*

By this time, from what you have already read, you know about *parentheses ( ), brackets [ ], asterisks* * * and other symbols such as *daggers* † †, *hashmarks* / / / / and *stars* ★★. A series of directions enclosed in them is either to be done all in one place, or to be repeated over and over again.

From here on the words begin to get fuzzy. Not eveyone always agrees on the same definition. The words "multiples," "clusters," and "groups" can all be synonymous, or different designers and editors can give each of them specialized meanings, sometimes using all three words in a single sentence. Don't get upset! Usually just making the thing and seeing it finished will make the meaning clear.

multiple(s) [mtpl(s)]: The number of stitches required to make a certain pattern. Also the result of multiplication, as "the pattern is a multiple of 6." A set of stitches.

cluster(s) [cl(s)]: a bunch of stitches, a group of stitches gathered or occurring close together, such as six double crochets all made into the same stitch.

group(s) [gp(s)]: a set of stitches that make up a unit of the design—"3 dc, ch 1, 3 dc all in the next st," might be considered a group.

In the specific instructions that make up this chapter, as much as possible I will give the "multiple" and the "plus" stitch numbers so that you can make however much of the fancy pattern stitch that you want to.

For clarity, so that you can see the details of the finished fabric, the following examples are made in #10 crochet cotton. This is not to suggest that it is the only kind of yarn to use. It is just that the camera can see it clearly.

MESH FABRICS

Sometimes I think God was asleep at the switch when She created me. She gave me more curiosity than energy, so when I saw a book of "500 Distinctive Crochet Stitches" advertised, my curiosity propelled me and I sent for it. "Think of it! 500 different pattern stitches all in one book. I can explore them all without going to the library or leafing through magazines," I said to myself as I waited for the new godsend to come.

When the book arrived, I felt cheated, exploited, and insulted all at the same time. Yes, there were 500 crochet pattern stitches in it, but most of them weren't "distinctive" or "different." Most were simple variations of the mesh fabric stitch.

What is mesh? It is " * chain one, skip one stitch, work one stitch in each of the next so many stitches, repeat from *." Row 2 and all the other rows are the same—just line it up and make a mesh on top of a mesh. That is all there is to it.

This example is made of double crochet and there are four stitches between meshes. There is a turning chain (which counts as one stitch) and a double crochet at the beginning of each row. At the end of each row there are two double crochet. The multiple is 5 + 7. (See Photo 1.)

Ch 32 (5 × 5 = 25 + 7 = 32);

*Row 1) Dc in 4th ch from hk, *ch 1, sk 1 ch, 1 dc in ea of next 4 ch. Rep from * across, ending ch 1, sk 1 ch, dc in ea of last 2 ch, ch 3, turn.*

*Row 2 and all following rows) Dc in first dc, * ch 1, sk 1, 1 dc in ea of next 4 dc. Rep from * across, ending ch 1, sk 1, dc in next dc and in top of t-ch, ch 3, turn.*

Rep row 2 for pat st.

Photo 1

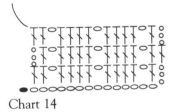

Chart 14

A chart for mesh fabric stitch would look as follows at left (see Chart 14).

Mesh is the simplest, easiest way to make an interesting fabric. It is relaxing and almost mindless because your fingers will soon memorize the spacing. The holes over holes will practically appear by themselves and you will have a lovely reversible fabric.

But mesh does not have to be just double crochet with four stitches between. It can also be any other stitch with however many stitches in between. That is why I was thoroughly disappointed in the book of 500 pattern stitches.

To help you understand why I felt so cheated, get out a pocket calculator, one that will go into the millions. Start figuring out for yourself how many kinds of mesh fabric there can be. Pattern #1 is one stitch between the mesh, pattern #2 is two stitches between the mesh, pattern #3 is three stitches between the mesh, and keep on going. Next, space the meshes out regularly but unevenly like "stitch-mesh-stitch-stitch-mesh" and put all that into the calculator. Now multiply that huge number of patterns by the number of kinds of stitches you could use. (Single crochet + double crochet + half double + triple + double triple + triple triple = 6). Got it? Does your calculator have any room left in it? Now put a plain row in between the mesh rows. Again you have six possibilities for each of the other patterns. Also, you can make mesh in geometric shapes such as squares and diamonds and such. The number you will come up with is phantasmagoric and mind-boggling, but *it is still all just mesh!* Hundreds of patterns in the book that was to satisfy my curiosity about fancy crochet stitches were just mesh.

I hope that this introduction to and explanation of mesh stitches will allow you, when you encounter it, to say, "Oh, this is just double crochet mesh with five stitches in between. Why didn't they just say so?"

FILET CROCHET

The next easiest of all pattern stitches, filet crochet, is just square spaces and places. The places are filled in solid with three double crochet, and the empty spaces are made by 2-chain spaces followed by a single post of one double crochet (which holds the hole upright). Marvelous patterns can be made by the placement of filled places and empty spaces. Birds and flowers and alphabets and scenes and geometric abstracts are just a few of the things you can do.

Some people insist that you must insert your hook into each of the chain stitches of the chain-spaces. Doing this takes time and dexterity. Other crocheters don't bother and are happy just to make double crochets in the holes of the chain-spaces themselves. On a swatch, try both ways and see for yourself which you prefer. Always remember that your crocheting must please you both in the doing and in the finished product. It is up to you to make yourself happy.

Usually, row-by-row instructions are not given for filet crochet. Instead, a chart of solid and blank squares is given and the printers of the pattern just expect you to know what to do. Sometimes you will be told how many stitches should be in the foundation chain. At other times you will be left to your own devices.

The basic multiple for filet crochet (see Photo 2) is three stitches plus three chains for a turning chain. First, decide how many squares you want. Multiply that number by three. Add three more for the t-ch. Let's try a checkerboard pattern of 9 squares with the first square a solid one; $9 \times 3 = 27$; $27 + 3 = 30$.

Ch 30. (But remember that it never hurts to make a few too many chains for the foundation. If you don't need them, you can cut them off.) A chart for filet crochet would look as follows:

Photo 2

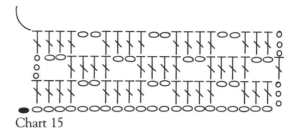

Chart 15

Row 1) Dc in 4th ch from hk, * dc in ea of next 3 ch (solid place made), ch 2, sk 2, dc in next ch (open space made) *, rep bet *s across, ending dc in ea of next 3 ch (final solid place made), ch 3, turn. (9 squares beg and ending with a solid one.)

Row 2) Ch 2, sk 3 dc, dc in next st, * dc in ea of next 3 sts, ch 2, sk 2, dc in next st *, rep bet *s across, ch 3, turn. (9 squares beg and ending with an empty one.)

Row 3) (This is just like row 1 except that we are making sts into sts instead of into chs. Some editors make the designer spell it out in abbreviated shorthand. Some crocheters think that this is an insult and wish the designer would just say it in plain English.) * Dc in ea of next 3 sts, ch 2, sk 2, dc in next st, * rep bet *s across, ending dc in ea of last 3 sts, fasten off.

If we were to start with an empty hole in making a similar checkerboard of nine squares, we would need to add two extra chains to our foundation to travel across the top of our empty hole. We would then make our first double crochet stitch in the eighth chain from the hook. 3 sts for the bottom, + 3 for the turning chain + 2 for the top of the empty hole = 8.

Not all charts for filet crochet have straight-up-and-down edges. Many get wider or narrower as you go along. If you will always remember that each square is three stitches wide and three chains tall, you will never get lost or wonder how many chains to make as your piece grows wider. To widen a piece, make sufficient extra chains at the end of a row to add on the extra squares. To indent and make the piece get narrower, at the beginning of a row, slip stitch over the top of the number of squares that you want to get rid of and continue on. To indent at the end of a row, simply turn the work around before you get to the end.

Household furnishings of filet crochet are traditionally made with rather fine cotton thread in white or ecru. Wearing apparel may also be made of filet in all kinds of yarn. Regardless of which you choose to make, remember that in order to be seen and appreciated, the design will need a contrasting background. "Light is only light when contrasted with dark," is an old art school adage. What you place *under* the filet piece will influence the effect that it gives. The effort put into a white piece on a white background may be lost for lack of contrast.

The fabric of filet crochet is reversible, but whether or not you choose to reverse it will depend on the design you have chosen. It lies flat and does not curl or roll, though a finish border is often added. Filet can be made in the round, forming a tube that will become a dress, blouse, or lampshade.

AN OPEN "V"

There are other kinds of open spaces that can be made in our crocheted fabric besides simple squares. One of the easiest things to do is to make a series of "V"s across a row. Two stitches of the base are skipped and then two stitches separated by a chain-one space are placed in the next stitch. This grouping is then repeated all across the row. You can use half double crochet, double, triple or even double triple stitches to make the series of "V"s. Let's do our swatch with double crochet because they are long enough to see what we are doing, but short enough to be quick to make.

The multiple of stitches is three, plus one extra chain for a post on the end of the row, and a turning chain of three (for double crochet) at the beginning of the row. If we want 10 "V"s we will need 3 × 10 = 30, + 1 + 3 = 34 for a foundation chain. (See Photo 3.)

Ch 34.

Row 1) Dc in 4th ch from hk, sk 1 ch, *[dc, ch 1, dc] in next ch st, sk 2 ch *, rep bet *s across, ending last rep sk 1, dc in last ch, ch 3, turn. (There is a post on each end of the row and there are 10 "V"s across.)

Row 2) (Make a new "V" in the ch-1 sp at the top of each old "V" across with a post at each end of the row.) * [Dc, ch 1, dc] in ch-1 sp *, rep bet *s across, ending dc in top of t-ch.

Rep row 2 for pat st.

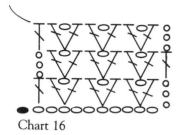

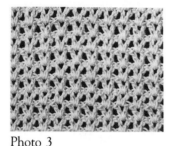

Chart 16

Photo 3

A chart for an open "V" would look as follows at left (see Chart 16).

A "V" fabric of single, half double, or double crochets, in a smooth classic worsted yarn of either sport or worsted weight, makes a nice fabric for sweaters. Made in triple crochet of a #10 crochet cotton, it is a lacy pattern. For variation, you can make a row of single (or double) crochet between the rows of "V"s for a heavier fabric that is still textured and airy. Regardless of the yarn you choose, "V"s can be made in the round forming a tube. (Of course, in making a tube you don't need the end-post selvage stitches.)

When a "V"d fabric is made flat, going back and forth, there will be no right or wrong side. If it is made in a tube, there will be a difference in the appearance of the inside and the outside.

If you choose to make your "V"s of one of the longer stitches, such as double or triple crochet, open space will show through the fabric and you will want to be choosy about the background for the item.

TWO SIMPLE DOUBLE CROCHET SHELLS

How can anything so common and so easy be so lovely? That is part of the beauty of crocheting. Even the simplest and easiest things are exquisite! And simple shell stitches are a good example.

Shells are made by putting a glop of stitches all into one place and then letting them fan out by skipping other stitches.

The glop can be solid or have a chain space in the center. The fan can be completely extended to make a half circle or it can be only partially opened. The variety is endless, but, for the sake of learning, let us play with shells of four double crochets separated in the middle by a chain-one space and then fastened down by a single crochet.

Our multiple is 6: (2 dc + 1 ch + 2 dc + 1 sc = 6). (We'll talk about what to do on the ends when we decide what the second row will be.) As for our foundation chain, I think that every designer in the world has a different idea. Some want you to skip one chain in between the cluster and the fastening down. Others say you must skip two. And still there are others who say that you skip two before the cluster and one after it. But let's make life easy and try two for this example. Later on you can do whatever you want.

Therefore, for this example our multiple is 6: 2 + 1 + 2 + 1 = 6. To make a swatch of 6 shells:

Ch 36.

*Row 1) * Sk 2 ch, [2 dc, ch 1, 2 dc] all in the next stitch (shell made), sk 2 ch, sc in the next st *, rep bet *s across, turn. (6 shells made.)*

Let's make a fabric that is *airy and light* by adding row after row of shells in the chain-one space. We'll need a turning chain of two or three to travel up to the next row. Here again designers differ on the number needed. Try three to start with, and if you find that it is too long to suit you, try two instead. (See Photo 4.)

*Row 2 and all following rows) Ch 3, * shell in ch-1 sp of previous row *, rep bet *s across, turn.*

A chart for this would look as follows:

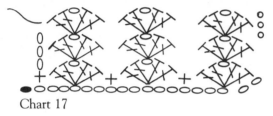

Chart 17

Photo 4

Made back and forth, a shell-on-shell pattern makes a reversible fabric. If you decide to make it tubular, there will be a definite difference in the two sides. I've seen lovely blouses and christening dresses made of shell on shell in fine cotton. I've also seen afghans in worsted-weight yarn made of it. Can you imagine a neck scarf of the finest wool in fingering or sport weight? I can.

A common variation is to make fastening posts of either double crochet or half double crochet in between the shells. That makes an even more airy effect.

But we can also make our shelled fabric *solid and sturdy* by making the second row of shells into the single crochet fastening of the previous row. (See Photo 5.) Here we will have a half of a shell at each end of the row to keep the edges even. It goes like this:

*Row 2) Ch 3, dc in last sc (½ shell), * sc in ch-1 sp, shell in sc*, rep bet *s across, ending sc in ch-1 sp, 2 dc in last st of the previous row, (½ shell), turn.*

*Row 3) (This is basically the same as row 1 except that we are working over an established row instead of a foundation chain. It differs from row 2 in that there are no half shells at the end.) Ch 3, * shell in sc, sc in ch-1 sp *, rep bet *s across, turn.*

Rep rows 2 & 3 for pat st.

Personally, I prefer to follow charts and photos. I hate going all through a row of abbreviated instructions only to find there is only one minor thing different on the whole row. The designer could just have told me that and saved the eyestrain of trying to keep my place on the page and do what the directions say on my piece, refocusing my eyes through my bifocals all the while. I think any pattern that doesn't give a photo or a chart is a cop-out and is almost as wishy-washy as a politician! A chart for the above shell variation would look as follows:

Chart 18

Photo 5

You don't even need a pattern to make an afghan of double crochet shells. You can make it small enough for a newborn baby in fingering- or sport-weight yarn. Or, you can make it large enough for your favorite football player in either worsted (4-ply) or bulky weight. Begin with a foundation chain approximately ⅓ longer than you want the finished piece to be wide. (The chain will shrink as you make the beginning row.) Set up your first row of shells until it is as wide as you want the finished afghan to be (30-36" for a baby, 40-45" for an adult). Now decide if you want the thing to be airy or more solid and make your second row accordingly. Just keep on going until the blanket is as long as you want it (30-45" for a baby, 72-82" for an adult).

Changing color and making different rows of shaded or contrasting colors dramatically alters the finished appearance of the afghan. You can change colors every row, every other row, every third row, or every six inches. So long as you are consistent, it doesn't matter what you choose to do. The result will be lovely, much appreciated, and uniquely yours. Try it and see; give your creativity a chance to blossom.

Please understand that shells are not limited to the formulas given above. Just as Mother Nature did not limit the creatures on the floor of the ocean to one kind, you are not limited to [2 dc, ch 1, 2 dc] shells. Think of the bounty of the sea and imagine what else you could do—more open with more than one chain in the chain-space in the center, more solid with 5-hdc shells, flowery [3 tr, ch 1, 3 tr] shells, spacious [(dtr, ch 1) 7 times] shells, are just a few. Have fun! Experiment!

If you choose to make a blouse of very long and very open shells, you will have to be careful of the kind and color of the undergarment you wear with it. Your slip or camisole will become a design element of the blouse.

COMBINING A SHELL AND "V"

Now that you are familiar with both shells and "V"s, what do you suppose would happen if you were to combine them across a row? You would get a very interesting and lovely fabric. And you have two very obvious options. You can make 1) shell on shell, and "V" on "V," or 2) shell on "V," and "V" on shell. Whichever you decide to do, the first row will be the same.

I am giving instructions for double crochet shells and V's, but they don't have to be limited to that. Half doubles, triples, and double triples can all be used. Each different stitch will have a different appearance. All will be beautiful.

When you know the basic geography of the pattern stitch, you can vary it all you want.

And that is what this chapter is all about, the basic geography and the maps, if you will, of pattern stitches. Your foremother in crochet had to figure out a lot of this for herself. You can build on the knowledge and the work of others.

Our shells will not fan out completely this time; they will sit right next to the "V"s without an attaching place. So let's try a multiple of 6 plus 8 for the turning chain and the end post.

Ch 38 (5 × 6 = 30 + 8 = 38.)

Row 1) (Beg with a "V") [dc, ch 1, dc] in 5th ch from hk, * sk 2 ch, (now make a shell) [2 dc, ch 1, 2 dc] in next ch, sk 2 ch, (and another "V") [dc, ch 1, dc] in next ch *, rep bet *s across, ending sk 2 ch, dc (for an end post), ch 3, turn. (5 shells and 6 "V"s, beg and ending with a "V.")

You are getting to be a pro at this. You take the shorthand instructions in stride, and you understand what is supposed to be happening. Next thing I know, you'll be inventing your own pattern stitches, leaving me standing at the gate post, yarn and hook in hand, writing out simple instructions. (Which is just what I want.)

Now try making *a new "V" in the old "V" and a new shell in the old shell.* (See Photo 6.)

Row 2) * [Dc, ch 1, dc] in next ch-1 sp, [2 dc, ch 1, 2 dc in next ch-1 sp *, rep bet *s across, ending [dc, ch 1, dc] in next ch-1 sp, dc in last st, ch 3, turn.*

Rep row 2 for pat st.

A chart for the above shell variation would look as follows:

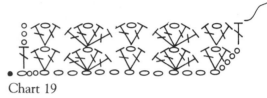
Chart 19

Photo 6

This pattern stitch gives a busy look, reflecting light and capturing shadow. It is more airy than just shells on shells, and it has a more interesting texture than just "V"s on "V"s. In a slightly fuzzy, heathery yarn, wouldn't it look lovely?

To make a *shell on "V," and a "V" on shell* (see Photo 7), the second row of the pattern would read:

Row 2) * [2 Dc, ch 1, 2 dc] (shell) in next ch-1 sp, [dc, ch 1, dc] ("V") in next ch-1 sp *, rep bet *s across, ending [2 dc, ch 1, 2 dc] (shell) in last ch-1 sp, dc in last st, ch 3, turn.*

Rep row 2 for pat st.

A chart for the above shell variation would look as follows:

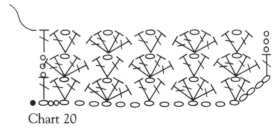
Chart 20

Photo 7

Strong vertical lines are produced by this pattern stitch. You could make up-and-down panels on the front or the sleeves of an otherwise plain sweater, and it would be outstanding.

Made flat, back and forth, shells and "V"s are a reversible pattern stitch. Of course, either of these two pattern stitches can be worked in tubular form without the end posts. The strong vertical effect is even more pronounced when you work in a tube, because all the stitches are made from the same side.

BRUNSWICK STEW

In Georgia, we are fond of our Brunswick Stew. It's a little of this; it's a little of that. And every cook will use a slightly different combination of ingredients. Like the cooks in Georgia, you can make a Brunswick Stew of crochet stitches.

To begin our recipe, let's take time out now to think about what you've already learned here, and also about that other book of 500 pattern stitches. You now know about plain stitch fabric, mesh, filet, "V"s, and shells. You recognize them for what they are when you see them in either printed instructions, charts, or photos.

Juggle those basic ingredients and you have the basis of most flat crochet pattern stitches.

Why is this important? When you know it, *the mystery and mystique of instructions is gone.* "There is no new thing under the sun." You can say, "Oh, this is just blah, blah, blah. No sweat!" And when you know this, you can change it.

"To make it wider, I can just throw in some extra mesh on each side."

"To make it narrower, I can just leave off some of the shells in the center."

And we also have already talked about combining shells and "V"s (sometimes with plain rows thrown in between). If I told you to make an afghan of [6 dc, 3 (2 dc, ch 1, 2 dc) shells, 6 multiples of 4-dc mesh, 6 "V"s, 6 multiples of 4-dc mesh, 3 shells, and 6 dc], you could do it with ease. You already know many more than 500 pattern stitches! You know what you need to know to make Brunswick Stew!

I don't mean to say that you will always, or even ever, have to invent your own designs (or recipes). That would be silly. There is no reason to reinvent the wheel or microwave ovens. If it suits your purposes, use what has already been figured out for you and done. Why waste time, effort, and energy starting over on something that works? But still, when you know what is happening, it is easier to do it, and if you need to, you can change it.

THE RIPPLE AFGHAN STITCH

A real winner and all-time favorite is the simple single crochet ripple afghan stitch. (See Photo 8.) It is special to me because it always looks good. Neatly folded, dumped in a lump on the end of the couch, artfully draped over the back of a chair, covering a sleeping body, it always looks good. There is no right or wrong side; there is no up or down. Whether made in a wonderfully wild and gaudy array of colors or in subtly blended tone-on-tone hues, it is always special, and there are no holes or spaces for toes or fingers to catch on.

Working into the *back loop only* of the stitches of the previous row gives it the same snuggly effect as a thermal blanket. The undulating ripples are made by an increase (of one into three) row after row, each falling directly above the one below, making some straight stitches, then skipping two stitches for an open decrease, then some more straight stitches. For this lesson, we are going to work with five stitches between the points.

Figuring out exactly how many chains to make to start a ripple afghan can be a headache! Often I just chain a "bunch" (at least one-half longer than the desired finished width), set up my first row, and then cut off the excess. Take my word for it that this multiple is 13 + 12 + 2. For the sake of learning, let's start with a small piece and

Ch 40.

*Row 1) Sc in 3rd ch from hk, sc in ea of next 4 chs. * Inc 3 sc in next ch, sc in each of next 5 ch, sk 2 ch, sc in ea of next 5 chs. Rep from * across, ending with 3 sc in next ch, sc in ea of next 6 chs. Ch 1, turn.*

*Row 2) Working thru the back loop only, sk next sc, * sc in ea of next 5 sc, work 3 sc in next sc (inc made), sc in ea of next 5 sc, sk 2 sc (dec made). Rep from * across, ending with sc in ea of next 5 sc, 3 sc in next sc, sc in ea of next 6 sc. Ch 1, turn.*

Just keep on repeating row 2 for pat st row after row after row.

A chart of the above ripple Afghan stitch would look as follows:

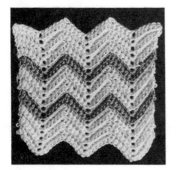

Photo 8

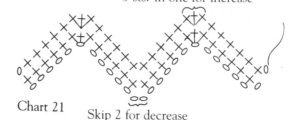

3 sts. in one for increase

Chart 21   Skip 2 for decrease

Beginning a ripple afghan is a time to dig into that pouch of supplies to save time and sanity. Remember to use safety pins when making the foundation chain, marking every 20th stitch so that you can count easily. When setting up the first row of your pattern, use knitter's slip-on thin plastic ring markers in the decreased stitches and in the center of the increased stitches. After you can see the pattern evolving, you can get rid of them.

You can vary this basic ripple afghan by changing the number of straight, even stitches between the increase and decrease points. With fewer stitches, it can be as sharp and definite as a needle-pointer's flame stitch. With more stitches, it can be as subtle as ripples on a pond in a gentle breeze.

But this is not the only ripple afghan pattern. It could also be worked in double crochet. There could be spaces and places in it. Next time you are in your favorite needlework store, leaf through the booklets. Many crocheters prefer to follow a tried-and-true set of directions. Others may want to make their own directions. After all, you are in charge of the direction of your life.

FISHNET

I do not really think that this is the way that fishermen from time immemorial have made their nets for fishing. Crocheting was not invented in immemorial times; fishermen more than likely used some sort of knot tying, which today we call macramé, to make their nets. Nonetheless, the finished product does look like fishnet and it is very easy to do. (See Photo 9.) * Just make a chain and then fasten it down in a previous row with either a slip stitch or a single crochet. *

These instructions are for a five-long chain with single crochet fastenings over a base of single crochet stitches.

Ch 25.

Row 1) Sc in 2nd ch from hk and in ea ch across. Turn. [24 sts rem.]

*Row 2) * Ch 5, sk 2 sc, sc in next sc*, rep bet *s across. Ch 8, turn. [8 lps.]*

*Row 3) * Sc in center of lp, ch 5 *, rep bet *s across, end ch 8, turn.*

Rep row 3 for pat st.

A chart of the above fishnet stitch would look as follows:

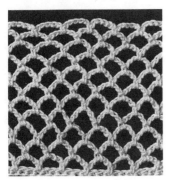

Photo 9

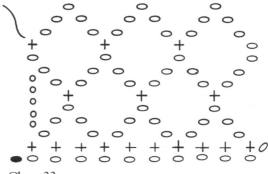

Chart 22

I could just as well have chosen a six- or seven- or nine-long chain. The longer the chain the looser and lacier the look. I could have used slip stitches for the fastenings instead of single crochet. Or I could have done as the Irish do, and thrown in lots of luxurious picots on the sides of the loops. But with this small example you get the idea of what fishnet is all about.

Usually fishnet is made of one color only, and though there is a slight difference in the sides if it is made flat, it is usually considered to be reversible.

ARCH STITCH

The basic idea of the whole family of arch stitches is the same as fishnet, that is, loops fastened down in the center of previous loops. But in this arch stitch the fastenings are thicker and fatter—four double crochets with a picot thrown in the middle of them to boot. The finished effect is still airy, but more refined and elegant than just plain fishnet. (See Photo 10.)

The multiple here is eight (one block and one open space) + three for the final block and three for a turning chain.

Chain desired number.

Row 1) (Begins and ends with a "block.") Dc in 4th ch from hk, 1 dc in next ch, [ch 3, sl st in 3rd ch from hk (picot made)], 1 dc in ea of next 2 ch, * ch 4, sk 4 ch, 1 dc in ea of next 2 ch, picot, 1 dc in ea of next 2 ch, rep from * across, end ch 7.

*Row 2) (Begins and ends with an open space.) * 2 dc in next ch-4 sp, picot, 2 dc in same ch-4 sp, ch 4, sk next 4 dc, rep from *, ending last sp ch 3, dc in top of t-ch. Ch 3, turn.*

*Row 3) (Begins and ends with a "block" the same as row 1 except that it is made over a completed row instead of a foundation ch.) 1 dc in first ch-4 sp, picot, 2 dc in same ch-sp, * ch 4, sk next 4 dc, 2 dc in next ch-4 sp, picot, 2 dc in same ch-sp, rep from * ending last block, 2 dc in last ch-4 sp, picot, 1 dc in same ch-sp, 1 dc in 4th ch of same ch-sp (to keep edge straight). Ch 7, turn.*

Rep rows 2 & 3 for pat st.

A chart for the above arch stitch would look as follows:

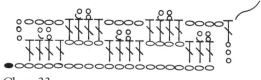

Chart 23

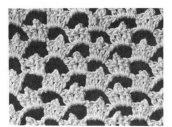

Photo 10

Arch stitches are usually made in one solid color, though there is no rule that says the rows couldn't be different colors if the crocheter chooses. Because of the holes of the arches you have to be careful about the background showing through. Depending on the particular arch stitch chosen, the fabric may or may not be reversible.

The variations for arch-type stitches are endless. When the vests made of Class C standard 4-ply came out in the early 1970s, there were many wonderful examples of it. You can single crochet over each arch before the next series of arches is made. You can double crochet down in a "V" to fasten the next row. You can fill the open space with crossed double crochet stitches. You can do anything that you want (and enjoy doing).

HERRINGBONE

Remember in Chapter 18 I said that you could work a stitch in another row rather than the one you were working on? Well, this herringbone pattern stitch does just that. (See Photo 11.) It is worked in double crochet, making a chain-one space instead of every fourth stitch. Two rows farther along, a long lazy double crochet is made into that chain-one space. When worked in three colors, two rows of each, it makes an especially lovely effect, the long stitch showing up on a different-colored background. I've seen it made into afghans and pillows with an ordinary tension. I can imagine a boxy jacket of it in a firm and tight gauge, in subtle tones of one hue.

This pattern stitch has a multiple of four + nine. Begin rows 1 and 2 with color A, change to color B for rows 3 and 4, change again to color C for rows 5 and 6, and then go back to color A again on the seventh and eighth rows.

These instructions are written with the turning chain at the beginning of the row instead of at the end, and that turning chain is two long instead of the ordinary three for double crochet. Why the person who devised the pattern wrote it that way, I don't know, but I've put it in here so that you can get used to the idea that not all directions will be written in the same way. If the chain-two turning chain is not long enough, change it to three-long. I also want you to get used to the idea that you don't have to follow directions exactly.

Ch 40.

Row 1) Ch 2, 1 dc in next 2 sts, * ch 1, sk next st, 1 dc in next 3 sts*, rpt bet *s to end, turn.

Row 2) Same as row 1.

Row 3) Ch 2, * ch 1, sk next dc, 1 dc in next dc, 1 dc in ch-1 sp of 2nd row below, 1 dc in next dc*, rpt bet *s across, ending ch 1, sk next dc, 1 dc in last dc, turn.

Row 4) Ch 2, * ch 1, sk next st, 1 dc in ea of next 3 dc*, rpt bet *s across, ending ch 1, sk next st, 1 dc in last dc, turn.

Row 5) Ch 2, * 1 dc in ch-sp of 2nd row below, 1 dc in next dc, ch 1, sk next dc, 1 dc in next dc*, rpt bet *s across, ending 1 dc in ch-sp of 2nd row below, 1 dc in last dc, turn.

Rpt rows 2 thru 5 for pat st.

A chart for the above herringbone stitch would look as follows:

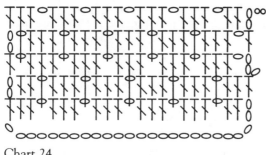

Chart 24

Photo 11

This pattern stitch has a definite right and wrong side to it. Still, in a fluffy mohair yarn with a rather large hook, it makes a lovely afghan.

DIAGONAL POPCORNS

Popcorn is a truly American product. The Native Americans taught the Pilgrims how to grow it, and it has become a national favorite. It was only natural that pioneer American women should incorporate this puffy delight into their handwork.

You will recall from Chapter 18 that a popcorn is created by making a bunch of stitches in one spot, then removing the hook from the last stitch, reinserting it in the first stitch of the group, and pulling through, sometimes making an extra slip stitch to keep the whole thing firm and tight.

In this pattern stitch on a flat double crochet background, puffy five-stitch popcorns make a raised diagonal pattern. They appear on every other row with three stitches in between. (See Photo 12.)

The multiple is four + one (for selvage edge) + three (for a turning chain), and there are four rows to the pattern.

Ch 24.

Row 1) (Wrong side) Dc in 4th ch from hk, dc in ea st across. Ch 3, turn.

Row 2) (Outside) * 5 dc into next st, pull up a lp and remove hk, reinsert hk into top of first dc, pull lp thru, sl st (PC made) (push the PC to the front of the work), 1 dc in ea of next 3 dc *, rep bet *s, dc, in top of t-ch, ch 3, turn.

Row 3) Dc in ea st across, ending dc in top of t-ch, ch 3, turn.

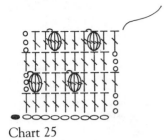

Chart 25

Photo 12

*Row 4) (Outside) 1 dc in ea of next 2 sts, * PC in next st (which is the middle of the 3 sts between previous PCs), 1 dc in ea of next 3 sts *, rep bet *'s across, ending PC in next st, 1 dc in last st, dc in top of t-ch, ch 3, turn.*

Row 5) (Same as row 3) Just dc across, ending dc in top of t-ch, ch 3, turn.

Rep rows 2 thru 5 for pat st.

Chart 25 illustrates the above popcorn stitch.

These are closely spaced popcorns and they are all made on the outside of the fabric. The popcorns could just as well be made on every third row and then pushed through to the front to make a less heavily embossed fabric. Also, there could have been five double crochets between the popcorns, which makes a less bumpy fabric. The background could have been other than just plain double crochet. It could have chain spaces in it or anything else the crocheter wished. Also, the whole thing could have been done in triple crochet instead of double. The marvel of crocheting is that it allows a simple, straightforward idea to be endlessly varied.

A few words of warning: popcorns add weight. Wearing a sweater of closely spaced popcorns will be like walking around in a suit of chain-mail. Popcorn bumps on table linens can cause spills and accidents. On bedspreads and pillows, they are ideal.

LOVERS' KNOTS

I thought I was in heaven when I discovered lovers' knots. (See Photo 13.) They were everything I thought crochet should be—light and lovely, sturdy and strong. They make an elegant open-work, forming an endless series of diamonds. The multiple for lovers' knots is usually 5 + 1 when they are to make a flat, non-rippled row. A skirt of lovers' knots, however, is often gathered onto a bodice of single or half-double crochet for baby garments. To achieve a gathered effect, the multiple would be smaller, skipping fewer stitches in between the single crochet fastenings on the original row.

Don't let the following instructions scare you. They are really very simple. I do suggest, however, that you have someone read aloud to you this unusual technique the first time that you do it so that you don't lose your place and your composure as well.

Ch 51.

*Row 1) Sc in 2nd ch from hk; * to work knot st, # draw up lp on hk ¼",
yo, pull thru lp, insert hk between vertical bar and long lp and draw up a
lp, yo, pull thru both lps on hk (knot st made); rep from # once, skip 4
chs, sc in next ch; rep from * across, turn.*

*Row 2) Work a knot st, sc in first lp of first knot st of previous row, sc in
2nd lp of same knot st, * work a knot st, sc in first lp on next knot st, sc in
2nd lp of same knot st; rep from *.*

Rep row 2 for pat st.

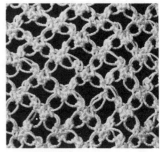

Photo 13

You'll be hard pressed to tell right and wrong sides in lovers' knot
fabric. The length of the loop drawn up will vary in size from ⅛" to
1" depending on the type of yarn, the size of the hook, and how you
want the fabric to appear. And there is no reason why you can't
make lovers' knots in the round. I've seen them used not only on
baby clothes, where they are lovely, but also on edgings for pillow
cases, and as the yoke of an exquisite blouse. Play with them. You
may come to love them as I do. But be aware that they are airy and
the background will show through.

SPIDER WEB

The works of the great architects of nature, spiders, were the
inspiration for this lovely pattern. (See Photo 14.) Long ago, some
foremother looked up at the delicate tracery in the corner of her
kitchen window as she washed the morning dishes and said, "I bet I
could capture that idea." Leaving the pans unscrubbed, she sat
down with her hook and twine and worked out a pattern. Perhaps
she first centered her spider web in a bed of double crochet. Then
she took a look at it and said, "It is a diamond pattern. I could place
one diamond beside and just above another and have spider webs
all over the place!"

And I have done that, too. I have placed isolated spider webs
amidst double crochet on sweaters. But I think the loveliest thing I
ever did with them was to make a triangular shawl in white sport-
weight wool of nothing but interlocking spider webs for one of my
daughters-in-law. I hope that she had as much fun wearing it as I
had making it!

These are the instructions for that triangular shawl starting at the
bottom back with just one web and getting bigger and bigger with

every row until it is the size you want it to be. But once you get the hang of it, you can do anything with the edges that you want to. You'll be able to make a rectangular piece with straight edges beginning on the bottom with half webs of half of the motifs and making half-width motifs on the sides.

Do you remember from Chapter 16 about increases, the method of making a new stitch at the end of the row in the bottom-most outermost loop of the last stitch? That technique is used in this shawl and you may want to refresh your memory about it before you begin.

This pattern requires that you make your slip stitches *very loose*. This is one instance in which you will have to insert your hook into those slip stitches and use them again. If they are made tightly, you'll end up fighting yourself all the way and end up hating the lovely spider web pattern. (I have seen examples in which the center of the web was made with single crochets instead of slip stitches. It is a good-looking solution to the problem of tight slip stitches, but not quite as effective as making loose slip stitches.)

Ch 6.

Row 1) Dc in 4th ch from hk, 1 dc in ea of next 2 sts. Ch 6, turn.

Row 2) (Each side gets wider.) Dc in 4th ch from hook, 1 dc in ea of next 2 sts. Ch 5, dc in ch-4 sp of previous row, [inc 1 dc in last st] 3 times, ch 6, turn.

Row 3) Dc in 4th ch from hook, 1 dc in ea of next 2 sts, ch 2, dc into ch-5 lp of previous row (the beg of the center of the web), ch 2, dc in top of t-ch, [inc 1 dc in last st] 3 times, ch 6, turn.

Row 4) Dc in 4th ch from hook, 1 dc in ea of next 2 sts, ch 5, sl st into ch-2 lp of previous row, sl st into dc, sl st into next ch-2 lp, ch 5, dc into top of t-ch, [inc 1 dc in last st] 3 times, ch 6, turn.

I'm sitting here at my word processor, typing in these instructions. As I look at them, I am aware that each row begins and ends in the same way—"Dc in 4th ch from hook, 1 dc in ea of next 2 sts . . . dc into top of t-ch of previous row, [inc 1 dc in last st] 3 times, ch 6, turn." And I'm thinking that it would save you a lot of reading and trying to keep your place while you work, save the printer the space on the page, and of course save me a lot of typing if I could simply say "Begin the row in the usual way. . ." and, "end as before." Shall we try it?

Row 5) *(This row begs a new web at the beg and the end of the row, and is the widest part of the original web.)* *Beg as usual, ch 7, 1 sl st in ea sl st, ch 7, end as before.*

Row 6) *Beg as usual, ch 5, 4 dc in next ch-sp (the center web is beg to get smaller), ch 5, 1 sl st in ea sl st, ch 5, 4 dc in next ch-sp, ch 5, end as before.*

Row 7) *Beg as usual, ch 2, dc in ch-sp (beg of center of new web), ch 2, 4 dc in next ch-sp, ch 2, dc in center sl st of previous row, ch 2, 4 dc in ch-sp, ch 2, dc in ch-sp, ch 2, end as before.*

Row 8) *Beg as usual, ch 5, sl in ch-sp, the dc, and the ch-sp, ch 5, 4 dc in next ch-2 sp, ch 4, 4 dc in next ch-sp, ch 5, sl st in the next ch-sp, the dc, and the next ch-sp, ch 5, end as before.*

Row 9) *(The center web is down to nothing and the two side webs are at their widest.)* *Beg as usual, ch 7, sl st in ea sl st, ch 7, 4 dc in ch-4 sp, ch 7, sl st in ea sl st, ch 7, end as before.*

Can you go on, on your own, from here?

Row 10) *Starts a new web at the beg, makes a dc down to the center of the first web, starts a new web in the middle, makes a dc down to the center of the last web, and starts a new web at the end of the row.*

A chart for the above spider web stitch would look as follows:

Photo 14

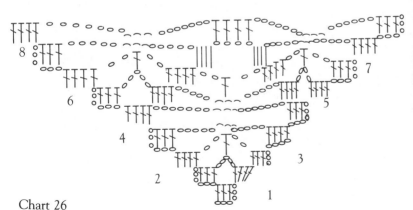

Chart 26

This pattern stitch is fully reversible.

I personally prefer to see a fabric of all spider webs in either a very light or a very dark color. When spider webs are interspersed on a solid double crochet background they stand out if the color is clear and vivid, like red or bright pink. They tend to get lost in muted or heather tones.

UP-AND-DOWN STITCH

Simply by making a stitch into every stitch of the previous row, but alternating the *kinds* of stitches we are making, a very different effect occurs. In this example we are making first two single crochets, then two double crochets across a row. On the next row we make single over double, and double over single, and so on. The variation in the stitches forms an interesting pattern on the fabric. (See Photo 15.)

Multiple = 4 + 1.

Row 1) Into 3rd ch from hk work 1 sc, 1 dc into ea of next 2 ch, * 1 sc into ea of next 2 ch, 1 dc into ea of next 2 ch, rep from * to end, ch 2. Turn.

Row 2) 1 sc into 2nd dc, * 1 dc into ea of next 2 sc, 1 sc into ea of next 2 dc, rep from * across to last 2 st, 1 dc into ea of last 2 sc, ch 2. Turn.

Rep row 2 for pat st.

Chart 27 illustrates the above up-and-down stitch.

Think of the variations possible with this simple idea. Two isn't the only number of stitches that you can alternate; it could also be three or four or more. Singles and doubles aren't the only kinds of stitches that you can choose to use; doubles and trebles could serve just as well. Try four doubles and four trebles and see the change with just a small difference. And the numbers of each of the stitches don't have to be the same! Try three of one and five of the other and see what happens. You could also use a sequence of all the stitches, going from short to long to short again (2 sc, 2 dc, 2 tr, 2 dc, 2 sc, and on the next row make the trs over the scs and vice versa).

When the rows are done in alternate or shaded colors, up-and-down stitch takes on a very special undulating appearance, making a superb reversible afghan or jacket fabric.

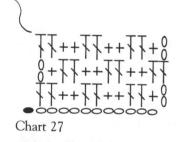
Chart 27

Photo 15

MY LADY'S FAN

My lady of long ago, in the days before air conditioning, fluttered her fan to give herself cooling breezes and to have a place behind which she could flirt. This pattern (see Photo 16) reminds us of the fluttering of that lady's fan. Rows of nine-stitch double crochet fans alternate across this lovely fabric pattern stitch. First they flare from the bottom as with any shell, and then, on the next row, they flare from the top by decreasing all nine stitches together into one. (If you need a reminder about how to decrease, go to Chapter 17.)

Multiple of 8 sts (1 fan) + 10 (2 half fans & t-ch).

Ch desired number.

*Row 1) (Fans spreading from bottom) 4 dc in 4th ch from hk (½ fan), * skp 3 ch, sc in next ch, skp 3 ch, 9 dc in next ch, (full fan made), rep from * across, ending skp 3 ch, sc in next ch, skp 3 ch, 5 dc in last ch (½ fan), ch 1, turn.*

*Row 2) (Fans spreading from top) Sc in last dc of previous row, * ch 3, make a 9-st dc dec down the next 4 dc, the sc at the bottom, and up the next 4 dc of previous row (full upside-down fan made), ch 3, sc in center dc of previous row, rep from * across, ending sc in top of t-ch, ch 3, turn.*

*Row 3) (This row is just like row 1 except that it is made over a row of completed fans instead of a row of chains.) 4 dc in first sc, * sc in 9-st dec of previous row, 9 dc in next sc, rep from * across, ending sc in 9-st dec, 5 dc in last sc, ch 1, turn.*

Rep rows 2 & 3 for pat st.

A chart for the above my lady's fan stitch would look as follows at right.

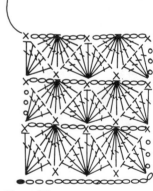

Chart 28

My lady's fan is a reversible pattern and when alternate rows are done in different colors, the effect is totally different.

This pattern stitch is included here for the purpose of explaining what you don't have to do. I love the look of this pattern, which I found in a Japanese book. Many, many times when I have been ready to begin a project, I have gotten it out and looked approvingly at it. Many, many times I have made a swatch of it in preparation to charting a garment, yet I have *never* made *anything* of it! Not that it doesn't look good. It does; it just takes more single-minded and devoted concentration than I am willing to give it. Each of us must know our own personality and what limits we are willing to go to for an effect. Not everything that is lovely is worth

Photo 16

doing, and, above all, crocheting should be enjoyable. If you don't enjoy doing it, don't do it! (But you never know until you try!)

QUEEN ANNE'S LACE

I've always liked to look at rich, elegantly embossed things. The wood carvings of Grinling Gibbons, the embellished salt cellars of Cellini, and the rococo designs of the American early Victorian walnut furniture that I collect, all thrill some nerve inside of my eyes and I stand in awe. Whenever I see Queen Anne's lace, I also stand in awe. And for me to be able to make such lovely lace in the air is both humbling and rewarding. I hope that you like it as much as I do. (See Photo 17.)

Originally I thought that the lace was named after Queen Anne. Not so. It is named after the lovely wildflower Queen Anne's lace, which blooms gloriously on roadsides and in sunny fields here in Georgia. As you look at the design, you can see the flower heads with their myriad tiny white blossoms. For my second grandchild, I made a white bassinette blanket of sport-weight yarn. For a shrimp-color raglan jacket, I made a long strip in a rich rust lustrous cotton that outlined the edges.

The standard directions take half a page and look intimidating and complicated. They are not. You make a chain circle and partially fill it with 13 double crochet. Next you turn and add a crown of single crochet and picots to the stitches to form the flower head. Each succeeding blossom is built on the base of the two previous flower heads and it is an interlocking exquisite array of blossoms.

I've taken these instructions from a 1940s leaflet for a baby blanket. I think the writer worked overtime making it seem hard. Don't let that stop you, and don't let her directions for the number of motifs limit you. All this business about the different strips is simply to make an indented top and bottom edge line!

Ch 6, join with a sl st to form a ring.

First Motif: Ch 3 to count as one dc, work 13 more dc into ring, ch 1, turn, work 1 sc in first dc, 1 sc in next dc, [ch 4, work 1 sc in ea of next 2 dc] 6 times, mark 3rd ch-4 lp with colored thread, ch 6, turn. (There are 6 ch-4 lps.)

Second Motif: Sl st in first free ch-4 lp, ch 3, turn, 13 dc in ch-6 sp, sl st to first sc of first motif, ch 1, turn, 1 sc in first dc, 1 sc in next dc, [ch 4, 1 sc in ea of next 2 dc] 6 times, sl st in next free ch-4 lp of previous Motif, ch 6, turn.

Third Motif: Sl st in first free ch-4 lp of just completed Motif, ch 3, turn, 13 dc in ch-6 sp, sl st in next free ch-4 lp of adjoining Motif, ch 1, turn, 1 sc in first dc from hk, 1 sc in next dc, [ch 4, 1 sc in next 2 dc] 6 times, sl st in next free ch-4 lp of adjoining Motif, ch 6, turn. Repeat Third Motif for pat, careful to leave 3 ch-4 lps free at ea side of strip, working until there are 34 Motifs. Work 1 more Motif, omitting last ch-6.
Fasten off.

Second Strip: (*The second strip is joined at the center of the crowning ch-4 loop.*) Marking 3rd ch-4 lp as before, work same as first strip until the 13th dc of 2nd Motif has been completed. Sl st to first sc of first Motif then join to first strip as follows: Ch 1, turn, 1 sc in ea of first 2 dc, ch 2, sl st in marked ch-4 lp of first strip, ch 2, 1 sc in ea of next 2 dc of 2nd Motif on 2nd strip, ch 2, sl st in first ch-4 lp of next Motif of first strip, ch 2, 1 sc in ea of next 2 dc, ch 2, sl st in 2nd lp of 2nd Motif of first strip, ch 2, (in other words attach to 2 ch-4 lps of first Motif and 1 of the second Motif) 1 sc in ea of next 2 dc, [ch 4, 1 sc in ea of next 2 dc] 3 times, sl st in next free ch-4 lp of previous Motif, ch 6, turn. Work 1 Motif same as 3rd Motif of first strip then continue in pattern until 13 dc of next Motif have been completed, sl st in next free ch-4 lp of adjoining Motif, ch 1, turn, continue working Motifs of second strip, joining to first strip as before until there are 34 Motifs in strip. Work 1 more Motif, omitting last ch 6.
Fasten off.

Third Strip: Marking 3rd ch-4 lp as before, work same as first strip until 13 dc of 2nd Motif have been completed. Sl st to first sc of first Motif then join to previous strip as follows: Ch 1, turn, 1 sc in ea of first 2 dc, ch 2, sl st in the marked ch-4 lp of previous strip. * [Ch 2, 1 sc in ea of next 2 dc, ch 2, sl st in next free ch-4 lp on previous strip] twice, ch 2, 1 sc in ea of next 2 dc, [ch 4, 1 sc in ea of next 2 dc] 3 times, sl st in next ch-4 lp of previous Motif, ch 6, turn. Work 1 Motif same as 3rd Motif of first strip, then continue in pattern until 13 dc of next Motif have been completed, sl st in next free ch-4 lp of adjoining Motif, ch 1, turn, 1 sc in ea of next 2 dc, ch 2, sl st in next free ch-4 lp on previous strip, repeat from * until 34 Motifs have been completed, then work 1 more Motif, omitting last ch-6.
Fasten off.

Following directions of 3rd Strip, work and join 6 more strips.

A chart for the above Queen Anne's lace stitch would look as follows:

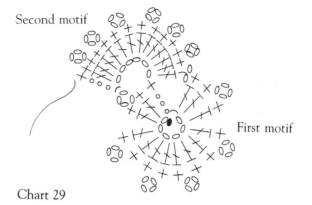

Second motif

First motif

Chart 29

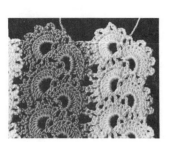

Photo 17

Queen Anne's lace is reversible, and I prefer to see it made in either a very dark or a very light color. Thread size doesn't seem to make a difference in the loveliness of it. I have used pearl cotton, yarn, and #10 thread all to good effect.

I hope that this short, abbreviated and limited collection of pattern stitches has served to initiate you into the wonders that are possible by varying the simple stitches of crochet. I hope that it has served to give you courage to try other wondrous things. But most of all, I hope that it has given you a thorough understanding of how pattern stitches and the instructions for them work, and that you will never ever be intimidated by the gobbledygook of abbreviations. If you choose to do more exploring with fancy pattern stitches, may I recommend to you "63 Easy to Crochet Pattern Stitches Combine to Make a Heirloom Afghan," Leisure Arts Leaflet #555 (26 pages, $4.00).

22
MAKING MEDALLIONS
AND MOTIFS

Crocheting isn't all just making flat fabric and circular pieces. Not by a long shot! One of the wonders of crochet is that we can make small geometric shapes and then join them together to form a large piece such as a bedspread or a tablecloth. Hauling around a heavy project in progress from the porch to the parlor to the peace and quiet of your own room is a hassle. It is much easier to make a series of small, lightweight, portable geometric shapes and then assemble them at a later date into the finished product. Our foremothers of crochet were not only creative and inventive, but also practical.

Though there is a technical dictionary-definition difference between the words *medallion* and *motif*, crochet designers and editors often make no distinction between the two words and sometimes use them interchangeably as I shall in this chapter. Either word means a unit of design, separate and complete in itself. The unit—medallion or motif—can then be joined to others shaped like itself.

Medallions and motifs in the shape of squares, equilateral (that is, equal-sided) triangles, and hexagons (six-sided shapes) can be endlessly joined on all sides to form a large flat piece. Large circles and octagons (eight-sided medallions) need to have an extra intervening motif to fill in the holes that will inevitably result in order to make the finished piece usable. Think of a tile floor to help you visualize this. If the tiles are squares, they can be abutted and you will have a solid floor. If the tiles are isosceles triangles or hexagons they will also abut perfectly and you again have a solid floor. If, however, the tiles are octagons, you will have to have a series of just-right-sized pieces to fit into the areas next to the 45-degree angles to make a smooth surface. (See figures at right).

(An exception to the circle-and-octagon rule is the black-eyed

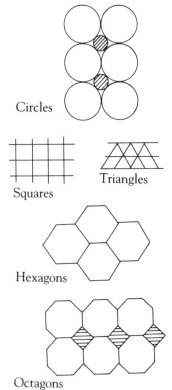

Circles

Squares

Triangles

Hexagons

Octagons

Susan pattern that follows. In this pattern you crochet tiny medallions and simply forget about filling in the holes because they are so small.)

The ways in which the geometric shapes are joined is creative and varied. Some are joined in the last row of the medallion. Often they are put together with a weaving technique (see Chapter 26) or sewing whipstitch. At other times they are joined with a row of single crochet on the outside of the article. In choosing a motif for a large piece it is wise to make a value judgment about your own temperament before you start; do you have the patience and skill to put those finished pieces together once they are all crocheted? For instance, I would never have the patience to put together the hexagonal spirals described below. I would have no trouble crocheting them, but I would not be able emotionally to join with a sewing whipstitch each side of each finished hexagon, cutting the thread, finishing in the tag ends, constantly threading a tapestry needle over and over again. The Irish rose square would give me no problem, because each motif is attached to others in the last row as you go along. Regardless of how lovely either the individual medallions or the finished piece may appear, remember that it will never finish itself—you must do it!

Whole encyclopedias of instructions for medallions and motifs could be written. There are thousands of them, each with its own lovely characteristics. This chapter is not intended to list them all; it is only a basic introduction to give you a feeling of how they work and why, how they can be joined, and what they can be used for.

BLACK-EYED SUSANS

I was still quite young when I first saw this pattern. It had been made in brown and yellow of about a #5 thread into place mats. They sat on a sun-drenched kitchen table in the home of a schoolmate with whom I was studying for a high school algebra test. Meals in my home were served onto plates at the stove and placed on a ragged oilcloth-covered surface with the admonition, "You better eat every bite or I'll tan your hide. Who cares what it looks like, think of all the starving children in China." The yellow daisies on the table, food spooned from pretty bowls, and happy conversation at my friend's home made an indelible impression on my young brain. I vowed that mealtimes in my *own* home would always be pretty, and crocheting such as this helps me keep my promise. It is not by bread alone, but by attractive settings as well, that man and woman really live.

But more than these memories led me to select this pattern for you as an introduction to circle medallions. These flowers are so tiny and so carefully contrived that they can be joined to one another without intervening motifs. The manner of joining to previously formed circles is to join the tip of the new petal with a slip stitch, that slip stitch replacing the middle chain of the chain-seven loop. Try the pattern out first with two colors as I first saw it, and then do it over in one solid color as it is done in the museum of the Historical Society in Stamford, Connecticut, and see what a difference there is without the color change. (Without the color change, it is much easier and quicker to do.)

FIRST STRIP: First motif: With brown, ch 10. Join with sl st to form a ring.

Rnd 1) Ch 1 (counts as 1 sc), work 23 sc into ring. Join to t-ch with sl st. Fasten off.

Rnd 2) With yellow, place a sl lp on hook, sc into any st, (ch 7, skp next sc, sc in next sc) 11 times; ch 7, join to first st and fasten off (12 lps).

Chart 30 illustrates the above black-eyed Susan motif.

2nd motif: Work as for first motif until rnd 1 is completed.

Rnd 2) Attach yellow and sc in joining, ch 3, sl st in any lp on first motif, ch 3, skp 1 sc on 2nd motif, sc in next sc, ch 3, sl st in next lp on first motif, ch 3, skp 1 sc on 2nd motif, sc in next sc, complete rnd as for first motif. Continue to join 2 lps of ea following motif, having 4 free lps at top and bottom between joinings until strip is desired length.

SECOND STRIP: Work in the same manner as first strip, joining motifs as shown in diagram, leaving one free lp between two joining motifs. Continue to join rows of motifs until piece is desired size. (See Figure 81 and Photo 18.)

This basic idea of tiny circles with 12 loops could be altered by making a shorter beginning chain and filling it with double instead of single crochet. Try it and see how this simple manuever changes the overall look of the piece.

Another variation is to follow the directions for rounds 1 & 2, and then lavish a coat of single crochet around each chain-loop for a more elaborate flower.

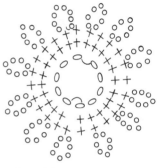

Chart 30

Figure 81

Photo 18

GRANNY SQUARES

Long ago, some granny took a look at the family scrap yarn heap and said, "I could make something useful out of this. There is not enough of one color or even one weight of yarn to make an afghan, but I could make it like a crazy quilt, using a different color whenever I ran out. If some of the squares were smaller because the yarn was thinner, I could just make extra rows until they were the right size." She did exactly that, making a wild and wonderfully colored coverlet. At the same time, she gave herself something to crochet without digging into the precious egg- and butter-money to purchase new yarn.

Today few of us are as thrifty as that granny was. It is more common for us to purchase new yarn in a special array of colors to do our crocheting. But we still use the pattern of squares that she devised. There are many variations of it, but basically it is a round checkerboard filet with corners. It begins with a circle. The first row sets up four corners interspersed with square blocks similar to filet places. The following rows make new corners in old corners and increase the number of filet places and spaces, until our squares are the size that we want them to be. A single square can be as large as a baby blanket or as small as three or four rows. (See Photo 19.)

When changing colors for a granny square afghan, I prefer to fasten off the old color after making a slip stitch joining at the end of a round and then putting a slip loop of the new color on my hook and just beginning in the air with a double crochet. It is faster changing colors that way, and when the time comes to finish in the ends, that part of it is faster, too, than if I had changed colors with the final two loops of an old stitch.

With Color A, ch 4, join with a sl st to form a ring.

Rnd 1) Ch 3 (counts as 1 dc), 2 dc into ring, ch 2 (for corner), * 3 dc into ring, ch 2, rep from * twice. Join with a sl st to top of t-ch. Fasten off.

Rnd 2) With Color B, work [3 dc, ch 2, 3 dc] into any corner to form new corner, * ch 1 (for new sp), work [3 dc, ch 2, 3 dc] into next corner, rep from * twice. Join with a sl st to first dc. Fasten off.

Rnd 3) With Color C, * [3 dc, ch 2, 3 dc] into any corner (for new corner), ch 1 (for new sp), 3 dc into ch-1 sp of previous row (new filet place), ch 1 (for new space), rep from * 3 times. Join to first dc with a sl st. Fasten off.

Rnd 4) With Color D, * corner in corner, ch 1, 3 dc in ch-1 sp, ch 1, 3 dc in next ch-1 sp, rep from * around. Join to first dc with a sl st. Fasten off.

Rnd 5 to Infinity) # Corner in corner, * 3-dc place in ch-1 sp, rep from * to next corner, rep from *3 times, join with a sl st. Fasten off, or if you want the next rnd to be the same color, ch 3 (which counts as 1 dc) to travel up and just keep on going.

A chart of the above granny square motif would look as follows at right.

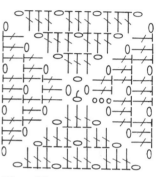

Chart 31

There are all kinds of variations to this simple square. Sometimes the corners have a chain-3 instead of a chain-2. Sometimes the chain-spaces in the middle are two-long instead of one. Occasionally I have seen double crochet places of four stitches instead of three. They are all just different designers' ideas of the same concept.

When they are all completed, granny squares can be joined either by weaving, by whipstitch sewing, or by single crocheting the pieces together on the outside. The crocheting will give a raised ridge, but that can become a design element, especially when made of a different color. I usually pin all of the corners together with my tiny coilless safety pins before I begin the attaching so that I won't get confused and mix up which goes next to what. With the safety pins keeping everything hanging together, I single crochet all the way across in one direction, knowing that when I finish all the squares in that direction, and go up and down in the opposite direction, any stretched places will get pulled together. It is easier for me to do it that way, because I tend to fret and get fractious when I have a hundred thousand ends of yarn to work in.

Photo 19

The only problem that I can possibly think of that anyone would ever have with the granny square is in getting off gauge. Stop periodically and check to make sure that the square you are working on is the same size as the one you started with. Change to a smaller hook if you have relaxed and your square has expanded.

SPIRAL PINWHEEL HEXAGON

Children of yesteryear played with pinwheels on sticks that spun marvelously as the youngsters ran in the breeze. They enchanted some foremother of ours and she captured the essence of them in a pattern to cover the bed of her sleeping child that he might have toys all night long. They are as lovely and intriguing today as they were long ago.

The center of this design (see Photo 20) is a set of six daisy petals. Each spoke of the wheel is divided by a longish chain-space. The offset spiral effect and the necessary increases are caused by skipping the first two double crochets of a previous round and then making four additional double crochets into the next chain-space. Every round, therefore, has more double crochets in it.

There is a very good lesson in options in this pattern. One can either keep on going making an endless spiral of stitches, or one can stop at the end of each round, join with a slip stitch, travel with slip stitches over 2 dc, and then chain 3 to travel up to the next round. In looking at the finished article, it will be hard to see which the crocheter chose to do. Since I haven't done it with the other motifs in this chapter, for a change I've written this one to be ongoing from round to round, not making a slip stitch joining and a traveling chain.

Ch 6, join with a sl st to form a ring.

Rnd 1) Ch 4 (to count as 1 tr), holding the last 2 lps of ea st on the hk make 2 tr in ring, yo, pull thru all lps to form cluster, ch 6, * holding last 2 lps of ea st on hook 3 tr in ring, yo, pull thru all lps to form cluster, ch 6, rep from * 4 times. Join with a sl st to first st of rnd. (6 petals and 6 ch-lps.)

Rnd 2) Ch 3, 7 dc in ch-6 lp, ch 6, * 8 dc in ch-6 lp, ch 6, rep from * 4 times. Mark the end of this rnd with a safety pin.

Remember that this is a continuous spiral with no stair-steps at the ends of the rounds; you just keep on going.

Rnds 3-9 [or however many rnds you want]) * Skp 2 dc, dc in ea dc, 4 dc in ch-6 sp, ch 6. (To finish the motif, count the ch-6 "ladders" to determine how many rnds you have made and stop at the "ladder" marked with a safety pin, joining to the next st with a sl st.)

A chart of the above spiral pinwheel motif would look as follows (see Chart 32).

A variation of this pattern is to scatter popcorn stitches in amongst the double crochets of the radiating arms. They change the surface from a smooth to a textured one. Of course that would not be a good idea if this is to be a tablecloth, but it is an excellent idea if this is to be a bedspread. This spiral pinwheel is also the basis of a cap or tam. Just keep going until the top of the cap is as wide as

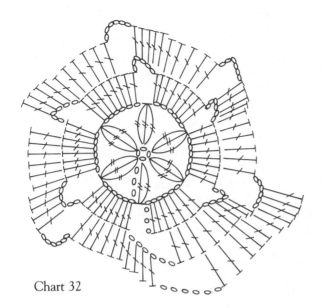

Chart 32

Photo 20

you want. Make only 2 dc in the ch-6 space to keep the cap the same diameter for a few rounds. Make no dc's in the ch-6 space to decrease to the size of the head. Finish the thing off with rounds of single crochet.

IRISH ROSE SQUARE WITH PICOTS

I was working as the needlework instructor at a large department store when I first encountered Irish crochet. (See Photo 21.) One of the women's bi-weekly magazines featured a blouse worked in Irish roses on the cover. I fell in love with the motif. It is everything that lace made in the air should be—exquisitely encrusted, daintily drawn together, and airy-light as a spring breeze. Traditionally it is made with very, very fine white thread—sewing-thread fine. Traditionally it is made over a loop rather than a chain ring, necessitating constant tightening and re-adjusting of the ring. But it is possible to revere and ape a thing without strictly following the tradition. My bifocaled eyes cannot see size #50 sewing thread, and my arthritic fingers cannot manipulate a size #14 steel hook. Nonetheless, I can adapt and capture the glory of these Gaelic flowers, shamrocks, and honeycombs to suit my abilities.

A rose begins very basically with a circle, sometimes open, sometimes with spokes, and sometimes closed. Next, a row of fishnet loops forms the base of the individual petals, and I have seen anywhere between 4 and 8 petals per round. These petals are made by making into each fishnet loop one single crochet, then one half-double crochet, an odd-number bunch of double crochets, another half-double crochet, and finally one last single crochet. When all the petals of that round are completed, another round of slightly longer fishnet loops is made, fastened down in between the single crochets in between the petals of the previous row. That row of fishnet is covered with the same sequence of stitches, but with more doubles thrown into the middle. And so on, making as many rounds of as many petals as the crocheter desires. There can be anywhere from one to four rounds of petals.

Next, rounds of fishnet are made. Pairs of picots are often thrown into the fishnet, and sometimes a third picot is added to the joining of the fishnet to make a three-leafed shamrock. Sometimes other decorative stitches are thrown in to give variety to the fishnet. Along the way, the circle is converted into a square. Squares are joined together on the last round by slip-stitching into the centers of fishnet loops.

The pattern given here is for a six-petaled rose with two tiers of petals around a spoked center, in an adapted non-traditional completely Maggie-ized manner. Please note that these directions may be somewhat different from other Irish rose patterns you may have seen in the lengths of the chain-ring and chain-spaces for the petals. My own chain stitches tend to be loose, and I find that I must shorten the number called for to keep a firm and tight rose. But that is the beauty of crochet-in-the-making. When we know what we are doing and what we are supposed to accomplish, we can adapt and change to suit ourselves!

FIRST MOTIF: Ch 7.

Rnd 1) Dc into beg ch, * *ch 3, dc into beg ch, rep from* * *4 times, end ch 3. Join with a sl st to 3rd ch at beg. (6 spokes.)*

Rnd 2) Into ea ch-3 sp work 1 sc, 1 hdc, 5 dc, 1 hdc, 1 sc. Join with sl st in next sc. (6 petals.)

Rnd 3) * *Ch 5, holding petals forward sc bet scs bet petals, rep from* * *around. Join with a sl st. (6 lps.)*

Rnd 4) Into ea lp work 1 sc, 1 hdc, 7 dc (2 more than last time), 1 hdc, 1 sc. Join with a sl st. (6 petals, ending bet petals.) (Rose completed.)

Note: We now have a six-petaled rose with two tiers of petals. At this point we need to get to a number divisible by four in order to become a square. Twelve is such a number so now we need to make two picoted loops for each of the six petals—one loop beginning between petals and one loop attached to the center of each petal. A picot is [ch 3, sl st in 3rd ch from hk (pc)]; a 2-picot lp is [ch 2, picot, ch 2, picot, ch 2, sl st to fasten.]

Rnd 5) * *Ch 2, pc, ch 2, pc, ch 2, (picot lp made),* * *sc in center dc of next petal, picot lp, sc in st bet petals, picot loop. Rep from* * *around. (12 2-picot lps.)*

Note: Now we need to define the corners of our square. In every third 2-picot loop we need to make a corner group of [3 tr, ch 4, 3 tr] instead of a new 2-picot loop to begin forming the corners as follows:

Rnd 6) *Sl st up the next 2-picot lp to one st past the first picot, ch 5 (counts as 1 tr), 2 tr, ch 4, 3 tr in this 2-picot lp for first corner,* * *make a 2-picot lp in ea of next 2 lps, another 2-picot lp (not fastened down) [3 tr, ch 4, 3 tr] in next lp, = corner #2, rep from* * *around, sl st in top of ch-5. (4 corners made.)*

Rnd 7) *Rnd 7 is just like rnd 6 except that it begs sl st across top of ch-5 and 2 tr, ch-5 (counts as 1 tr), 2 tr, ch 4, 3 tr in this lp, and so on.*

SECOND MOTIF: Work the same as before to rnd 7. Rnd 7 is joined to the previous motif with a sl st at the corner center, and in the middle of each 2-picot loop.

A chart for the above Irish rose motif would look as follows:

Photo 21

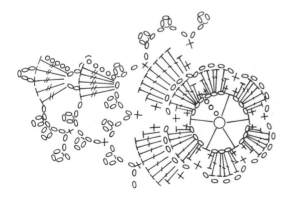

Chart 33

Detail #1
first row of petals

Detail #2
second row of petals

This is not the only kind of a rose to make. We could have made three tiers of petals. Also, in this example, all of the tiers of petals lie directly behind one another. Be aware that roses can also be made with the second tier of petals sitting between those of the first tier and the third tier. An example is given in Chapter 24.

Irish rose crochet makes up into wonderful blouses. Make one square to find out what your gauge is, and then plot it out. The center front, center back, and top of the sleeve panels are usually squares. After the thing is joined together on the final round of each square, rows of plain or picoted fishnet are added at the under-arms until the desired size is reached. Often a simple 5-dc shell edging is added to the finished blouse. (See Figure 82.)

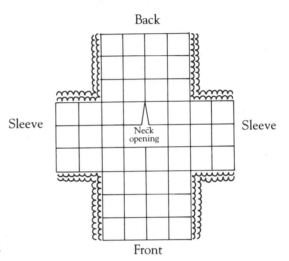

Figure 82

Like filet crochet, Irish crochet often needs a darker background to set it off to perfection. I once made an ecru Irish rose blouse and wore it over a brown camisole with a long, narrow, brown crepe skirt. It made an exquisite formal outfit.

A four-petaled rose in a semi-granny square makes a gorgeous afghan. Squares of eight-petaled roses in fine thread make a lovely yoke for a summer cotton nightie. Roses alone can decorate a ring-bearer's satin-covered pillow to become an heirloom wedding re-membrance. There are so many possibilities! The only trouble with crochet is that there aren't enough hours in a lifetime to make even just one of everything.

PINEAPPLE IN THE SQUARE

In American folklore, the pineapple is the symbol of hospitality, of welcoming others to the warmth of hearth and home. Representations of pineapples in print, wood, cloth, and thread are traditional housewarming gifts. They are easy to do in crochet, so make some.

Each of these squares is made up of four pineapples separated by fishnet with fans in the diagonals. (See Photo 22.) The medallions are joined in the final round of fishnet as you go, so there is no final crocheting or sewing later.

FIRST MOTIF: Ch 6, join with a sl st to form a ring.

Rnd 1) Ch 3, 3 dc into ring, (ch 2, 4 dc into ring) 3 times, ch 2, 1 sl st into 3rd st of ch-3. (A square has been made.)

Rnd 2) Sc into sp just formed, (ch 7, 1 sc into next sp) 3 times, ch 7, sl st into first sc. (4 loops).

*Rnd 3) (The beg of 4 pineapples [9 dc] with posts [ch-1, tr, ch-1] in between.) Ch 5, * 9 dc into next lp, ch 1, 1 tr into next sc, ch 1; rep from * 2 times more, ending 9 dc into next lp, ch 1, sl st into 4th st of ch-5.*

*Rnd 4) (A ch stitch is added to each side of each dc.) Ch 6, * (1 dc into next dc, ch 1) 9 times, 1 dc into next dc, ch 2, tr in next tr, ch 2; rep from * 2 times more, ending (dc in next dc, ch 1) 8 times, dc in next dc, ch 2, join with a sl st into 4th of ch-6.*

*Rnd 5) (The pineapples change from dc to [ch 3, sc]. Shells and diagonals beg bet the pineapples as those pineapples start to get narrower.) 1 sc into same place as sl st, * ch 3, sk next ch-2 sp, (sc into next ch-1 sp, ch 3) 8 times, ch 3, 1 sc into tr; rep from * 3 times omitting final sc. Sl st into first sc.*

*Rnd 6) (Beg fans at diagonals.) Ch 3, 3 dc in same place as sl st, * into next lp work 1 sc, ch 3, 1 dc, (ch 3, 1 sc into next lp) 7 times, ch 3, into next lp work 1 dc, 3 ch, and 1 sc, 7 dc into next sc; rep from * omitting 7 dc at end of last rep, 3 dc into same place as first 3 dc, sl st into 3rd of ch-3.*

*Rnd 7) 1 sc into same place as sl st, * ch 5, into next lp work [1 sc, 3 ch, 1 dc], ch 3, skp next lp, [1 sc into next lp, ch 3] 6 times, ch 3, skp next lp, into next lp work [1 dc, ch 3, 1 sc], ch 5, skp next 3 dc, 1 sc into next dc; rep from * omitting final sc, sl st into first sc.*

Rnd 8) Ch 4, 3 tr into same place as sl st, * 1 sc into next lp, ch 5, into next lp work [1 sc, 3 ch & 1 dc,] ch 3, skip next ch-3 lp [1 sc into next lp, ch 3] 5 times, ch 3, skip next ch-3 lp, into next lp work [1 dc, 3 ch, 1 sc], ch 5, sc into next lp, 7 tr into next sc; rep from * omitting 7 tr at end of last rep, 3 tr into same place as first 3 tr, sl st into 4th of ch 4.

Rnd 9) 1 sc into same place as sl st, * ch 5, sc into next ch-5 lp, ch 5, into next lp work (1 sc, ch 3, 1 dc), ch 3, skp next lp, [1 sc into next lp, ch 3] 4 times, ch 3, skp next lp, into next lp work [1 dc, ch 3, 1 sc], ch 5, 1 sc into next lp, ch 5, skp next 3 tr, 1 sc into next tr; rep from * omitting final sc, sl st into first sc.

Rnd 10) Ch 5, 3 dtr into same place as sl st, * [1 sc into next lp, ch 7] twice, into next lp work [1 sc, 3 ch, 1 dc], ch 3, skp next lp, [1 sc into next lp, ch 3] 3 times, ch 3, skp next lp, into next lp work [1 dc, ch 3, 1 sc], [ch 7, 1 sc into next lp] twice, 7 dtr into next sc; rep from * omitting 7 dtr at last rep, 3 dtr into same place as first 3 dtr, sl st into 5th of ch-5.

Rnd 11) Sc into same place as sl st, * [ch 7, 1 sc into next lp] twice, ch 7, into next lp work [1 sc, ch 3, 1 dc], ch 3, skp next lp, [1 sc into next lp, ch 3] twice, skp next lp, into next lp work [1 dc, ch 3, 1 sc], [ch 7, 1 sc into next 7 ch-lps] twice, ch 7, skp 3 dtr, 1 sc into next dtr; rep from * omitting 1 sc at end of last rep, 1 sl st into first sc.

Rnd 12) Ch 6, 3 trtr into same place as sl st, * ch 5, [1 sc into next lp, ch 7] 3 times, 1 sc into next ch-3 lp, ch 7, skip next 4 lps, 1 sc into ch-3 lp, (ch 7, 1 sc into next lp) 3 times, ch 5 into next sc work [4 trtr, ch 3, 4 trtr]; rep from *, omitting 7 trtr and ch-3 at end of last rep, 4 trtr into same place as first trtr, 1 dc into 6th of ch-6.

Rnd 13) Into lp just formed, work [1 sc, ch 5, 1 sc] (a corner lp made), * [ch 7, 1 sc into next lp] 10 times, ch 5, 1 sc into lp as last sc, (another corner lp made); rep from * omitting 1 sc, ch 5 and 1 sc at end of last rep, sl st into first sc. Fasten off.

SECOND MOTIF: Work the same as the first motif thru rnd 12. Rnd 13) Sc in lp just formed, ch 2, sc into corresponding corner lp on first motif, ch 2, sc into same lp on 2nd motif, [ch 3, sc into next lp on first motif, ch 3, sc into next lp on 2nd motif] 10 times, ch 2, sc into next corner lp on first motif, ch 2, sc into same lp on 2nd motif, and complete as first motif.

On subsequent motifs join in the same manner on 2 sides.

A chart of the above pineapple motif would look as follows:

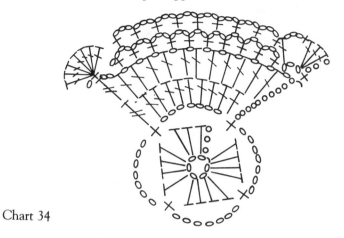

Chart 34

Photo 22

If you choose, you may edge the finished piece with a simple shell of (3 dc, ch 1, 3 dc).

People are always moving to new living quarters; situations are always arising where a gift that denotes hospitality is in order. The making of a pineapple pattern is quick and easy. Give the traditional gift. Who cares what the recipient does with the gift? It is my philosophy that a gift is always for the giver, not the receiver. Allow yourself to feel good in the giving.

A MEDALLION OF MANY USES

I have chosen this Marguerite-like circular flower motif (see Photo 23) for a number of reasons. Like the ripple afghan of Chapter 21, it uses the raised work-in-back-loop-only technique. The multiple increases make a rippled circle that does not lie flat, and will later become the fold line of pleats.

Also, on this motif you may stop in different places. It is complete after the fastening down of the pleats, after the first series of popcorns, or after the second set. The instructions call for working-in-the-back-loop-only on many rounds. I dislike doing this for two reasons. 1) It is more time consuming and 2) it makes for a less firm finished piece. When making this pattern for myself, I choose to work through both loops of the sts of the previous round. You may do as you please. Besides the options of size and back or front loop, you have options of color. If you want, you can make a dark center for the flower, changing colors after completing the round of loops following the popcorns at the center, and the round that secures the pleats in place could be of still another color.

Ch 9, join with sl st to form ring.

Rnd 1) Ch 1, 18 sc in ring. Join to first sc with a sl st.

Rnd 2) (Make a ring of popcorns separated by ch-2's.) Ch 3, 4 dc in back lp of next st, drop lp from hk, insert hk in top of ch-3 and draw dropped lp thru (starting popcorn [pc] st made); * ch 2, skp 1 sc; 5 dc in back lp of next sc, drop lp from hk, insert hk in first dc of 5-dc group and draw dropped lp thru (pc st made). Rep from * around (9 pcs), end ch 2. Join to top of first pc st.

Rnd 3) (Make a ring of holes that are dc's separated by ch-2's.) Ch 5, * dc in next lp, ch 2, dc in next pc, ch 2. Rep from * around, end dc in last sp, ch 2 (18 sps). Join to 3rd ch of ch-5.

Rnd 4) Ch 1, sc in joining, * 3 sc in next sp, sc in next dc. Rep from * around, end with 3 sc in last sp, join with a sl st to first sc. (72 sts.) (The circle is now ruffled and will not lie flat.)

Rnd 5) Ch 1, sc in joining: Work in back lp of ea st only, sc in next sc; * 3 sc in next sc (3-sc group made) sc in ea of next 3 sc, rep from * around, end sc in last sc. Join. (18 3-sc groups.)

Rnds 6 thru 16) Ch 1, sc in joining, working in back lp of ea st only, and making 3 sc in center sc of ea 3-sc group, sc in ea sc around. Join. At end of last rnd, fasten off. With a tiny safety pin, mark center st bet 3-sc groups. (Row 16 ends with 25 sts bet the 3-sc groups.) (18 pins.)

Rnd 17) Fold and fasten the tapered pleats as follows: Overlap the 5 sc following any marked sc over the 5 sc before same marked sc; make a lp on hk, working through both thicknesses, sc in next 5 sc, ch 4, * overlap the 5 sc following next marked sc over the 5 sc before the same marked sc; working thru both thicknesses, sc in the 5 sc, ch 4. Rep from * around. Join to first sc. (18 pleats.)

Rnd 18) Working in back lp only, sc in first 2 sc, * 3 sc in next sc, sc in next 2 sc, sc next 4 ch, (sc in 5 sc, sc in next 4 ch) twice; sc in 2 sc. Rep from * around, end with sc in last 4 ch. Join. (6 3-sc groups.)

Rnds 19 thru 23) Working in back lp only, sc in ea sc around making 3 sc in center sc of ea 3-sc group. Join. At end of last round fasten off.

Rnd 24) Join thread to center of any sc of any 3-sc group, working thru both lps of sc, ch 4, dc in same place, * [ch 1, skp 1 sc, dc in next sc] 18 times; ch 1; in center sc of next 3-sc group make [dc, ch 1, & dc]. Rep from * around, end with ch 1. Join to 3rd ch of ch-4. (120 sps).

You can stop at the end of this round if you choose, or you can go on and add rounds of popcorns to make a larger medallion. (For the photograph, we stopped at this point.)

Photo 23

Rnd 25) (A round of dc, ch-1 sps with extra dc's in the corners.) Sl st in sp, ch 4, dc in same sp, * [ch 1, dc in next sp] 19 times; ch 1; in next sp make [dc, ch 1, dc]. Rep from * around, end with ch 1. Join with sl st to 3rd ch of ch-4. (126 sps.)

We now make rounds of pc's separated by 5 plain sts with 3 sc's in the 6 corners. There is a plain sc round (with corners) in between the pc rounds.

In the original instructions, directions were given for half motifs to be used at the top and bottom of a bedspread. If you worked through the back loop only of many rows and have raised ridges on the front, it is necessary to break off the thread at the end of each half round and start again at the beginning. (What a mess of tail ends—ugh!) Those original instructions took up another page and a half. I think that you are by now clever enough to figure it out on your own.

Also, the original instructions called for a five-strand, 10-inch-long fringe. You will find instructions for fringing in Chapter 27.

As I said in the beginning of this chapter, whole encyclopedias of instructions for medallions and motifs could be written. The directions here are just a small sampling to whet your appetite and get you hooked into the joys of making them. If you run across a pattern that suits you almost but not exactly, don't hesitate to change it and make it uniquely your own. Too big? Leave off a few rounds. Too small? Add a few rounds more with increases.

If you want to design your own medallions, here are a couple of simple guidelines:

It is what you want to happen on the second round that will determine how you begin the center. The length of the starting chain and the number and kind of stitches worked into it depend upon whether you want a square, a hexagon, an octagon, or a circle to take shape on the second round. A square needs a number of stitches (or groups) divisible by 4; a hexagon requires a number of stitches divisible by 6; an octagon has to have a number divisible by 8; and the circumference of a circle is usually divisible by 12. Your beginning chain will be however long it takes to get all those stitches in on the first round.

This next bit goes back to high school geometry. By and large, with fudging allowed, every time the radius of a circle doubles, the number of stitches in the circumference doubles also.

The beauty of crocheting is that you can see what is happening *as you go.* If the round isn't working, rip it out and do it over so that it does work. You can easily count and duplicate whatever you did right on the next medallion. Crocheting is so wonderfully flexible; you can make definite rounds or continuous spirals; you can take out or throw in a few extra stitches so that they will be there on the next round when you need them. You can be the Absolute Ruler, the Queen by Divine Right, the Creator of your own world of crochet, which is more than most of us can say about other aspects of our lives. I cannot control the Post Office's delivery of mail, or decide that the supermarket must carry my favorite brand of jam. I cannot determine the thread count of the blue jeans that I wear, but I certainly can create and control my crocheting. It makes life more tolerable to know that I'm on top of *something.*

23
LAVISHING LACES
ON LINENS

Once upon a time, not so long ago, in the days before permanent press, automatic washers and dryers, and the throw-away culture, linens played an important part in the household and in housekeeping. Linen sheets and down pillows and cotton towels were passed from generation to generation. Their care consumed hours of back-breaking labor: soaking in cold water; boiling in soapy water to clean; hanging in the sunshine to remove stains; and ironing with stove-heated irons. Linens were important to our foremothers of crochet.

It was only logical that items that were so costly and that required so much care should receive special attention and decoration. With the discovery of crocheting, of making lace in the air in the nineteenth century, women found that they could easily and inexpensively adorn these possessions with lace that was as lovely as any costly imported stuff from Brussels or Venice. A small crochet hook could make a tiny opening in any cloth and lace could be crocheted right on anything. Wide bands decorated towels of all kinds; handkerchiefs were embellished; sheets and pillow covers were bedecked; undergarments were trimmed; crocheted finishing touches were added to everything that stood still.

Along the way, in doing this, our foremothers discovered that, more often than not, the crocheted trimming lasted longer than the thing to which it was added. It must have greatly pained women to have the cloth disintegrate with wear and tear, bleaching and scrubbing, leaving the crocheting still intact but unusable. Women soon set about to make crocheted lace that was removable.

Edgings can be made in three ways. 1) You can crochet directly into the cloth; 2) You can make a long starting foundation chain and work your edging into that, later sewing it to the fabric; or 3) You can make an edging that is complete with every pattern repeat and simply make a sufficient length of repeats necessary for the project. This type, too, will be attached by sewing.

Quickly women found that either of the two latter ways were preferable, because when the cloth item wore out, the edging could be salvaged for another similar article.

Each of the three ways of making edgings has its disadvantages.

1) In working directly into the cloth you must first prepare the cloth. I like to draw a thread about one quarter of an inch from the cut edge to make sure that the area to be crocheted is true to the grain of the fabric. Next I take the piece to the sewing machine and sew a single row of tight stitches (about 12 to the inch) directly on top of the drawn thread so that the first row of preparatory single crochet will not unravel the cloth. Now I take the scissors and cut the fabric very close to that line of stitches. As I crochet my chosen edging, I know that the trimming I am making will outlast the cloth, but if the thing is small, such as a handkerchief or a face cloth, it is no great loss. If the item is large, however, for example, the edge of a blanket, I will have not only the loss of the effort but also the cumbersomeness of the size of the item to contend with.

2) If I decide that I want the lace to be detachable and have chosen a pattern that starts with a chain the length of the item, I have a very real problem in determining just exactly how long to make that beginning foundation chain. *As you work over a long foundation chain, each stitch you put into that chain will shorten it.* Instructions that tell you to "make a chain of desired length" are way out in left field dreaming about the daisies. You cannot tell how much that foundation chain will shorten until you have done at least two rows. Then it is too late to add or remove a few inches that may make all the difference in whether or not if fits that fine linen nightie hem. Also, I hate the tediousness of whipstitching by hand the finished lace to the parent item. And it seems a sacrilege to attach it with the sewing machine after all of the fine handmade crocheted stitches. (Any printed pattern calling for a foundation chain can also be made over a preparatory row directly onto the cloth.)

3) If I make a pattern that is complete in its width with every pattern repeat, I no longer have the problem of guessing at the

length of a foundation chain, but I still have the problem of attaching it by hand.

Regardless of how it is done, making edgings for woven (or knitted) articles is rewarding. It is like planting blooming annuals along a walkway or wallpapering the bathroom; it is quick and easy and the effect is immediate and long lasting. Have you longed for pillowcases like Grandmother's that were lavished with lace? Do you know a bride who would treasure hand-decorated sheets, or a special friend who would appreciate a set of hand towels encrusted with handmade lace? How about a lace-edged handkerchief as a special "Thank You"?

As with the preceding chapters of specific instructions, I cannot do more here than begin to open the first page of the book of edgings. What follows is merely an introduction to the concept of adorning fabric with handmade lace. If you find that you like the idea, go and explore; there are many specialty books of nothing but edgings. If you dislike the idea, you don't have to make edgings; just know that it can be done.

Of course edgings can apply to crocheted fabric as well as woven cloth. It is very common to apply a simple edging to both crocheted clothing and pieces made up of medallions. There is more in Chapter 26 about finishing edgings.

PICOTED DOUBLE CROCHET SHELLS

The simplest kind of an edging to make is an easy two-row pattern of picoted double crochet shells. (See Photo 24.) It can be made over either a base of single crochet worked directly into fabric, or over a long foundation chain. One of my first girlhood projects in crochet was to edge a white linen handkerchief with pastel variegated thread. At this stage of my life, my taste would run to dark ecru color edging on off-white fabric, but the pattern itself is still a favorite. All it is is a shell of four doubles with a three-long picot thrown in the middle. In this case the shell is fastened down with a single crochet.

For crocheting directly onto cloth, if the item is not already finished with a rolled hem, prepare it as directed on page 156. Check to see that the hook you have selected is small enough to separate the fibers of the cloth to make a tiny hole to insert the hook. You do not want to just punch through and break any of the fibers. Still the hook must be large enough to easily hold the chosen thread in making the stitches.

Base Row) Beg just after a corner, place a sl lp on the hk and, close to the edge, work one row of sc evenly spaced all around, making 3 sc into the very corners so that the edging will lie flat. Join with a sl st.

*Row 1) * Skp 2 sc, [2 dc, (ch 3, sl st into 3rd ch from hk—picot made), 2 dc] all into next sc, skp 1 sc, sc into next sc, rep from * to corner. Finagle and juggle sts so that corner will occur in the center of the 3 sc of previous row. [3 dc, picot, 3 dc] in corner. And just keep on going around.*

A chart of the above picoted double crochet edging would look as follows at left (see Chart 35).

When doing this pattern along a foundation chain, the multiple is 5 + 4. (But you know that you can cut off any excess chain.) (You also know that the length of the foundation chain will be longer than the finished edging.)

Ch desired length.

*Row 1) * Skp 2 ch, [2 dc, (ch 3, sl st into 3rd ch from hk—picot made), 2 dc] all into next ch, skp 1 ch, sc into next ch, rep from * across. Fasten off.*

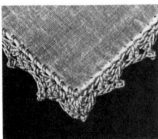

Chart 35

Photo 24

For variation, to make a deeper edging, rows of open-space filet could be worked before the shell row. (Remember the formula for open-space filet: Ch 3 to travel up, * ch 2, skp 2 sts, dc in next st, rep from *.) Or one or more rows of open shells of [2 dc, ch 1, 2 dc] could be worked before the final picoted-shell row.

Another variation is to make the shells of [3 dc, picot, 3 dc] and fasten them down with slip stitches. Feel free to do whatever pleases you and complements the cloth.

MORNING SUNRISE

Like a rising sun peeking just above the horizon, these crowned half circles (see Photo 25) will brighten the edge of napkins on the breakfast table. Though the instructions given are for beginning with a long foundation chain (in order to sew the finished lace on later), it could just as well be done over a base of single crochet worked directly into the fabric. A lustrous Mercerized pearl cotton would be an ideal thread to use.

The pattern is a multiple of 12 sts + 1.

Row 1) Ch desired length, ch 1 (to turn), sc in 2nd ch from hk, sc across. Turn.

*Row 2) * Ch 5, sk 5, [shell of 2 dc, ch 3, 2 dc] in next sc, ch 5, sk 5, sc in next sc; rep from *. Turn.*

*Row 3) * Ch 1, [7 tr with ch 1 bet trs] in ch-3 sp of shell. Ch 1, sc in ch-5 lp, ch 2, sc in next lp; rep from *, ending last rep with 7th tr. Turn.*

*Row 4) Sc in first ch-1 sp, * [ch 5, sc in 4th ch from hk (picot made), sc next sp] 5 times, sc in ea of next 4 sps; rep from *.*

A chart for the above morning sunrise edging would look as follows:

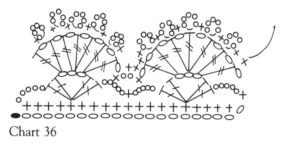

Chart 36

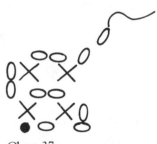

Photo 25

SIMPLE AND SWEET

The easiest example of a crochet edging that is made without a foundation chain or a base of single crochet, and is complete with every repeat, is this handmade rickrack. (See Photo 26.) It is just the perfect little touch to add to small items such as baby dresses and insulated pot holders.

*Ch 3, [shell of 1 sc, ch 2, 1 sc] in 3rd ch from hk, * ch 2, turn, shell in ch-2 sp of previous shell, rep from * to desired length.*

A chart for the above simple and sweet edging would look as follows at right (see Chart 37).

Chart 37

INSERT OR APPLY WITH LOVE

Inserted between strips of fine linen or lawn cloth on a blouse or nightie, or applied across the width of a Turkish towel, this lovely lace (see Photo 27) is an excellent example of complete-as-you-go

Photo 26

edging. For the blouse or nightie, make it in a fine thread; for the towel, make it in thickish thread.

Row 1) Ch 18, [shell of 2 dc, ch 2, 2 dc] in 4th ch from hk, ch 6, sk 9 chs on foundation ch, [dc, ch 3, dc] in next ch, ch 6, shell in last ch. Ch 3, turn.

Row 2) Shell in ch-2 sp of first shell, ch 5, 7 dc in ch-3 sp, ch 5, shell in next shell, ch 3, turn.

Row 3) Shell in first shell, ch 4, dc in first dc of 7-dc group, [ch 1, 1 dc] in ea of next 6 dc, ch 4, shell in shell, ch 3, turn.

Row 4) Shell in shell, ch 1, dc in first dc on fan, [dc in next sp, dc in next dc] 6 times, ch 1, shell in shell, ch 3, turn.

Row 5) Shell in shell, ch 6, [dc, ch 3, dc] in center dc of fan, ch 6, shell in shell, ch 3 turn.

Rep rows 2 through 5 for pattern until the strip is as long as you need, making sure to end after completing row 4.

A chart for the above insertion edging would look as follows:

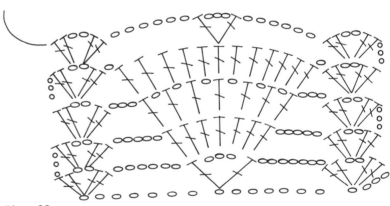

Photo 27   Chart 38

FESTIVE FANS

The finer the thread and hook you choose to use, the more exquisite these overlapping fans will appear. (See Photo 28.) Since they will become an heirloom to cherish, it is a good thing that they are worked as a complete-as-you-go pattern. Over and over they can be attached to special items, just waiting to be removed and used again.

Ch 13.

Row 1) (Beg at straight edge) Dc in 6th ch from hk and in next 2 chs, ch 7, sk 4 chs, sc in last ch. Ch 3, turn.

Row 2) (Beg at fan edge) Work 11 dc over ch-7 loop, ch 2, 3 dc over t-ch. Ch 5, turn.

Row 3) (Straight edge) Work 3 dc in first ch-2 sp, [ch 1, dc in next dc] 11 times; ch 1, dc in top of t-ch. Ch 5, turn.

Row 4) (Fan edge) Dc in first ch-1 sp, [ch 2, dc in next sp] 11 times; ch 2, 3 dc over t-ch. Ch 5, turn.

Row 5) Work 3 dc in first ch-2 sp, (ch 3, dc in next sp) 12 times. Ch 5, turn.

Row 6) Sc over first ch-3 loop, [ch 5, sc over next lp] 11 times; ch 5, 3 dc over t-ch. Ch 5, turn.

Row 7) Work 3 dc over first ch-5 lp, [ch 5, sc over next lp] 12 times. Ch 4, turn.

Row 8) (Fan edge) (We will be making picot-lps over the part of the fan that will hang free, and simple ch-lps over the part of the fan that will be used as a base for the next fan.) Sc in 3rd ch from hk (picot made), ch 1, sc over first ch-5 lp, [ch 4, make picot, ch 1, sc over next lp] 7 times; [ch 5, sc over next lp] 4 times; ch 5, 3 dc over t-ch. Ch 5, turn.

Row 9) (A partial row) Work 3 dc over first ch-5 lp, ch 7, sc over next lp. Ch-3, turn.

Row 10) (Like row 2) Work 11 dc over ch-7 lp, ch 2, 3 dc over t-ch. Ch 5, turn.

Row 11) (Like row 3) Work 3 dc in first ch-2 sp, [ch 1, dc in next dc] 11 times; ch 1, dc in top of t-ch; sc in next loop on previous scallop. Ch 5, turn.

Row 12) (Like row 4) Dc in first ch-1 sp [ch 2, dc in next sp] 11 times; ch 2, 3 dc over t-ch. Ch 5, turn.

Row 13) (Like row 5) Work 3 dc in first ch-2 sp, [ch 3, dc in next sp] 12 times. Sc in next lp on previous scallop. Ch 5, turn.

Row 14) (Like row 6) Sc over first ch-3 lp, [ch 5, sc over next lp] 11 times; ch 5, 3 dc over t-ch. Ch 5, turn.

Row 15) (Like row 7) Work 3 dc over first ch-5 lp, [ch 5, sc over next lp] 12 times. Sc in next lp on previous scallop. Ch 4, turn.

Row 16) (Repeat row 8) Sc in 3rd ch from hk (picot made), ch 1, sc over first ch-5 lp, (ch 4, make picot, ch 1, sc over next lp) 7 times; (ch 5, sc over next lp) 4 times; ch 5, 3 dc over t-ch. Ch 5, turn.

Rep rows 9 thru 16 for length desired, ending after completing row 16. Fasten off.

A chart for the above festive fan edging would look as follows:

Photo 28

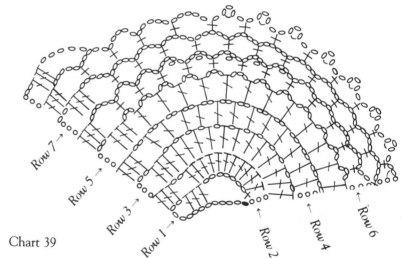

Chart 39

PLENTY OF PINEAPPLES

My secretary, Betty, insisted that I include this complete-as-you-go pineapple pattern. (See Photo 29.) She remembers her mother making yards of it to edge bleached flour-sack pillowcases, chicken-feed-premium towels, and Indian Head cotton tablecloths. The bleached flour-sack fabric and the chicken-feed-premium towels may be a thing of the past, unknown to those born after the Great Depression and World War II, but this lovely edging remains alive and well in today's world. It can be made of fine thread with a fine hook to make a special gift of a fine linen handkerchief, or with pearl cotton and a larger hook to adorn thick and fluffy towels. Each example will take on its own charm.

The pattern is nothing more than fishnet and pineapples with a heading of single crochet over a chain. There is no getting lost on this one, because as each pineapple tapers, the amount of fishnet gets larger—the kind of easy work to do when the TV is on but not worth watching.

Row 1) (Beg at heading edge) Ch 33, sc in 2nd ch from hk, 1 sc in ea of next 6 ch, [ch 5, skp 4 ch, sc in next ch of foundation ch] 5 times, ch 5, (6 ch-5 lps), [shell of 3 dc, ch 2, 3 dc] in last ch.

Row 2) (Beg at outer edge) Ch 5, turn, shell in ch-2 sp of previous shell, ch 5, (1 dc, ch 6, 1 dc) in 2nd lp (head of pineapple), ch 5, skp 1 ch-5 lp, shell in ch-5 lp, sc in next lp, ch 5, sc in next lp, ch 5, 1 sl st in ea of last 6 sc.

Row 3) (Heading edge) beg all odd rows ch 11, turn, sc in first lp, ch 5, sc in next lp, ch 5, shell in shell, ch 4, 14 tr in ch-6 lp, ch 4, shell in shell.

Row 4) Ch 5, turn, shell in shell, ch 4, sc in ea of 14 tr, ch 4, shell, [ch 5, sc in next lp] twice; end all even rows with ch 5, sk 2 chs on ch-11, sc in each of next 6 chs.

Row 5) Beg heading edge as before, then [ch 5, sc in next lp] twice, ch 5, shell in shell, ch 5, sk first sc, 12 sc, ch 5, shell in shell.

Row 6) Ch 5, turn, shell in shell, ch 5, sk first sc, 10 sc, ch 5, shell in shell, [ch 5, sc in next lp] 3 times, then end as before.

Row 7) Beg as before, then [ch 5, sc in next lp] 3 times, ch 5, shell in shell, ch 5, sk first sc, 8 sc, ch 5, shell in shell.

Row 8) Ch 5, turn, shell in shell, ch 5, sk first sc, 6 sc, ch 5, shell in shell, [ch 5, sc in next lp] 4 times, then end as before.

Row 9) Beg as before, then [ch 5, sc in next lp] 4 times, ch 5, shell in shell, ch 5, sk first sc, 4 sc, ch 5, shell in shell.

Row 10) Ch 5, turn, shell in shell, ch 5, sk first sc, 2 sc, ch 5, shell in shell, [ch 5, sc in next lp] 5 times, end as before.

Row 11) Beg as before, then [ch 5, sc in next lp] 5 times, ch 5, shell in shell, sk 2 sc, sc in center of shell.

Row 12) Ch 5, turn, shell in shell, ch 5, [1 dc, ch 6, 1 dc] in 2nd lp, ch 5, shell in 4th lp, sc in next lp, ch 5, sc in next lp, end as before.

Rep rows 3 thru 12 for pattern. When edging is desired length, end after completing row 11. FINAL ROW: Ch 5, turn, shell in shell, [ch 5 in next lp] 6 times, then end as before. Fasten off.

A chart for the above pineapple edging would look as follows:

Photo 29

Chart 40

VIOLETS

A friend of mine adores these sweet violets. (See Photo 30.) She wants me to scatter them everywhere. We found the pattern in an edging booklet, but we have used rows of them sprinkled in among rows of plain double crochet.

After optional rows of an openwork heading, the flowers themselves are made in two rows of triple crochet puffs. If you wish to use the edging as an insertion across flat double crochet work, you:

Ch desired length.

Row 1) *(Optional heading) Sc in 8th ch from hk,* * *ch 7, sk 4 ch, sc in next ch, rep from* * *across, end ch 3, sk 1, dc into last st, turn.*

Row 2) *(Optional heading)* * *Ch 7, sc in next ch-7 loop, rep from* * *across, ending ch 3, dc into last lp, ch 1, turn. Fasten off.*

Row 3) *(First half of flower row) (All trs are made as puff sts, that is, you retain the last 2 lps of each st on the hk and then when all trs are done in this manner, yo and go thru all lps on hk.)* * *Ch 5, 3 tr into base of ch, 3 tr into center st of next ch-7 lp, ch 5, sl st into same ch of same ch-7 lp, ch 5, sc into center st of next ch-7 lp* *; rep bet* *s across ending last petal of last flower with 4 trs, turn.*

Row 4) *(Second half of flower row) (All trs are made as puff sts.) Ch 5, 2 tr into center of flower of previous row, ch 5, sl st into center of flower (first horizontal petal made), ch 5, 2 tr in center of same flower, ch 5, sl st into center of same flower (vertical petal made), ch 5, 3 tr into center of flower (first flower complete),* * *ch 1, 3 tr into center of next flower, ch 5, sl st into center of same flower (horizontal petal made), ch 5, 2 tr into center of same flower, ch 5, sl st into center of same flower (vertical petal made), ch 5, 3 tr back into center of same flower, rep from* * *across.*

A chart for the above violet edging would look as follows:

Chart 41

Photo 30

If you use this as an insert, the following row is just chains between the vertical petals with a sc into the edge of the petal.

I'm not hardnosed about these "violets." They can be made in any color. In fact, in yellow they become common cinquefoil, the lovely "green and gold" wildflower. And they are completely reversible, back and front, up and down.

I grew up in an age when it was uncommon for a woman to be employed outside the home. Peeling potatoes, cooking foods, then handwashing the dishes all took hours. Laundry alone consumed two full, long, hard days—one to wash and one to iron. Now, thanks to prepared food, no-iron clothing, and countless appliances, we have time and energy in the evenings to once again lavish laces on linens.

24
PRECIOUS LITTLE
JEWELS TO ADD

I love an old-fashioned flower garden helter-skelter with blossoms of all colors and kinds, a lovely riot of the exuberance and hope of Mother Nature. I want to bring bouquets in with me to admire close up, but I can't bring myself to cut them off from their source of sustenance. A solution for me is to conjure up reproductions in thread and yarn that seem to take on a life of their own. There are hundreds that we could make. But the point of this chapter is not to list all of the possibilities and variations, but to introduce you to some of the special techniques in making precious little jewels to add as decorations.

CABBAGE ROSE

You were introduced to roses in the chapter about medallions and motifs, with an Irish rose square. I said that it was possible to vary the flower and this is such a variation. (See Photo 31.) Here we are working around an open center and making three rounds of eight offset petals. The finished effect is a full-blown, crowded, fluffy flower.

Ch 8. Join with sl st to first ch to form a ring.

Rnd 1) Ch 1 (counts as 1 sc), work 15 sc into ring. Join with sl st. (We need 16 sc so that we can make 8 lps on the next rnd.)

*Rnd 2) * Ch 5, sk 1 sc, sc into next sc, rep from * around. (8 loops.)*

Photo 31

Rnd 3) Into ea lp work 1 sc, 1 hdc, 5 dc, 1 hdc, 1 sc. Join with sl st. (8 petals.)

*Rnd 4) Tilting the petals forward, loosely sl st at the base of the sts to center dc of first petal, * ch 6, sc in the back of center dc of the next petal, rep from * around. (8 lps offset behind first rnd of petals.)*

Rnd 5) Into ea lp work 1 sc, 1 hdc, 7 dc, 1 hdc, 1 sc. Join with sl st. (8 offset petals.)

*Rnd 6) Tilting flower forward, loosely sl st at base of sts to center dc of first petal, * ch 7, sc in the back of center dc of petal, rep from * around. (8 offset petals.)*

Rnd 7) Into ea lp work 1 sc, 1 hdc, 9 dc, 1 hdc, 1 sc. (We could go on forever and ever making more rnds of lps and petals, but let's stop here.) Join with a sl st. Fasten off.

In thread, this pattern makes a wide, flat flower. In a yarn that has more loft, it makes a fluffier flower. There are several things you can do to make it even fluffier and floppier. 1) Make the chain-loops shorter, thereby cramming more stitches into a shorter space. 2) Add more stitches to each petal. 3) On Rnds 6 & 7 you could change the center dc's to [3 dc, 3 tr, 3 dc].

Without changing the stitches, if you wished, you could make each round of petals a different shade of the same hue, going either from light to dark, or from dark to light. The completed roses could decorate household items such as napkin rings or tissue box holders or toilet paper covers. Or they could decorate your crochet work-basket to carry around with you as an example of your skill. (Depending on the yarn or thread used, they could be a bit too heavy to use as clothing decoration except maybe as neck scarf ends or such.)

PRETTY PANSIES

These are the flowers that caught my childish eye so very long ago. (See Photo 32.) They are as pretty today as they were then. I have included them here, following the rose, because they are a variation of the same technique—an open center around which loops for the petals are made. There are five loops for the five petals. The petals themselves vary in size as real pansies do. Another variation from the preceding rose is that an additional round is worked to enlarge the size of each petal.

FLOWER: *Starting at center with yellow, ch 5. Join with a sl st to form ring.*

Rnd 1) Ch 1; [sc in ring, ch 3] 4 times; 5 dc in ring, drop lp from hk, insert hk from front to back in first dc of 5-dc group and draw dropped lp thru, ch 1 to fasten, ch 3. Join to first sc, fasten off. (5 lps and 1 cluster).

Rnd 2) (Make petals) Attach variegated purple with sl st at joining, [in next lp make 1 sc, 5 dc, 1 sc] 3 times; [in next lp make 1 sc, 2 dc, 3 tr, 2 dc, 1 sc] twice. Join to first sc. (3 small and 2 large petals).

Rnd 3) (Enlarge each petal) Ch 1, sc in joining, ch 3, make 2 dc in ea of next 4 dc, 2 sc in next dc, sc in next sc, sl st in next sc, ch 3, 2 dc in ea of next 5 dc, ch 3, sl st in next sc, sc in next sc, 2 sc in next dc, 2 dc in ea of next 4 dc, ch 3, sl st in next sc, (sc in next sc, 2 dc in next dc, 3 tr in next 5 sts, 2 dc in next dc, sc in next sc) twice. Join, fasten off.

LEAF: *With green, ch 9 (which will be center vein of leaf).*

Rnd 1) Sc in 2nd ch from hk, sc in next ch, hdc in next ch, dc in next 3 ch, hdc in next ch, in last ch [sc, ch 2, sc]; working back along opposite side of foundation ch, hdc in next st, dc in next 3 sts, hdc in next st, sc in next 2 sts, join to first sc.

Photo 32

Rnd 2) (Make the leaf wider) Ch 1, 2 sc in joining, sc in ea st to ch-2 sp, sc in ch-2 sp, ch 2, sl st in 2nd ch from hk, sc in same ch-2 sp (for point of leaf), sc in ea rem st. Join. Fasten off. Attach to back of pansy wherever desired.

I personally feel that tampering with the color scheme of these pansies would be like tampering with the Holy Writ. They are *purple* pansies and that is that! If the color is limited, the usage is not. They can decorate blouses, hankies, nighties, baby and children's things, pot holders, luncheon mats, and on and on. The finished flower needs to be smallish, and I'd hesitate to make them in Class C knitting worsted, but they do well in any thread or yarn that you can find in variegated purples.

SWEET DOUBLE DAISY

Twenty-eight chain-loop petals, half made in the front loop of the single crochets at the open center and half made in the back loop of those same stitches, form this frilly daisy. (See Photo 33.)

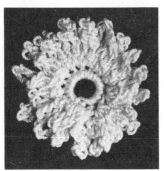

Photo 33

Ch 6 and join with a sl st to form a ring.

Rnd 1) Work 14 sc into ring, sl st in first sc.

Rnd 2) (Front rnd of ch-lp petals) Working in the front lp of ea st, [sc, ch 6, sc into same st] 14 times, sl st in first sc.

Rnd 3) (Back rnd of petals) Tilting first rnd of petals forward and working in back lp of ea st of Rnd 1, [sc, ch 8, sc into same st] 14 times, sl st in first sc. Fasten off.

Adventuresome crocheters may wish to experiment with color on this flower. The center could be golden yellow, the front round of petals could be light pink and the back round could be dark pink. The finished daisies could ring the neckline of a simple half-double crochet shell-type blouse or tank top. In blue with purple centers, the flowers could become bachelor's buttons to frame a face beneath a cap that warded off winter winds. Or how about daisies with lime green centers with just a single round of white petals scattered over a simple yellow double crochet baby afghan?

SPLENDID CHRYSANTHEMUM

Again two rounds of petals encircle an open center, but this time after we chain out, we make a sort of picot and work back on the chain we have just made to form a broader curling petal. The process is time-consuming, but elegant. (See Photo 34.)

Photo 34

Ch 5, join with a sl st to form a ring.

Rnd 1) Work 13 sc into ring, sl st in first sc.

Rnd 2) (Front rnd of petals) Working in the front lp of ea st, [sc, ch 5, sc in the 2nd ch from hk (to form point of petal), hdc in the next 2 chs, dc in next ch, sc in next sc at beg of ch (petal made)] 13 times, sl st in first sc.

Rnd 3) (Back rnd of petals) Tilting the front rnd of petals toward you and working in back lp of ea st, [sl st, ch 6, sc in 2nd ch from hk, sc in next 4 chs (petal made)] 13 times, sl st in first sc. Fasten off.

From the leftovers in your yarn stash, you could whip up a marvelous bouquet of chrysanthemums, each of different color and size depending on the yarn and hook you used. With the beginning and ending tail ends taped with floral tape to stems that can be purchased at your favorite craft store, you can produce an everlasting floral arrangement for your home or someone else's. Or wrap a gift package with brown wrapping paper, tie it with yarn, and, instead of a bow, use three of these flowers. Who knows, the handmade package decoration may be treasured as much as the gift inside.

There is nothing to stop you from varying this flower. A larger beginning ring and more single crochets in it would mean more petals. A longer chain-out, a few slip stitches on it before the single crochet(s) begin and you have a spider mum. When you understand what is going on in your craft, you are the mistress of it. When I was a teenage beginner, I followed instructions like the Word of God. When I understood what was happening, I was free to create and had dominion over my world of crocheting.

STAR WITH FIVE POINTS

Does your Christmas tree need more decorations? Does a child's room need a mobile of shining stars? Would someone like a star-studded costume? Make a closed-center circle, enlarge it on the next round, then chain out for the points, working back along the chain with increasingly longer stitches toward the center. (See Photo 35.)

Ch 2.

Rnd 1) Work 5 sc in 2nd ch from hk.

Rnd 2) Work 3 sc in ea st of rnd 1. (Remember to watch for the place you began and don't go past it).

Rnd 3) [Sc in next st, ch 6, sl st in 2nd ch from hk (for point), sc in next ch, hdc in next ch, dc in next ch, tr in next ch, tr in side of first sc, sl st in next 2 sts] 5 times, sl st in very first sc. Fasten off.

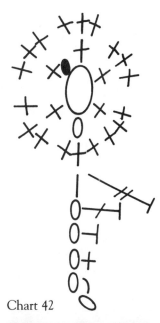

Chart 42

A chart for the above star design would look as follows at right (see Chart 42).

The number of different kinds of stars that can be made is endless. Another plain round of single crochet after round 1 will give you more places from which to begin points. All of the points do not have to be either the same length or width! Snowflakes follow the same basic idea. Though all snowflakes are six-sided, stars can have as many points as you can crowd in. Investigate the possibili-

Photo 35

ties; if you are a pattern follower, there are lots of pamphlets and booklets at your friendly local supplier's store. (And pick up some metallic thread while you are there; stars were meant to shine!)

LUCKY FOUR-LEAFED CLOVER

Remember in Chapter 17 on decreasing you were taught how to make a puff stitch by *starting* to make either a double or a triple crochet, and then another and another in the same place, finally finishing off the last step of all the stitches in one fell swoop? Well, a puff stitch of three triples forms the centers of the leaves of this lucky shamrock. (See Photo 36.) From an open single crochet center, you chain four stitches up, make a puff stitch, chain four stitches down to the center again and fasten with a single crochet. When you have completed four of these full and rounded leaves, you make a longer chain and single crochet back along it to form the stem. It is simple and easy, so don't let these horribly complicated instructions send you running for the aspirin bottle. I have printed this misbegotten mess of asterisks and brackets and parentheses just to show you how cumbersome things can get in this lovely world of making lace in the air.

When you encounter gobbledy-gook such as round 2 below, stop and look first at the picture. See what it is the designer wants you to do. Are puff stitches or popcorns or groups and clusters called for? Once you can recognize the blob within, you can relax and settle back and just do it, muttering under your breath, "Why didn't they just say so in plain English?" Everything from ". . . yarn over twice, insert . . ." to ". . . pull through 4 loops on hook, . . ." is just a puff stitch, which is a decrease of three triple crochets made in the same spot!

Try it with green Class B smooth classic sport-weight yarn and a size G hook.

(Please note that these four-leafed clovers are not to be confused with true Irish crochet shamrocks. They are made by an entirely different technique.)

Ch 5, join with a sl st to form ring.

Rnd 1) Work 14 sc into ring. (Where did we get the number 14? 3 for each of 4 leaves, 3 × 4 = 12 + 2 for the stem.)

Rnd 2) 1 sl st into ea of first 2 sc, to make one leaf, [ch 4, yo twice, insert hk in next st, (draw up a lp, yo, pull thru 2 lps on hk, yo, draw thru 2 lps

on hk), * yo twice, insert hook in same st that you just worked in, rep bet
( ) *, rep bet *s twice, yo, pull thru 4 lps on hk, ch 4, sl st in next 2 sts],
rep bet [ ] 3 times, to make a stem, ch 6, turn, sk first ch, sc in ea ch, sl st
in first sc. Fasten off.

A chart for the above four-leafed clover design would look as
follows at right (see Chart 43).

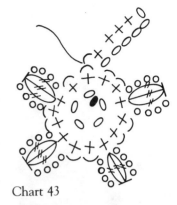

Chart 43

How many places can you think of to scatter these lovely lucky
four-leafed clovers? Sitting on place mats, napkins, and scarves,
decorating blouses, accenting tams and coasters, perched on a
Christmas tree, they sing out in pearl cotton; they puff up in worsted yarn.

BUTTERFLY

Photo 36

This is a thoroughly Maggie-ized invention. I wanted a butterfly
to decorate a bridal shower gift. I spent more than an hour looking
through my reference books and past issues of crochet magazines
and didn't find what I was looking for. "Nuts!" I said, "In this
amount of time I could have just made one up. There are thousands
of kinds of butterflies in the world and no one will ever know
whether or not mine is authentic. A butterfly is a body tapered at
both ends, four wings that resemble leaves rounded at the ends and
chopped off at the body. They can be any color combination in the
world. There is nothing to it, but to do it." (See Photo 37.)

*With dark color, ch 13 for the base of the body. Sl st into the 2nd ch from
hk to make a point at the end, sc in next ch, hdc in ea of next 8 ch, sc in
next ch, sl st in last ch, fasten off. (Body complete.)*

The body you choose to make can be longer or shorter with more
or fewer chains. It can be made fatter with dcs in the middle, or
skinnier with all scs.

*(Upper wing—make 2) With any color, ch 9, join with a sl st to last hdc
of body, ch 1, working out along the ch-9, 1 sc in ea of next 3 sts, 1 dc in
ea of next 3 sts, 1 tr in ea of next 2 sts, make enough tr in last st to turn a
flat corner, and then work back toward the body on the opposite side of the
ch with 2 tr, 3 dc and 3 sc. Join with a sl st to body. Fasten off. With any
new color, join at body and work around wing enlarging it with increasingly longer sts and increasing when necessary to keep it lying flat. When
that row is finished, do another one (with the same or a different color) in
the same manner. (Upper wing is fat and wide).*

Your upper wings can be any size or shape you choose. Make one and see if you like it. (You can always rip it out!) Just count and copy for the matching wing on the other side.

Photo 37

(Lower wing—make 2. Top edge of lower wing will be overlapped by upper wing.) Ch 11, join with a sl st to hdc at other end of body. Ch 1, working out along the ch-11, 1 sc in ea of next 10 sts, 1 dc in next st, enough dc in last st to make a flat corner, working back toward body on ch-11, 1 dc in next st, 1 sc in ea st, join with a sl st to body. Fasten off. Add a new color and enlarge wing as before. (Lower wing is longer and skinnier).

Adventuresome crocheters can even figure out a swallowtail butterfly. Play with it. Create your own and have fun.

As I said when I began, this is only a small handful of the splendid little jewels that you can make. There are also petunias and poinsettias, lilies and lotuses awaiting you, to name but a few. You can follow instructions or you can make up your own designs as surely as a jeweler can set a stone. Who cares whether or not the flowers and birds and bees are anatomically accurate; if they are attractive, and you are so inclined, do it!

25
MULTI-COLOR JACQUARD CROCHET

Early in the nineteenth century, a man by the name of Joseph Jacquard invented a loom that would produce an intricately woven pattern of many colors. As the fabrics made on this special kind of loom became available, women took a look at them, lusted after them, and said to themselves, "I could do something like this with my crocheting. It wouldn't cost anything. Just change colors in special patterns, and wouldn't they be pretty!"

The man's name has stuck to multi-colored crocheting, and today we call "jacquard" any of a whole family of distinctive effects. Checkerboards, geometrics, argyle-like diamonds, plaids, balloons, animals, houses, and all kinds of scenes are all examples of what inventiveness has given to us. Jacquard is a wonderful way to use up bits and pieces of leftover yarn, making a bunch of balloons on the front of a child's otherwise plain sweater, a house and tree on a hotpad, or a plaid coverlet when there is not enough of any one color to make any one thing.

It is the changing of color that is the most important element of jacquard patterns, not the variation and placement of the stitches as with shell or up-and-down patterns. Usually the background is solid and flat, and usually of only either all single, half-double, or all double crochet. Occasionally a mesh of "make one stitch, chain one, skip one stitch" is made where a "top chain-stitched" vertical line will be worked later.

Remember from the earlier chapters that we considered single crochet stitches to be one stitch tall—as tall as they are wide—making a square. If you work your color pattern over a background bed of single crochet, each separately colored stitch will turn out to be almost square. If you use a background bed of double crochet, however, each stitch will be slightly more than twice as tall as it is wide. So the kind of stitch you decide to use will depend upon what you want the finished project to look like. You'll have a hard time making balloons look round in double crochet and the roofline of a house may look funny, too. But in single crochet you'll have no problem with those designs. Argyle-like diamonds will usually look better in double crochet because we think of long-and-narrow areas of color rather than square ones.

Depending on the effect desired, instructions for jacquard crochet can be written in two ways. We can do it with words or we can do it with pictures. If we are working with a repeating instruction across a row, for instance, for a row of a diamond pattern, we can simply say, "Row 3) 1 st of color A, 5 sts of B." If we are working with specialty shapes, such as balloons, we are much better off to draw it and make a chart or graph. Regardless how the designer has chosen to write the directions, the finished effect can be lovely.

(If you have in mind a particular motif, a snowman for a Christmas stocking, for instance, and do not choose to design it yourself, look into the wonderful wealth of square charted designs created for needlepoint and cross stitch. If they are not too complicated and do not call for a lot of colors, they work up marvelously in single crochet!)

As in so many endeavors—cooking or cleaning or crafting— there are little tricks to ease the process. Tricks such as, "How do you change to a new color?" Remember in Chapter 15 we talked about changing color, and that there were two ways to do it. For jacquard crochet it usually works better to

make the last step of the last stitch of the old color in next color. Before the last loops are worked off, just drop the old color and finish the stitch with the new. Let the old color hang there and go on with the new. When (and if) you pick up the old color again on the same row, be careful not to pull too tightly on the old color as you begin to work with it. You must leave enough yarn between the stitches for the fabric to lie flat and smooth. If you pull too tightly, your fabric will gather and ruffle up.

Because of the loops along the backside of the row, many crocheters find that their gauge in jacquard crochet is smaller than their gauge with the same yarn in solid color work. If that is true for you, use a larger hook on the areas of jacquard.

With a little forethought, even if you are working flat, that is, back and forth, you can make all of the strands fall to the same side of the fabric. Which side of the fabric the loops fall on will depend upon how you insert your hook. You have two choices of what to do with those loops. Many people are content to let them hang. That is a little messy for my standards. I solve the problem in the following way:

If your fabric is reversible, and/or if you don't want loops of thread on the back of your fabric, on next row take extra pains and work over the strands from the row below. That is, insert your hook from underneath the loop-strands, let the strands simply sit there, and work over them as you make the new stitch. (See Figure 83.)

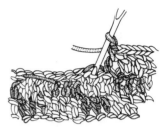

Figure 83

I find it slow and tedious to hide those loop strands, but I find it even more distressing to leave them loose. I can't have my pizza without the calories!

A BUNCH OF BALLOONS

A symbol of joy and delight, childhood and freedom, balloons are easy to make. They are just circles of color worked against a background of single crochet. (See Photo 38.) And though the shape cannot vary, the size can. Often I make larger balloons toward the bottom and smaller ones near the top, though there are no rules about it. And I like to use odd numbers of balloons in a grouping to avoid any thought of confining geometry, to keep them free and wholesome. When I am finished, I thread a tapestry needle with a darker-than-the-background color. With simple backstitch or chain stitch I embroider strings to make sure that the eye knows that these are balloons tied with strings, and not just spheres of color. A chart for this design would look as follows:

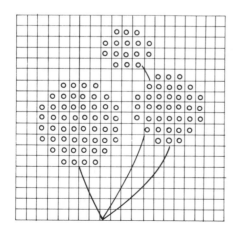

Chart 44

Photo 38

A sky-blue place mat made of thick, absorbent cotton yarn with a huge bunch of colorful balloons tied down to one corner would brighten the peanut butter and jelly sandwich lunch of any child.

NEVER-ENDING TRIANGLES

Alternating triangles of color can change a flat dull crocheted fabric into an exciting one. (See Photo 39.) With closely related colors such as blue and turquoise you get an almost iridescent effect. With unrelated colors such as black and yellow you get a bold modern look. You can do this simple pattern with either double or half-double crochet stitches depending on what you want to use the fabric for.

The multiple is 6 stitches and the full repeat is 6 rows.

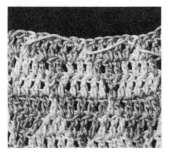

Photo 39

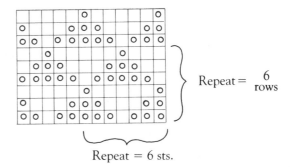

Chart 45

Repeat = 6 rows

Repeat = 6 sts.

Can you imagine a woolen jacket of half-double crochet in black and white to wear with slacks? Or rectangular cotton hand towels of double crochet to brighten a guest bathroom?

PLAIDS

Plaids are perhaps the showiest example of jacquard. I prefer to make plaids in double crochet because of the speed, though they can be made equally effectively in single or half-double crochet. Whole rows are made of one solid color according to a pre-planned scheme. Where the scheme calls for a vertical line to be added later, a mesh of chain-one is made instead of a double crochet stitch.

The vertical lines are added after the straight-across rows of the fabric are completed. Often they are made with a *doubled* strand of yarn. (And sometimes a larger hook may be required to carry the doubled strand.) As the vertical chain stitches are made over the front of the mesh spaces, the working yarn(s) are held at the *back* of the work so that both sides of the fabric are covered.

It is true that when making plaids you are actually working the fabric twice, and it is more time-consuming. (It also makes for a heavier fabric.) But the results can be spectacular! Your plaid can be subtle and almost iridescent, or it can be bold and bright, all depending on your choice of color and spacing.

TWO-COLOR PLAID

A multiple of 11 stitches and a repeat of 8 rows. (See Photo 40 and chart below.)

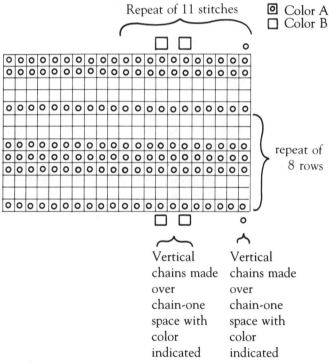

Repeat of 11 stitches

☐ Color A
☐ Color B

repeat of 8 rows

Photo 40

Vertical chains made over chain-one space with color indicated

Vertical chains made over chain-one space with color indicated

Chart 48
When making horizontal solid-color rows, be sure to make a chain-one space instead of a stitch where vertical lines will be added.

THREE-COLOR PLAID

A multiple of 12 stitches and a repeat of 6 rows. (See Photo 41 and chart below.)

Photo 41

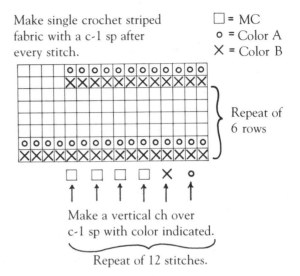

Make single crochet striped fabric with a c-1 sp after every stitch.

□ = MC
o = Color A
✗ = Color B

Repeat of 6 rows

Make a vertical ch over c-1 sp with color indicated.

Repeat of 12 stitches.

Chart 47

Please don't be limited by these two plaid suggestions. Make up your own! Plaids have no stern and hidebound rules. You can have as many rows and stitches between colors as you choose. Plaids can be whatever you want them to be. Have you ever thought of using three or four colors of yarn in different plaids to make scatter pillows for a plain-colored couch or bed? Various sizes of pillow forms can be purchased at fabric stores and, presto, you become an original decorator.

III

AFTER THE LAST STITCH IS FINISHED

26

PUTTING IT ALL TOGETHER

One especially nice thing about doilies is that when you are through, you are through. Just fasten off, hide in the beginning and ending tail ends of yarn, and the piece is finished. Unfortunately the same cannot be said about many medallions and most articles of clothing. Pieces have to be put together to make a usable item. This is not my favorite thing to do, and I am not alone; many crocheters hate it. But how we complete a job is as important as how we begin it.

When my four boys were growing up, I was a mean mother. Though I could have afforded to hire many necessary yard and household jobs done, I chose to make the boys do most of them. I felt that learning to do a job, and doing it well, were part of their basic education, as vital as reading and arithmetic. And I insisted that the job of cleaning and sweeping the carport was not finished until boxes were placed where they belonged in the storeroom, sweepings were dumped in the trash can, and brooms and dust pans were put away. Half-done jobs were not acceptable, and to ensure completed projects, I enforced the credo, "Every lousily done job means that you have to do two more." Slowly and surely they learned to do the bothersome finishing work.

Though the bothersome finishing work of any job may not be much fun, in crocheting especially, it is vitally important. The effect of the loveliest pattern in the world, the most perfectly made stitches, the finest design concept can be ruined by thoughtless and sloppy finishing techniques.

The words *thoughtless* and *sloppy* in the paragraph above were chosen with care because we really do have to *think* about how to go about putting all of the pieces together, and we have to join them with *care* because there are no hard and fast rules and techniques that *always* work on everything. What is a good idea for one article may not work at all for another. You need to know a whole bag of handy techniques to be prepared for different situations.

The object of finishing work in crochet is to enhance the loveliness of the article and ensure that it will wear well. The most elegant bedspread in the world is of no value if the motifs come apart the first time it is washed. A jacket that has ugly seams and botched joinings is no source of pride and joy.

The object of finishing work in crochet is *not* that the finishing be done in any certain way, but that whatever way you choose *works* for that particular item. I recently made myself a vest in a diamond mesh pattern of glossy, slippery yarn. In the "idea" stage I had envisioned a saw-tooth edging of [sl st, sc, dc, tr, dc, sc, sl st]. By the time I got the thing half-finished, I realized that it would need a firm, hard edging of three rows of single crochet to make the vest hold its boxy shape. In another yarn the saw-tooth edging might have worked. However, it was inappropriate in the yarn I was using.

THINGS TO THINK ABOUT IN JOINING

IS THE SEAM A DECORATIVE ELEMENT?

Many times we want our seams to be hidden and invisible— letting the fancy pattern stitch stand out on its own. Yet there are times when we want to make the seam prominent and visible. A raised seam on the outside may reinforce the shape of the medallions and make them even more appealing. We may even want to use a different colored thread to make an outside seam, as I did with my granny square afghan. Or think of how dark, solid-color outside seams would emphasize the shapes of pieces of a tweed jacket. Knowing whether or not you want your seam to be visible will help you determine what kind of a seam you want to make.

Seams made by either slip-stitching or single crocheting the edges together from the inside will always show from the outside. There will always be a visible valley on the public side.

HOW MUCH BULK AND WEIGHT
DO YOU WANT IN SEAMS?

*As far as I am concerned, the less weight and bulk in seams the better.
The object of putting the pieces together is to get an attractive and usable
item. Heavy, bulky seams do not make an article any nicer to look at.*

In fact, wide or thick joinings detract from the lovely effect of all of
our carefully made stitches.

*Crocheted and backstitched seams always add unwanted bulk and weight
to the finished item.*

The one exception to this is when seams are deliberately made on
the outside of the piece to enhance the shape of the pieces. In that
case, the bulkier the better. But when your crocheted fabric is light
and fragile-looking, you have to be careful to avoid weighty seams
that may cause drooping or sagging. Single crocheted or back-
stitched seams may do just that. Try invisible weaving instead.

WHETHER TO WORK FROM
THE OUTSIDE OR THE INSIDE

If you make seams on the inside, the side not seen by the public,
it is very hard to be certain what is going on on the outside, the side
that will be seen by the public, until the seam is completed. And,
when all is said and done, it is the public side that counts. In making a seam from the inside, it is easy to wander a bit with your
stitches, a bit farther out here, a bit farther in there. You may not
notice the meandering as you are doing it, but it may show up
horribly on the outside when you are finished. Also, working a
backstitch, in particular, you may be splitting the yarn or thread as
you move along the inside of the piece. When you are finished, the
split yarn may show up on the outside and look ugly.

*Whenever possible I prefer to make seams from the important side, the
public side, because I can see the finished result as I go.*

THE KINDS OF JOININGS
YOU MAY ENCOUNTER

*The manner in which you choose to make the seam or joining will depend
upon the kinds of pieces you have to put together.*

There are five possible kinds of joinings that you will encounter in putting crocheted items together:

1) *Vertical to vertical.* Up-and-down edges joined to other up-and-down edges. The side seams that join the back of a jacket to the front, or two long strips of an afghan that need to be attached are examples. It may be very important that rows of one side abut perfectly to matching rows of the other side as you move along vertical edges. If this kind of seam is to be inconspicuous, I prefer to use invisible weaving. If the seam is a design element, I prefer to use single crochet on the outside, often with a contrasting color.

2) *Horizontal to horizontal.* Final row stitches abutted to final row stitches. The edges of a hexagon medallion or a granny square, or flat, straight-across shoulder seams are examples. In this case, you want to join and hide the back loop of the edge stitches, carefully fitting each stitch of one piece against the corresponding stitch of the other piece. And you want the front loops of both pieces to nestle close to each other. Many instructions will tell you to use a sewing whipstitch from the backside on these. Again I prefer to use invisible weaving from the front.

3) *Horizontal to vertical.* The up-and-down edge of one piece fits up against either the first or the final row of another piece. Crosswise ribbing attached to the bottom of a sweater and the underbelly of a stuffed animal joining the sides and legs are examples that come quickly to mind. Here, you want to hide the back loop of the horizontal edge (if there is one), and use as little as possible of the vertical edge. In the case of the sweater ribbing, you may want some flexibility and elasticity in the seam. Backstitching from the inside is not a good idea if you need stretch; it is not elastic. Whipstitching is better, but invisible weaving is best.

4) *Diagonal.* Raglan sleeve joinings and pieces of novelty articles are the best examples. On these edges, if you used decreases for shaping, they may be treated just the same as other vertical seams. If you made your pieces narrower by simply avoiding the end stitch, you will have a series of steep stair steps. Read on to where I discuss the problems of shoulder stair steps. (One time of putting together awkward and mismatched stair steps may be sufficient to convert you to using decreases instead of skipping end stitches.)

5) *Stair-step shoulders.* There is no way around it; human shoulders always slope down from the neck to the arm. If we make straight, flat-across shoulders in our garments, particularly sleeveless ones, we can get an unflattering, fly-away batwing effect. The better answer is usually to make partial or short rows to taper the shoulders. Unfortunately, this will result in ugly little triangular shapes to get rid of when making the seam. My favorite way, again,

is to do invisible weaving from the front. An alternative is to back-stitch or even machine-stitch the seam from the inside. Any way you do it, it often takes a little bit of touch-up steaming to get rid of the mess.

PREPARE YOURSELF FOR THE JOB WITH THE RIGHT TOOLS

We talked about all of the following tools in the chapter called "Supply and Demand" and suggested that you keep a little pouch of necessary tools, but I feel it is important to remind you of them before you begin to put your project together. You will need:

A *tapestry needle* with *a blunt point*. In making seams, your needle should slide alongside the fabric yarn. It should not spear or pierce it. The needle should be the smallest size that you can successfully thread with *the same yarn that was used in working the piece*, because that is what you will use to make the seam.

Pins. I use *safety pins* when I am doing invisible weaving from the outside, and *long plastic-coated hair-roller fastener pins* when I am backstitching from the inside. Make life easy for yourself; fasten together each end of the area to be seamed with pins. If it is more than a few inches long, fasten it together in the middle, and maybe even in quarters. Usually you will want to match rows to rows. If you don't use pins, you can easily get close to the end only to find that one piece is longer than the other. Then the whole seam has to come out and be redone.

A *tape measure* so that you can double-check that the seam (or added border) will be the correct length. It is easy to make a back-stitched seam shorter than the rest of the piece if you don't measure as you go. An underarm seam that hikes up is ugly. It is also easy to make an added border longer than the body of the article, causing an unwanted ruffle if you don't measure as you go. Only by check-ing yourself frequently can you be sure that you are getting the desired length.

And *scissors* of course. (I know that cavewomen cut threads with their teeth, but they didn't wear lipstick.)

USE THE YARN THE ITEM WAS MADE WITH TO MAKE THE SEAMS

It is almost always best to use the yarn or thread the item was made with to make the seams. If you use a different thread, it may have different washing, wearing, stretching, and fading qualities than the original with which the article was made. The only time I get into trouble with this bit of advice is when I use a very nubby yarn. The nubs give me problems in weaving invisible seams; they won't always go through the small openings of the stitches. When they just won't budge, I first try picking out the nubs by hand and getting rid of them. If that doesn't work, I will purchase a small skein of pearl cotton, which comes in a wide array of colors, and make my seams of that.

YARN WEARS OUT AS YOU MAKE SEAMS WITH IT

I know that constantly joining in new yarn to finish a seam is bothersome. And I know that it is tempting to use a piece of yarn or thread long enough to make the whole seam. But the friction caused by pulling yarn or thread in between the crocheted stitches causes it to wear out rapidly when making woven, backstitched, or whipstitched seams. For the sake of good wearing qualities, please use short pieces, not more than twenty inches long, to make your seams. It is even more bothersome to repair a seam that gives out than it is to keep joining in new yarn.

SOME OF THE MOST COMMON WAYS OF JOINING:

INVISIBLE WEAVING

I first learned *invisible weaving* for knits. I thought it was magic, for suddenly I was able to make narrow, lightweight seams that were almost imperceptible to the eye. The next time I had to put together a crocheted garment, I tried it and it worked wonderfully. It is now my favorite way to join crochet and I rarely use any other method.

Besides the advantage of making a non-bulky joining, it is done from the outside, the public side, of the article and you can see what the finished thing will look like *as you do it.*

If you have never tried invisible weaving, don't be frightened by the thought of learning something new. Even old dogs can learn new tricks. Charlie, my standard poodle, was no longer a puppy-child when I bought a new car. He was used to riding in the back seat of the old car, entering through the back door, and he loved to go for rides. To ride in the new car, he had to learn to jump into the hatchback from the rear. Rather than stay home, he quickly learned. And rather than continue to have ugly seams, you can quickly learn to make invisible ones. Give it a try!

But just reading about it with your eyes isn't enough. Your fingers need to learn it, just as they needed to learn to make the stitches themselves. Please take time now to make three swatches of double crochet, each about four inches square, to practice with. Any yarn will do, but I suggest a Class C smooth, classic worsted—good old standard 4-ply—because the openings in the stitches are large enough for beginners to see. Once you know how, you can do invisible weaving on anything.

VERTICAL WOVEN SEAMS

Thread a tapestry needle with a strand of yarn about twenty inches long. On a flat surface, lay two of the swatches side by side, starting slip loops on the left, foundation edges at the bottom, and final row at the top. You will immediately notice that when they are aligned row for row, the end posts are not the same. On the first row, on the right-hand piece, the first end post is a dc, and on the left-hand piece, the end post is a ch-3. On the second row, the situation is reversed; on the right-hand piece, the second end post is a ch-3, and it is a dc on the left-hand piece. Our object in invisible weaving is to join the dc to the ch-3 so neatly that they will look like one stitch.

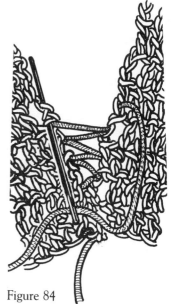

Figure 84

With safety pins, pin the pieces together. From the back, insert your needle into the outermost, bottom-most chain stitch of the left-hand piece. Leaving a six-inch long tail end dangling at the back, pull the yarn through. Go across the space between the two swatches and from the front insert your needle down into the outermost, bottom-most chain of the right-hand piece. Pull the thread through to the back and tie a square knot.

On the left-hand post, from the back, bring the needle up in the second chain stitch of the end post. Pull the yarn through. Go across the gap, and from the front insert the needle down in the same spot where you went in before and bring it up in the middle of the double crochet. Pull the yarn through.

* Go back across the gap, insert your needle back into the same spot you came out of before, and bring it up on the same piece a short distance higher up *, which in the case of double crochet, will be the top of the stitch. (See Figure 84.)

Just keep on going, repeating the words between the *s in the paragraph above over and over.

After you have made about four or five weaving stitches, stop and pull firmly but gently on the weaving yarn.

The two swatches will pull together, and the opposite edges will abut each other.

Holding the top of the seam in your left hand, pull down on the bottom of the seam with your right hand to adjust the tension so that the seam is just as tight or just as loose as the swatch stitches are.

See how easy it is, and isn't it lovely to look at. I wish that the printer could make the paragraph above that begins with an asterisk leap out of the page at you by printing it in Day-Glo orange. The words between the asterisks are important ones. Memorize them with both your eyes and your fingers. They are the formula for invisible weaving, regardless of the kind of stitch involved. Sure, there will be differences, but the formula remains the same. You will probably need only one vertical weaving stitch for single crochet, and you may need three for a triple, but you do them in the same manner.

Students often ask me, "But what if the two pieces aren't the same? What if there are more vertical rows on one side than on the other?" Well, you just fudge a little, that's all. Not in the middle of the seam, but near an edge, you finagle and on the longer piece, bring your needle up farther along than on the short piece. I won't tell if you don't.

And students will try to get me to make a hard and fast rule. "From which direction should I weave the seam, bottom to top or top to bottom?" they will ask. The answer is that it doesn't matter. What matters is that you begin the seam from the point that will be most exposed. On an underarm jacket seam, people will see the hemline. Any mismatched rows will be concealed by the arm.

HORIZONTAL SEAM WEAVING

When you are weaving horizontally, you will insert your needle *between the front and back loop* of final-row edges. But the formula is the same. Pick up the third swatch, place it above the first swatch with the final row on the bottom so that you are joining horizontal final row to horizontal final row.

With safety pins, pin the piece together. At the right-hand edge, from the back, insert your needle into the outermost, edge-most place on the lower piece. Leaving a six-inch-long tail dangling at the back, pull the yarn through. Go across the space between the two swatches and from the front insert your needle down into the outermost, edge-most place on the upper piece. Pull the thread through to the back and tie a square knot.

On the lower swatch, from the back, bring the needle up between the front and the back loop in the first stitch. Pull the yarn through. Go across the gap, and from the front insert the needle into the same spot where you went in before and bring it up in between the front and the back loop in the middle of the first stitch. Pull the yarn through.

* Go across the gap and, from the front, insert your needle between the front and back loops, back into the same spot you came out of before and bring it up in the next stitch between the front and back loops *. (See Figure 85.)

Keep on repeating the instructions between the asterisks.

After every four or five stitches, stop and adjust the tension.

Figure 85

See how snugly and perfectly the two swatches nestle together. The back loops of the edges of each piece disappear to the inside and you have a lovely seam. The front loop of the bottom piece is butted to the front loop of the top piece.

In weaving medallions together, it is usually easiest to weave the seam in the same direction the final row was made, whenever possible. Never forget that fudging is allowed. If somehow there is an extra stitch or two on one piece, take an extra long stitch on that piece near one edge.

(If you come to an area where there is only a chain-length, you can often make a sewing running stitch through the chain-length until you come to the next solid area. That is a lot easier and quicker than fastening off at the end of a solid space and joining in new yarn again at the next solid space. If the running stitch shows, you'll just have to grit your teeth and contend with lots of short seams.)

If you are joining a foundation row to a foundation row, or a foundation row to a final row, you use the same formula of * Go across the gap, and, from the front, insert the needle back in the same spot you came out of and up in the next stitch. * Of course, if you are working with a foundation row, you have only the bottom loop and not a top loop to bother with.

WEAVING HORIZONTAL TO VERTICAL

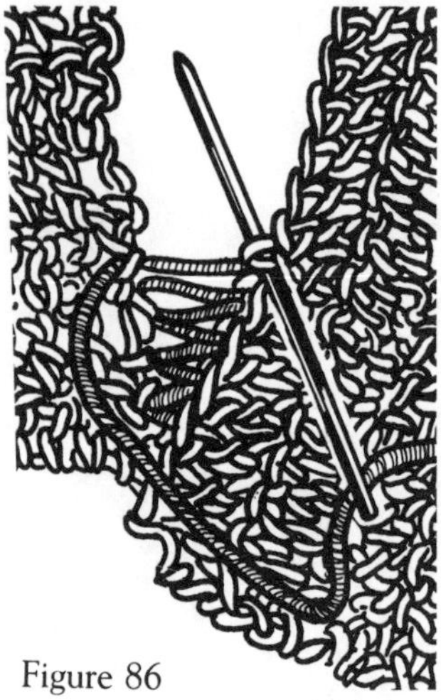

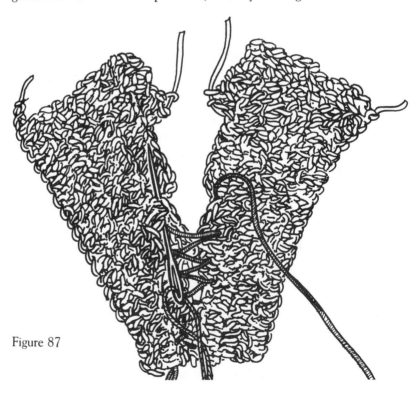

Figure 86

Now pull the third swatch down to meet the second swatch and you have a different situation to deal with. You will be joining a horizontal edge to a vertical one.

On the horizontal edge you will place your needle between the front and back loop, stitch for stitch, and you will make your stitches on the vertical edge however long as is necessary to make the pieces join smoothly. (See Figure 86.)

STAIR STEPS

When dealing with stair steps you simply cut corners. Not with scissors, but just by avoiding them. When I was a beginner at weaving seams, I used to make a diagonal line by basting a sewing thread where I wanted the seam to be. (See Figure 87.) I then made my invisible weaving seam from the front, using the basting as a guideline. With more experience, I now just wing it.

Figure 87

SINGLE CROCHET

To make a seam of single crochet on the inside:

With straight pins, first pin the area together. Place a slip loop on the hook. Holding the fabric between your left thumb and forefinger insert your hook under one strand of the front piece and under one strand of the back piece, and make a single crochet stitch. Move on and make another. (See Figure 88.)

Piece #1 →

Piece #2 →

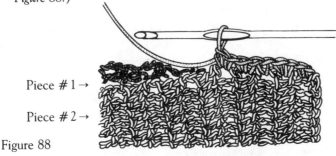

Figure 88

You have to be very careful to catch only the very edge single strand of yarn. It is easy to get off course and take more width than necessary, so go slowly and patiently.

If you try to make a single crochet seam on an article that has lots of end posts of double crochet, triple crochet, or long chains, you will have to make more than one single crochet seam stitch for every row. If you don't, the seam will pucker. And only fiddling with it, stopping and inspecting it from the outside, will determine how many extra seam stitches you will have to make for each row. Sometimes I think that life, and raising children in particular, would be much easier if the rules were hard and fast without requiring personal judgment and adjustment. But if that were true, we would be ants and not people. There is no way to avoid thinking and remain a person.

There is no difference in making a single crochet seam on the outside. Just be very careful with every stitch; they are going to show.

SLIP STITCH

Crocheters who are afraid to try to learn how to do invisible weaving may be saying, "I could do a loose slip stitch instead of a single crochet on the inside and it would be lighter-weight." That is true, but you still have the open split space problem on the front of

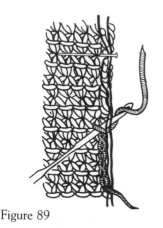

Figure 89

the article. And you have a new difficulty in keeping the slip stitches loose enough so that the seam does not draw up too tight and shorten the item. Slip-stitch seams at your own risk. (See Figure 89.)

WHIPSTITCH

Crocheters who have never heard of invisible weaving from the front often use whipstitching as a better alternative than making single crochet seams. It is better in many cases, but it is not as good as the weaving. Instructions will often tell you to put medallions together with whipstitching. Carefully done, it makes a pretty good seam.

Whipstitching is usually done from the inside of the article.

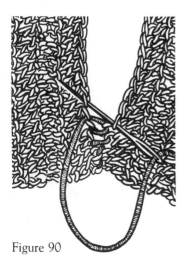

Figure 90

Pin the area together with straight pins. Hold the two pieces together in your left hand. From the back to the front, insert your threaded tapestry needle into the edge-most, outermost loop of both pieces. Leaving a six-inch-long tail end, pull the yarn through to the front. Tie a square knot.

* Take the needle to the back of the work, and from the back to the front, as close to the edge as you can get, insert it a short distance to the left of the last stitch. Pull the yarn through to the front *. (See Figure 90.)

Be sure that you work as close to the edge as you can get. If you are working across the final row of stitches, catching only the back loop of each stitch is sufficient. Stop frequently and admire your work. Turn the work over to the front and check the tension of the seam. It should be just as firm and just as giving as the fabric itself.

BACKSTITCH

Backstitching is usually done from inside, unless, for some reason, you are overlapping the pieces. You have to be careful to get far enough away from the edge to have a solid base, and still stay close enough to avoid extra bulk. This is particularly difficult if the edges to be seamed are made of double or triple crochet. I use backstitching only when there is no other way to get the job done.

A sewing technique that embroiderers are familiar with, backstitching is called just that because, as you move along from right to left, you insert your needle *in back of* where it last came out. It enables you to make stitches closer togther than if your needle was just doing a running stitch. (See Figure 91.)

Figure 91

SEWING MACHINE

Using a sewing machine to put together crocheted pieces may be a better solution than you might think at first glance. Of course, it is not handmade, but it sometimes works out very well. If you are having trouble joining stair steps you might want to give it a try. (If your piece is thick, you may have to adjust the presser-foot tension.)

GETTING RID OF THE TAIL ENDS

You already know from Chapter 15, Joining New Yarn, how to hide tail ends in the middle of a piece. When tail ends occur at the edge of a piece, you have other options. You can hide them in a seam or in the first row of single crochet of a border.

On any kind of seam, you can whipstitch tail ends at the edge of the piece to *one side* of the seam on the inside. Space it out and don't make the whipstitches too close together. Please don't whip the tail ends to *both* sides of the seam together, because that will make a bulgy-bulky spot.

When I have made a border, I often slide the tail ends under the first row of single crochet on the private side of the piece.

Occasionally, when working with a glossy, slippery-smooth, downright slimy yarn, the knots just won't stay tied and the ends won't remain where you hid them. When that happens, step into the twentieth century and up to the check-out counter of your favorite fabric store. Ask the clerk for either a textile glue or something like Fray Check™ to make those pesky ends stay put.

WORKING EDGINGS ON CROCHET

Often a border is an ideal way to finish an unseamed edge of crocheting. It is common to add decorative borders to bedspreads, additional-width borders to place mats, and stabilizing borders on the edges of clothing. If you listen carefully, usually each piece will tell you what kind of a border, if any, it wants. "I want a narrow edging of simple picots or crab stitch," it may say, or "I am so plain; I need a wide lacy border to look finished." Try different things. The piece will let you know when it is happy.

(Remember that, in Chapter 23 about edgings, I said any border worked either directly into cloth or over a foundation could be worked at the edge of a crocheted piece as well. Complete-as-you-go borders may be added to anything.)

But to do any of these borders, we usually need to make a foundation row of single crochet first.

Though printed directions don't usually tell you to do it, when making a border, be sure to make increases at the corners and on the curves (and decreases on the inside curves).

How many increases will you need? Enough so that the piece will lie flat. Stop and lay the article on your lap, love it and pat it down. If it doesn't want to just sit there and smile at you, you didn't make enough. If it leaps up and wants to play, you made too many increases.

Borders almost always work out better if you work in rows not rounds.

Single crochet is particularly nasty about curling up when worked in rounds. It behaves itself when you join the end of a row to the beginning with a slip stitch, chain one, turn and work back the other direction.

I often change hook sizes for different rows of the edging. Frequently, I make the initial single crochet foundation row with the hook that was used to make the article. Then for the second row, I often change and use a size smaller hook. If I don't change hook sizes, my borders are often too loose.

A border made of rows and rows of single crochet, as on the front of a jacket, often will curl at corners in spite of anything that the crocheter does. A gentle steaming of the finished, cleaned piece is usually the best answer to get rid of the curl.

A job isn't finished until it is finished. Until all the parts are put together and the ends tidied up, a thing isn't done. If finishing is done poorly, the effect of the whole project is diminished. If the bothersome finishing is done well, we have a thing of lasting pride and joy, and we all need more pride and joy in our lives.

27
FINISHING TOUCHES

Most of our crocheting today is done for fun, not of necessity. And part of that fun is decorating our finished crocheted articles with bits of humor—a pompom on the top of a clown doll's hat, a luxurious fringe on a feathery shawl, a monk's cord tie on a pretty blouse. All of these things and more are just plain fun to add when we are finished. They are all easy to do and should be a part of any crocheter's bag of tricks.

FRINGE

It was probably for its added weight that fringe was invented, for it is nothing more than groups of strands of yarn pulled through the edge of a fabric to cause it to hang better. Heavy fringe makes a bedspread stay in place; fluffy feathers of fringe keep a delicate shawl from creeping up our back. There are lots of uses for fringe.

All fringes are made in exactly the same way and yet all fringes differ in length, the number of strands used for each grouping, and how close the groupings are placed. I can tell you only the basic rules. You will have to fiddle and fuss to get just the effect you want.

The only general rule of thumb I can give is that the strands should be cut approximately the finished length you desire *plus* two inches *times* two. For instance, if you want a six-inch-long finished fringe, add two inches to the six and then multiply by two ($6'' + 2'' = 8'' \times 2 = 16''$). You'll need:

- Yarn or thread

- Long scissors or shears
  A wastebasket to catch the mess

- A hardback book that measures however many inches around that the strands need to be cut

- A crochet hook large enough to hold all of the strands, but small enough to push through the base fabric

To make a six-strand fringe six inches long:

Select a book that measures approximately sixteen inches around. Beginning at an open edge of the book, loosely wrap the yarn around the book about thirty times. Cut the yarn along the open edge of the book.

Select three strands of the yarn. Hold them together to align them and then fold them in half. With the inside, the private side, of the article facing you, insert a crochet hook through the article close to the edge. Catching the fold of the strands with the crochet hook, pull them back through the hole an inch or so. (See Figure 92.)

Spread the fold open and pull the ends of the strands through the loop that is created. (See Figure 93.) Pull the ends gently until the fringe is securely seated against the article.

Pull strands halfway through piece to form a loop.

Figure 92

Repeat this procedure as often as specified or as you please, stopping to wrap and cut more yarn as needed. When you are finished, grab the wastebasket to catch the mess as you trim the ends. Using the index and second fingers of your left hand as guides, trim the ragged ends of the fringe so that they are even.

When I am ready to make a fringe, I get three or four different size books off the shelf and cut different lengths of yarn. First I try three strands per group, then four or five or six or more. I then go make myself a cup of coffee, and when I come back, the fringes will have held an election among themselves and announce which is the preferred one. And that is the one I will make.

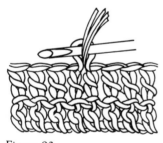

Figure 93

TASSELS

Tassels are simple and easy to make. They are fun to add to the corners of pillows as an accent. They also give added weight to ties and belt ends. The supplies you will need are:

- Yarn or thread

- Shears or long scissors

- A piece of stiff cardboard one inch longer than the desired finished length of the tassel

- A wastebasket

To make the tassel:

Cut two strands of yarn about twenty inches long to use as ties. Wrap the yarn around the cardboard until you have a nice tidy bundle of it.

Run a doubled strand of the tie-yarn under the bundle at the top of the cardboard and tie it securely. (You will use this tie-strand to fasten the completed tassel in place.) Cut the yarn at the bottom of the cardboard.

Take the other tie-strand and wrap it around the bundle ½ to 1 inch below the gathering point. Tie this strand securely, wrap it around the same spot several times more, and then tie it again. (The knots will disappear by themselves.) Comb the loose ends smooth with your fingers.

Using the index and second fingers of your left hand as a guide, trim the ragged ends. (See Figure 94.)

cut

Figure 94

POMPOMS

Pompoms are just attractive little puff-balls of yarn. The more loft there is to the yarn, the more attractive they will be. (They just don't come off at all well with threads that have no loft.) Pompoms are often added to hats, slippers, toys, and such.

Many yarn and craft supply stores have handy-dandy commercial pompom forms for sale that minimize the normal wastage of yarn, and produce uniform-size puff balls. If you are going to be making many pompoms, I recommend you purchase such a device and follow the instructions on the label. If you make a pompom only once in a blue moon, this is the way it is done:

Have handy:

- A piece of stiff cardboard

- Long scissors or shears

- A wastebasket

- If you are going to make more than one matching pompom, have a pencil and paper to take notes.

Cut 4 strands of yarn about 18 inches long to use as ties. Take a piece of stiff cardboard about 4 × 6 inches and wrap it round and round on the shorter side with yarn—perhaps about 25 times. (Remember to count the wraps so that you will know for the next time.)

Pull the yarn together at the top and bottom of the cardboard and tie the yarn in each area with a doubled tie-strand.

With scissors, cut the wrapped yarn between the ties. (Two puff balls will result.) (See Figure 95.)

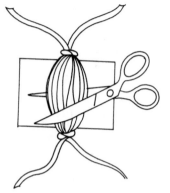

Figure 95

If the balls are thin and flimsy, tie them together. If they are puffy enough singly to please you, get ready to trim and "groom" them. Grab the pair of long shears and the wastebasket to catch the mess. Holding on to the long tie-strands that will be used to attach the pompoms, begin trimming the uneven ends to make a round and uniform ball.

I wish I could give you more exact instructions, telling you exactly how many times to wrap around exactly the right size of cardboard. Alas, yarns vary in density and loft; humans vary in how tightly they wrap and stretch the yarn. You'll just have to experiment with each different yarn to determine the number of wraps and the size of the cardboard.

TWISTED MONK'S CORD

Sometimes a twisted rope belt will add just the right finishing touch to a garment. I've used them on lace dresses for belts, ponchos for neck-tying strands, and on purses for drawstrings. They look especially handsome in nubby yarns and are the simplest kind of a rope or strong cord known to man.

I hate to say it all the time but, again, experimenting with the number of strands and the tightness of the twist put into them is the only way to achieve exactly the effect you're after. You'll need:

- *Lots* of yarn or thread

- A tape measure and scissors

- An area to work in that is three times as long as you want the finished cord to be

● A door knob or a strong fastening point at the other end of the area in which you are working.

To make a cord 6 feet long: Cut ten strands of yarn 18 feet long. Tie the ends together to form a large loop. Thread a small piece of yarn through the loop and fasten it to the door knob or strong fastening point.

Slip a pencil or small dowel into the opposite end of the loop and twist the pencil round and round in the same direction until the yarn gets tightly twisted. Lay a heavy object on your end of the twisted loop and another halfway to the door knob.

Walk to the other end of the area and detach the yarn from the knob. Carry it back to the other end of the room to fold the twisted strands in half.

Remove the heavy object and allow the torque of the strands to twist themselves together around each other to form the rope. Tie a simple knot about 4 inches from each end to secure the strands.

Cut and unravel the threads at these knotted ends, comb them out with your fingers, and trim the ragged ends with scissors. (See Figure 96.)

Back in the "olden days" when I was a Brownie and then a Girl Scout, everybody had hand egg-beaters or hand drills around the house. They were great little tools to help with the twisting of the yarn. In these "modern times," I have in my house an electric mixer, a blender, a wire whisk, and a power-driven screwdriver. None of those things seems to work very well for the twisting of the yarn; their speed makes it difficult to control the amount of twist. I now use a good old pencil and do it the hard way. Such is modern American life.

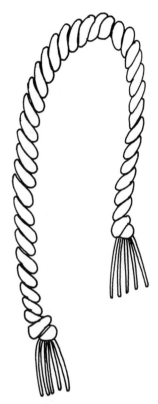

Figure 96

CROCHETED CORDS

Sometimes a twisted monk's cord is too heavy for ties on your light and lacy crocheting. When we want to use the same yarn that the item was made of instead of resorting to ribbon, we have two choices. We can make either a *slip-stitch cord* or a *single crochet cord*. They are both just a single row of stitches made over a foundation chain. In both instances, be sure to make the foundation longer than you want the finished cord to be, because it will shrink as you work the row.

Regarding the slip-stitch cord, I have trouble keeping my stitches loose enough so that the cord does not pucker. Therefore, I use a larger size hook for the slip stitches than I do for the foundation chain.

You will remember from when you were just learning to make single crochet stitches, that one row of single crochet over a foundation chain will curl up in a never-ending spiral. There is nothing that you can do about it. Just be aware that, if you use it for a tie, the ends will not hang straight.

YARN BUTTONS

When I have made a pretty blouse or sweater, I usually hate to put store-bought buttons on it. They seem to detract from the lovely hand-made look. Frequently I will take time to make crocheted buttons of the same yarn or thread that the garment was made of to adorn it. There are basically two types to choose from: round ball buttons stuffed with the thread itself, and buttons made over round "bone" ring forms available at yarn, craft, and yardage stores. Which I choose to use will depend upon which kind the sweater likes best, because I make up all four of the following examples and see which looks just right.

There are two important things you need to be told about the making of either ball or "bone" ring buttons. The first is that it is imperative that you remember what you do in the making of the first one, so that you can make all the buttons for one garment identically. (My pencil comes in handy here, because if I don't write it down, sure as the phone rings when I'm in the shower, I'll be interrupted before I can make three identical buttons.) Secondly, both ball and "bone" ring buttons need to be made *very firmly and tightly*. It is necessary to use a crochet hook that is several sizes smaller than would normally be used for a particular yarn.

BALL BUTTONS

These are just rounds of single crochet worked from a closed center. Stitches are increased until the button is the desired circumference. Then one round is worked without increases. Finally the stitches are decreased until you have a sphere. The sphere is stuffed with thread and voilà! you have a usable button. But remember, use a smaller than normal hook.

Make a sl lp 18" from the end of the yarn. Ch 2, join to first ch with a sl st, ch 1.

Rnd 1) Make 8 sc into ring, join with sl st, ch 1.

Rnd 2) Sc into sl st, * sc in next st. 2 sc in next st *, rep bet *s around. Join with sl st, ch 1 (12 sc rem).

Rnd 3) 1 sc in ea st. Join with sl st, ch 1.

Rnd 4) Dec 2 sts into 1 around as follows: * Insert hk into next st, yo and draw up a lp, insert hk into next st, yo and draw up a lp, yo and pull thru 3 lps on hk, * rep bet *s around.

Cut yarn 18" long. Fasten off. Stuff ball with as much of the beginning 18" piece as possible. Thread ending yarn on a tapestry needle and use doubled to fasten button closed and to sew to garment.

COVERED "BONE" RING BUTTONS

You have to experiment with different size rings that will suit the yarn. (They come in sizes from ¼" to ⅞".) Only after you have covered the ring and drawn the stitches to the center will you be able to judge if you have the appropriate size. Be sure to work with a smaller than normal hook so that the stitches will be very tight.

Place a sl lp on hk and, working thru the center of the ring, make as many sc around the ring as possible, crowding them tightly, but not overlapping them. Join with a sl st. Cut yarn 18" long and fasten off. Thread ending yarn on tapestry needle. Going thru the outer loop only of every other sc, make a running stitch to gather the stitchess together. Pull firmly to the back side to fill in middle of ring. Make a few darning stitches across center to secure. Use tail ends to sew button to garment.

The appearance of covered bone ring buttons can be changed by pulling the basting stitch to the *front* instead of to the back. Also, four-leafed clovers can be made by omitting the basting thread, pushing the stitches to the front, and making darning stitches across the center from outer loop to outer loop in two places at right angles to each other.

28

THE CARE AND
FEEDING OF
CROCHETED ARTICLES

All across the country, museum textile curators agree on how you should preserve your crocheted articles. "Keep them away from light; ultra-violet light destroys both color and the fiber itself. Wrap the article in acid-free paper; acid causes the fiber to disintegrate. Store the article flat or rolled around an acid-free tube; do not hang or fold. Avoid extremes of humidity; some fibers actually require a moderate amount of humidity and all fibers resent a completely dry environment. Protect the articles from rapid temperature changes. But most of all, make sure that the article is completely clean without a trace of acid, oil, dirt, sweat, soap or detergent."

It is nice and accurate advice, but it is almost impossible to follow. If an item is wrapped in acid-free tissue paper in a dark place, you can't even see it, much less use or wear it and enjoy it. And I like to enjoy my crocheting.

If I tell you of my feelings about antiques, you'll understand where I stand about conserving crocheted articles. There are certain types of old furniture, tools, and accent pieces that I fell in love with when I was young. I thought that they were beautiful. Growing up in California, where almost nothing was old, antique pieces cried out to me, singing of a past that was absent from my life. I wanted their age and continuity to surround me. I didn't inherit any antiques, so I went out and bought them. Slowly, piece by piece, I acquired a lovely collection. The only new furniture that I have in my house are contemporary couches, innerspring mattresses, and adjustable-shelf bookcases. Our foremothers simply didn't have those advantages! The rest of my furnishings are about a hundred years old. I keep my clothing in old dressers; my perfume and tissues and dusting powder sit on top of them. I sit on old chairs with a kitty on my lap; sometimes that kitty scratches the upholstery. I place my coffee cup on old tables; sometimes liquids make a ring on the surface. Every new puppy that comes into the house adds a few new teeth marks to the runners of rocking chairs. I carefully polish my antiques with lemon oil, protect them from direct sunlight with lace curtains, and try to keep them from harm, but I know that I am not taking museum-quality care of them. I use them daily and I love them, and they make my day-to-day living richer and warmer. I am willing to put up with normal wear and tear for the enjoyment that they give me.

So, too, it is with my crocheted things. I gladly put up with the unavoidable abuse of daily living for the pleasure of their company. They may not last forever, but life is here and now. Clothing was meant to be worn even if sunlight strikes it. An afghan was meant to cuddle in even if hot chocolate gets spilled on it. Tablecloths are going to get stained; you can't avoid spills. Children are going to destroy, through over-loving, the very toys that they care the most about. These things I gladly take in stride. Still, we can try to make our crocheted items last as long as possible. Some things we should do; some things we should try to avoid.

CLEANING

Keeping a thing as clean as possible will help it to last longer. But there is a catch-22. The action involved in cleaning it will cause it to wear out faster.

It is impossible for humans or crocheting to exist without acquiring dust and grime. Just the making of a piece can get it dirty. Stop and think about it; look at your hands. When God created us, She gave our hands protective coatings; our skin exudes both helpful acids and softening oils. If we didn't have the proper acid balance, we would fall prey to all kinds of bad germs. If our skin were not lubricated, it would crack and bleed. When we crochet, the yarn or thread runs through our fingers, and our hands hold the fabric as we make it. There is no way to avoid getting acids and oils on our piece, save working with gloves on. It is dirty even before it is finished. If we have areas that have had to be ripped and redone, these parts will have run through our fingers three times—once to crochet, second to rip, and third to crochet again. And depending on how big a project is and how long we worked on it, it may need to be cleaned immediately. Certainly if we intend to block it, to apply steam to it, it will need to be free of soil before blocking.

Your choices to remove soil are dry cleaning and washing by hand or machine. Regardless of which method you choose, just the saturation of the fabric with the fluid, the sloshing of it around in the liquid, and the lifting of the soggy article will all cause wear and tear on the item. It seems that you are damned if you do and damned if you don't. But don't throw up your hands and scream. A careful cleaning is better than allowing dirt to remain.

Remember, way back in the beginning of this book, we talked about the information on yarn labels. Often the label will tell you whether to dry clean (and with what) or wash (and how).

DRY CLEANING

If the label tells you not to wash, to dry clean only, that is what you will have to do. Take the item *and the label* to your favorite dry cleaner for treatment. And pray! Pray hard that they will take proper care of it, and that they will remove all traces of the cleaning fluid as well as the accumulated soil. You may want to have them block the item after it is cleaned. Blocking is discussed later in this chapter.

WASHING

In the nineteenth century, washing meant soaking the article overnight in cold water, building a fire under the kettle to slowly bring it to boiling, adding lye soap and simmering the stuff, then rinsing in cold water three times, wringing thoroughly between rinsings. Sometimes coffee or tea was added to the final rinse for a cream or ecru tint. At other times, "bluing" was added to white items to make them reflect the light better. Often they were dipped in starch. After that the items were laid out in the sun to dry. (I'm glad that I wasn't alive then, because it was an awful lot of backbreaking work.) The cold water softened the set-in soil. There were no abrupt changes in temperature. Boiling with soap cleaned the items. There was more gentle sloshing than there was rugged movement. The thorough rinsing removed all traces of the soap. The sunshine bleached out any remaining spots. It is a shame that so much work was involved, because it really was a very good system of cleaning. Many old crocheted fabrics have survived in surprisingly good condition.

I don't want to go back and live in the nineteenth century. I'm happy in the twentieth and looking forward to the twenty-first. But stop and think about how our great-grandmothers kept their linens clean, and how we can bring the good parts of what they did into the present. The soaking in cold water to soften the soil we can still do. We even have packaged enzymes available to help us. We no longer need the boiling temperatures, because we have kinder, more gentle, soaps and detergents that are active in cool water. The three sloshing clear water rinses we can still do. Coffee, tea and bluing we can do without, because our threads are made with better dyes or bleaching agents. We can avoid the sunlight, because we now know that it destroys both the fibers and the colors. Instead, we have mounds and mounds of clean, dry, fluffy towels to quickly pull the moisture out of the soggy-wet fabrics. Thank goodness for automatic clothes dryers to dry the towels!

HAND WASHING

Wool and other animal fibers, lofty synthetics, and most cottons and rayons respond beautifully to a loving hand wash.

Usually, a careful hand washing followed by careful forming and drying is all the blocking most crocheted items ever need. This loving care will smooth any uneven stitches or seams and give the article a fresh and soft appearance, enhancing the pattern stitches.

The knowledge of the fine art of hand washing seems to have disappeared from our culture sometime in the early 1950s with the introduction of the automatic washing machine. It is surprising how many people do not know how to do it. The process is a little time-consuming, but it is not at all hard to do. I'm not talking about the women of the village carrying the clothes on their heads to the local stream and beating them with stones. I'm talking about something you can easily do at your own kitchen sink with the assistance of your automatic clothes dryer. You'll need to have on hand:

- A completed article with all the seams woven and loose ends worked in

- A colander (or dish-drying rack) to set the garment in to drain

- Gobs of clean dry towels, beach towels or those super-big towels called bath sheets, if you have them

- One of the enzyme pre-soak powders, if the item has lots of soil worked into it

- One of the specialty cold-water, hand-wash cleaners or pure mild soap powder

- A clean kitchen sink or a large dishpan, or, in the case of a large heavy afghan, you may want to use the bathtub

- A flat, airy place to lay the garment undisturbed while it is drying

- A plastic trash bag to protect the surface of the drying area

- About an hour's time

- And a happy, loving attitude. (Inanimate things *do* reflect our attitude.)

If what you are washing is a garment, try it on the intended wearer and measure it. Make a note of the present measurements *and* the desired measurements. If it is a shaped article such as a toy, you will want to have the stuffing handy. For things like booties, wad up tissue paper into the shape of the baby's feet. If it is a hat, find a bowl about the size of the head of the intended wearer. You may wish to mark any badly soiled areas with basting thread.

If you plan to use the pre-soak enzyme, dissolve it in a small amount of warm water, and then add it to a sink or basin full of *cold* water, mixing it with a stroke or two of your hand. Immerse the garment for ten to twenty minutes (according to the instructions on the label), and then check the soiled areas you outlined. If necessary, squeeze them a bit to help the enzyme carry away the soil. Then wash as follows:

If you are not planning to pre-soak, fill the basin with cold water and add the proper amount of specialty cold-water cleaner, mixing it gently with your hand. (You don't want to create a lot of suds.) Immerse the article for ten minutes. Do not wring or twist the fabric as you wash or rinse it. The fibers are at their weakest when wet, so handle gently!

At the end of the soaking time, roll up your sleeves and gently slosh the article around a bit. Have the colander handy. With your two hands, scoop up the garment from the soaking water and lift it up from underneath to the colander to drain. Let the dirty soak water out of the basin, rinse it, and fill it with cold rinse water.

Press down firmly on the article as it rests in the drainer to remove excess water. Then, from the colander, dump it into the cold rinse water. Slosh the article around a bit and remove it from the rinse as you did before.

Do two more rinse baths in the same manner until the rinse water is clean, clear, and free of suds. If you choose, you may add a fabric softener to the last rinse. Some people like fabric softeners, and they can work wonders. They vary so much from one manufacturer's product to another, however, and the products themselves change so often, that I hate to make firm and forever statements about them. Be aware also that some people swear by adding hair conditioner in the last rinse for wools and animal fibers. It makes sense—hair is hair—but the products all differ, so choose wisely.

When the last rinse is finished, dump the garment into the colander to drain while you prepare for the next step.

Some articles will need a detour here if they require starch. When I was a little girl almost everything was starched and ironed. Doilies were starched by dipping them into a sugar solution. That is no longer advised. It attracts bugs and can make the fibers so brittle that they are fragile. Some of the old crochet books that I researched advised a home brew of "pure wheat starch, gum Arabic and salts of sorrel, which are available from your pharmacist." That is part of yesterday, too. A commercial laundry starch from your supermarket is better. Just follow the directions on the label of your favorite brand. Starched articles should be laid out on plastic to dry and fastened with rust-proof pins to the desired shape, and it is hoped they will dry before they mold. Here in humid Georgia, it can be a real problem.

If the article is not starched, proceed as follows: Press down on the article several times as it rests in the colander to remove as much water as possible, and then dump it onto a waiting towel. Arrange the article flat and cover it with another towel. Fold the edges of the towel toward the center, and then, very firmly, roll up the towels. Bang it a couple of times on the edge of the sink, and then let it rest for about fifteen minutes.

Unroll the towels, remove the article, place it in another dry towel, roll, and let it rest again. When you unroll it this time, you will have to make a decision, a value judgment, as to whether or not most of the moisture has been removed from the article. (That's why I previously spoke of a clothes dryer. The towels don't need washing, but it sure is nice to have a dryer to dry them in. You can use lots of them without worry.)

DRYING FLAT

At this stage of my life, I use my guest room bed to spread the article out to dry. Before I had a guest room, I used my dining room table. Before I had a dining room table, I used my bed. Select and use a safe, airy (but not outdoors) place where children, kittens, puppies, bugs, and sunshine cannot reach. Whatever flat surface you choose to use, it is wise to protect it from moisture with a plastic trash bag. Then spread out a layer of towels, one or two deep depending on the thickness of the towels and of the article.

Remove the article from its last towel wrapping and arrange it *lovingly* on the towel, working with your gentle hands those areas that need a bit of evening-up or stretching or compressing. Gently pull first across the item from side to side and then up and down to "seat" the stitches and enhance the pattern relief and texture.

Doilies, place mats, and the like should be laid public-side down on the towel(s) to enhance the pattern stitches. If it is a sweater that you are working with, get out your tape measure and notes and tenderly adjust the sweater as you please to the size you desire. Minor adjustments in width and length can easily be made. Gently stuff booties with tissue paper and arrange the hat over the bowl-form. Ease stuffing into toys. Whatever it is you are doing, let it dry, untouched, undisturbed, with the windows opened or a fan blowing. Come back in an hour or so and change the towel(s) under the article. If it is double-thick, like a sweater, flip the article over to the opposite side and remeasure it to assure yourself that it is the size you desire. If your article is extra-heavy, you may want to repeat the towel-changing maneuver until the item is dry.

Now aren't you proud of yourself? You have learned a nearly lost art, the article is clean and fresh, smooth and evened, the seams are invisible, and you have just what you want. Moreover, the item is free of damaging soil with as little injury as possible.

MACHINE WASHING

I wouldn't want to have to go back to all hand washing. I'm glad that there is an automatic washing machine in my house. Properly used, it can be a great time and effort saver, even for hand-crocheted articles. Just remember the catch-22 of washing: rough handling of wet fibers can damage them, and all trace of the cleaning agent must be removed.

If the yarn label says it is okay, and if your machine has a "delicate" or "gentle" cycle, feel free to go ahead and use your machine. But first stop off at your local supermarket and purchase a couple of mesh laundry bags. They resemble a pilllowcase and are made of sturdy nylon net with a zipper or drawstring across one end. Placing your crocheted article in a mesh laundry bag prevents both the wear and tear of excessive movement, and snags from other items in the wash. (If you are washing an afghan, which is often too large to fit into a mesh laundry bag, you may want to toss in something smooth and small, such as pillowcases or hand towels, to help balance the weight.) Whether or not you use the mesh bags, always turn an article such as a sweater inside out before washing.

You may wish to use an enzyme "soak" cycle first if the item has accumulated either lots of human body soil or food stains, as well-loved afghans are apt to do. Use cool water and be sure to dissolve the powder in the water before you add your washables.

Follow the same advice for your "delicate" cycle as well. Use cool water, add the cleaner first, then the washables. Hot water is only for fibers that can stand it, and only after the soil has been softened by cooler water. Use pure soap or gentle detergent. A word of caution: The "delicate" cycle of my machine is so delicate that it does not remove all of the cleaning agent. Since rinsing is so important, so that no trace of the cleaner is left in, I run my things through the gentle cycle again in plain cool water.

MACHINE DRYING

Some modern manmade fibers actually do better with machine drying! If the label says so, I'm all for it. The only problem is the additional wear and tear of the tumbling movement. To minimize that, I will often dry the crocheted article separately, still in its mesh bag. Along with the crocheting, I throw in extra, dry towels to quickly pull out the moisture. And I keep the time short so as not to overdry the item.

BLOCKING

Now that the thing is clean, we can consider blocking. The nice part is that if you have carefully washed it, it may not need blocking at all. Thank goodness! Home blocking has ruined more things than it has ever improved.

Blocking means the infusion of heat or steam into the fibers of a fabric to smooth or shape it.

Sometimes blocking can do wonders. More often than not, blocking can ruin a garment. Every crocheting instructor in the world has had clients, blind with tears, bring in home-blocked articles that were now a stretched, shiny mess. You see, when heat and/or steam is applied to yarn and thread, the fibers themselves are temporarily weakened so that they can be restructured into (hopefully) the shape that you desire. While they are thus weakened, they are terribly vulnerable. If not supported properly, they can stretch from here to Timbuctoo. Unwanted shiny spots can occur. The heat necessary to do the desired shaping can cause fibers to mat down or felt, and become hard blobs instead of lofty threads.

Let me list the *don'ts* of blocking first. If you are then still convinced that blocking is for you, you can read the dos.

Mohair and angora and many man-made fibers should never get anywhere near heat or steam; they will turn into felt—hard and firm like a felt hat.

Never let an iron touch the fabric directly. Use a heavy wet press-cloth between the fabric and the iron. (Of course, if you use a heavy press-cloth, you cannot see what you are doing.)

Do not apply steam or heat to an item that will have to be moved before it is dry and cool.

Do not use an ironing board to block anything that is larger than the board. As you move the item over the edges, the weight of the already hot wet fibers will pull the thing all out of shape.

Do not use pins that will rust to fasten an item down. Often you don't know that the pins are going to rust until they do.

Above all, please remember: do not apply heat or steam to an article that is not absolutely clean. The heat or steam will permanently seal in the soil.

If the thing absolutely has to be blocked, do think of letting a professional do it. A yarn shop that has a steam machine and lots of flat surface, or a dry cleaner that has a vacuum steam table are to be considered professionals. They have distinct advantages over you. In both cases they can *see* what they are doing. Hopefully both will be familiar with the fiber content that they will be working with. In the case of the yarn shop, they can infuse steam from the steamer and then let the piece dry unmoved. In the case of the dry cleaner, they can vacuum out the steam and heat with a flick of the wrist, and the thing is ready immediately. Considering the time, money, and effort you have already invested in making the item, the cost of paying a professional to give it the finishing touch is minimal.

If you just want to put a touch of steam on the corner of a border to make it lie flat or if you want to touch up a stair-step shoulder seam, go ahead and give it a try. Heat your iron to medium. Saturate with water an old scrap of Turkish toweling to use as a press-cloth. Lay a fresh, dry towel on the flat surface. Place and shape the article on top of it. Cover the item with the wet towel. Gently set the iron on the towel. If the area is larger than one iron-space worth, lift up the iron and set it down again. When the article is steamy-hot, remove the press-cloth and, with your hands, shape the article the way you want it. *Let it dry completely without moving it.*

NEVER HANG CROCHETED ARTICLES

If you need to be told never to hang a crocheted article, you do not appreciate your own craft! You should know from working with it that the stitches are always movable. Only with real fuzzy yarns are the stitches permanently set in place. You should know from working with it (and from purchasing the thread) that weight is involved. If you hang it up, gravity is going to pull it down and out of shape.

Make whatever reassignment of space that you have to, but store your work as flat as you can, with as few folds as possible.

If you have inherited a fine piece from your great-grandmother and do not wish to keep it out on display, give it museum-quality care so that your great-granddaughter can inherit it from you. Other than that, love your crocheted pieces and live with them. May they bring joy to your life.

IV

LEARNING LESSONS

29
BELL PULL SAMPLER WALL HANGING

My students usually want something permanent and tangible to show for their learning efforts, and I like to leave them with a reference guide to remind them of all that we have covered. Therefore, I devised this learning lesson bell pull sampler wall hanging. It can be used either for a class project or as an individual experience. Long after it is finished, when specific instructions are encountered, the student can look at the directions and the sampler and say, "Oh, of course, I've done that before. This is what it looks like."

I have used this learning lesson many times to teach rank beginners, to re-teach students that "crocheted a little bit a long time ago" but have forgotten most of the basics, and even experienced crocheters who may never have come across some of the techniques. The instructions are written in a very careful way so that the first time a word is used, it is spelled out in full followed by the abbreviation in parentheses. All of the material here has been covered in the body of this book, but I've included little incidental notes in the instructions in case students need to refresh their memory.

Materials:

- One skein each of two colors of Class C Smooth Classic Knitting Worsted (standard 4-ply) 50 gr each

- Size F crochet hook (for main part)

- Size D or E crochet hook (for button)

Photo 42

- Scissors

- Tapestry needle

- Commercial pompom and tassel forms

Using color A, place a slip loop (sl lp) on the hook (hk). Chain (ch) 16. (See Chapters 8 & 9 for sl lp and ch.)

Make a row of *single crochet* (sc) as follows: sc in the 2nd ch from hk and each (ea) ch across, [15 stitches (sts) + original turning ch (t-ch)], ch 1, turn. (Note that the t-ch counts as one st, therefore you have 16 sts.) (See Chapter 10 for sc.)

Work even in sc until piece measures 2½" long. Cut yarn 20" long and fasten off (see Chapter 10). Note: *Always* leave at least a 6-inch-long tail end when changing yarns so that it can be hidden invisibly when the project is finished. In this case, we are going to come back later and make a seam, so we might just as well plan for it now and make our tail end longer than 6".

Also, please note that there are two ways to change yarns at the beginning or end of a row. (See Chapter 15.) 1) You may make the final yarn-over-pull-through-two-loops of the last st with the new yarn, or 2) you may complete the last st of the old color and fasten off, then place a sl lp of the new color on the hk and just begin working with it. I have chosen to use method #2 in these instructions.

With B, place a sl lp on the hk, *double crochet* (dc) in ea st across, ch 3, turn. (See Chapter 12 for dc.) You still have 16 sts across. Instructions (insts) will say "16 sts remain (rem)."

Work even in dc 1 row more, fasten off. (15 sts + t-ch. Total 2 rows dc.)

With A, *half-double crochet* (hdc) in each dc across, ch 2, turn. (See Chapter 11 for hdc.)

Work even in hdc 1 row more, fasten off. (Total 2 rows hdc.)

With B, *triple crochet* (tr) in ea hdc across. (See Chapter 13 for tr.) (1 row tr and 16 sts rem.)

With A, *double treble* (dtr) in ea tr across. (See Chapter 13 for dtr.) (1 row dtr and 16 sts rem.)

With B, *treble treble* (tr tr) in ea dtr across. (See Chapter 13 for tr tr.) (1 row tr tr and 16 sts rem.) Notice how though the number of sts is still the same, the piece has expanded in width. It is just the nature of these longer sts.

Attach A and work 1 row sc. (Note: In filet crochet, 3 dc = a solid space (sp), and ch 2 + 1 dc = an open sp, and ea *group* (gp) is a multiple of 3 sts.) (See Chapter 21.) We are going to make 5 gps and a selvage st at ea end. 3 × 5 = 15 + 2 = 17. One selvage st will have to be added at the end of the row. Beginning (beg) and ending with a solid sp, work *filet* checkerboard across as follows:

Row 1) ch 3 (= end post), * 1 dc in ea of next 3 sts (= solid sp made), ch 2, skip (sk) 2, dc in next st (= open sp made) *, repeat between (rpt bet) *s across, ending make 1 dc in ea of next 3 sts & dc again in last st for selvage st. Ch 3, turn. (5 gps + 2 sts rem.)

Row 2) Work solid over the holes and make sps over the solid areas, end dc in last dc. Fasten off B (17 sts rem).

Attach B. Make 2 rows of *simple dc "V"* pattern (pat) st. (See Chapter 21) as follows:

Row 1) Dc in first st (for selvage st), sk 1 st, * dc in next st, ch 1, dc in same st, sk 2 sts *, rep bet *s, end dc in top of t-ch (for selvage st). (5 "V"s made.) Ch 2, turn.

Row 2) * [Dc, ch 1, dc] in the chain 1 (ch-1) sp of row below *, end dc in top of t-ch, cut yarn 20″ long. Fasten off.

Make a *granny square* (see Chapter 22) as follows: With A, Place a sl lp on the hk, ch 6, join with a slip st (sl st) to form a ring.

Round (rnd) 1) Ch 3 (counts as 1 dc), into ring work 2 dc, ch 2, * 3 dc, ch 2 *, rep bet *s twice. (4 3-dc gps made.) Join with sl st in top of t-ch. Fasten off.

Rnd 2) With B, place a sl lp on hk and into any corner ch-2 sp work * [3 dc, ch 2, 3 dc], ch 2, sk next 3 dc *, rep bet *s around, join with sl st in top of first dc. (8 3-dc gps.) Fasten off.

Rnd 3) With A, [3 dc, ch 2, 3 dc] in corner, * ch 2, 3 dc in ch-2 sp, [3 dc, ch 2, 3 dc] in next corner sp, rep from * twice, 3 dc bet next ch-2 sps, ch 2, join in top of first dc. Fasten off.

Take a break from crocheting. Fold the top section of A sc's in half and whipstitch in place to form a rod pocket for bell pull holder.

Fasten in some of the ends (see Chapter 15).

Weave granny square in place (see Chapter 26).

With right side of granny square facing, with B, working in the back loop (bl) only, make 15 sc across top of granny square, ch 3, turn.

Make 3 simple *4-dc shells* (see Chapter 21) across as follows:

Row 1) Sk 1 st, dc in next st, * [2 dc, ch 1, 2 dc] in next st, sk 3 sts *, rep bet *s across (3 shells), end dc in last st. Ch 3, turn.

Row 2) [2 dc, ch 1, 2 dc] in ch-1 sp of previous row, end dc in post. Fasten off.

With A, even tops of shells to a straight line as follows: Hdc in first st, ch 2, * sc in ch-1 sp, ch 2, hdc bet shells of row below, ch 2, rep from * across, end hdc in last st. Ch 3, turn.

Make a row of 5 *popcorn sts* (PC) (see Chapter 18, Crossed Stitches) across as follows: Ch 2, sk 2 sts, * 5 dc in next st, draw up a long lp and remove hk. Insert hk in first dc and pull long lp thru, sl st, ch 2, sk 2, rep from * across ending dc in last st. Fasten off.

With B, make a row of 5 *puff stitches* (PS) (see Chapter 17): Dc in edge st, * 2 dc in ch-2 sp, PS in top of PC, rep from * 4 times, end 2 dc in ch-2 sp, dc in last st. Fasten off.

With A make a row of *crossed tr's* (CTR) (see Chapter 18, Crossed Stitches) as follows: Dc in first st. * Sk 2 dc, tr in next PS, ch 1, tr back into first skipped dc, rep from * across, end dc in last PS. Fasten off.

With B work one row of 15 sc across.

(See Chapter 17.) Making rows of sc, *decrease* (dec) one st at beginning and one st at end of each row until a center point is formed. Fasten off.

Along diagonal edge, attach A and make one sc in each row to center point, make 3 sc in center point, sc in each row up other diagonal edge, ch 1, turn.

Make a *classic sc ripple afghan st* (see Chapter 21) as follows: *working in back loop only of sts of row below*, sc in first st, dec 2 sts into 1, sc in each sc to point, 3 sc in point, sc in ea sc until 3 sts rem, dec, sc in last st, ch 1, turn. Rep this row once more.

With A make a ball button (see Chapter 27). Attach to center of bottom triangle.

Finish in all tail ends of yarn.

Steam lightly.

Decorate top rod pocket with pompoms and embellish the bottom with a tassel made according to directions on purchased forms (or see Chapter 27).

Slip bell pull hanger through top rod pocket.

30
THE EASIEST SWEATER

The easiest of all possible crocheted sweaters, this elegant cap-sleeved pullover sweater is a joy to make and wear. Two simple rectangles, one for the back and one for the front, both worked diagonally, are all there is to it. Follow the directions and it is guaranteed to fit. Make it in cotton for a summer topper, and again in wool or mohair to wear in winter over a blouse or turtleneck. This pattern is reprinted with permission from *Crafts 'n Things Magazine*, 14 Main Street, Park Ridge, Illinois 60068. The magazine is published bimonthly, $8.00 per year.

Measure the actual body bust of the intended wearer. Add 2 inches to this number, divide the new number by 2. The result is the *magic number* to make this sweater fit correctly. For instance, if the bust measurement is 36" add 2" = 38", divide by 2 = a *magic number* of 19.

Note: You can use these instructions for any size person and any type of yarn. Of course, the amount of yarn needed will vary according to the desired size of the garment and the kind of yarn used. Naturally hook size will vary with the type of yarn, just *be very sure that you are getting a perfect right-angle triangle instead of a diamond shape.* Depending on your gauge and the yarn you choose, you may have to try several sizes of hook to get the right-angle triangle.

You may also vary the color striping pattern to use up bits of yarn left over from previous projects, making a "Chinese menu" sweater.

Photo 43

CROCHETED SWEATER INSTRUCTIONS:

Suggested Materials:

- Yarn: Esslinger "Ingrid" (50% cotton, 30% Mohair, 20% acrylic), 50 gr balls, approximately 81 yards each, for a size 34″ bust with stripes on the front only:
  Main color (MC) blue #21, 6 balls
  Color A (A) white #01, 1 ball
  Color B (B) coral #57, 1 ball

- Hook size: F (3.5 mm)

- OR ANY YARN AND ANY HOOK THAT WILL RESULT IN A TRUE SQUARE

Abbreviations used:

ch = chain, dc = double crochet, hdc = half-double crochet, sc = single crochet, sl lp = slip loop, sp = space, st = stitch, t-ch = turning chain, tr = treble crochet, yo = yarn over, ea = each, rep = repeat, rem = remain.

Directions for front:

Row 1) With MC place a sl lp on the hk, ch 4, [tr, ch 1, dc, ch 1, 2 tr] in last ch from hk, ch 3, turn.
Row 2) Dc in 2nd tr of previous row, ch 1, dc in ch-1 sp, dc in dc, dc in next ch-1 sp, ch 1, dc in next tr, dc in top of t-ch, ch 4, turn.
Row 3) Tr in 2nd dc of previous row, ch 1, 2 dc in ch-1 sp of previous row, dc in ea dc across, 2 dc in ch-1 sp (thus making 4 more dc on row), ch 1, tr in next dc, tr in top of t-ch, ch 3, turn. (Note, this row has 2 tr posts at ea end of row.)
Row 4) Dc in 2nd tr of previous row, ch 1, dc in ch-1 sp of previous row, dc in ea dc across, dc in ch-1 sp (thus making 2 more dc on ea row), ch 1, dc in next tr, dc in top of t-ch, ch 4, turn. Note: This row has 2 dc posts at ea end of row.
Check to make sure the piece is a perfect right-angle triangle.
Rep rows 3 & 4 until piece measures 6″ along diagonal edge. Do not ch 4 at end of row. Cut off MC, turn.
Begin color striping pattern: * 1 row A, 2 rows B, 1 row A, 4 rows MC *; rep bet *s.
Continue to work in pattern as established until the diagonal edge measures the same as the magic number.
Maintaining color striping pattern and continuing to alternate rows with dc and tr posts, begin to decrease as follows:

Row 5) Make a t-ch of 4 from previous row, or with new color, tr in 2nd dc, sk ch-1 sp and next 2 dc, dc in ea dc across until 3 st rem, sk 2 dc and ch-1 sp, tr in last dc, tr in top of t-ch, ch 3, turn. (4 sts dec'd across row and there are now no ch-1 sps.)

Row 6) Dc in 2nd tr, sk first dc, dc in ea dc across row until 2 sts rem, sk next dc, dc in tr, dc in top of t-ch, ch 4, turn. (2 sts dec'd across row.)

Row 7) Tr in 2nd dc, sk next 2 dc, dc in ea dc across until 3 sts rem, sk 2 dc, tr in last dc, tr in top of t-ch, ch 3, turn.

Rep rows 6 & 7 until 4 sts and t-ch rem. Draw up a lp in ea st across, yo, draw through all lps. Fasten off.

Make back same as front with (or without) striping pattern. Fasten off.

Sew shoulder and underarm seams according to Figure 97. Finish in all tag ends of yarn.

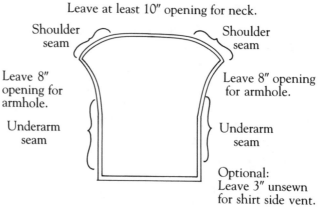

Leave at least 10″ opening for neck.

Shoulder seam   Shoulder seam

Leave 8″ opening for armhole.   Leave 8″ opening for armhole.

Underarm seam   Underarm seam

Optional: Leave 3″ unsewn for shirt side vent.

Figure 97

31
ADDITIONAL PROJECTS

TABLE/TRAY MAT

A Quick and Easy Beginner's Project
No experience necessary

I'm opinionated! I believe that our daily living should be surrounded by practical, exquisite loveliness. The ordinary everyday things we do and see and use should be a delight to the eye and the touch without being a fragile botheration. Eating is a case in point. Whether it is a tray that I carry into the living room to eat from while I watch the evening news, the wooden kitchen table set for sharing supper with a friend, or the table outside in the garden room when I take a break for lunch, I believe that both the food and the setting should be pleasant to look at. To help achieve that end, I use lots of washable, no-iron table and tray mats. A pretty plate set on a lovely mat makes any meal more enjoyable. Such a mat is the one shown on the following page (see Photo 44).

Practical because it is made of DuPont Comfort 12, a machine-washable, machine-dryable yarn that looks and feels like cotton, beautiful because it is light and lacy and lets the under-surface show through, endearing because it is handmade, even an unsure beginner can whip up this easy project in a few hours. It is just a turning-chain of three for an end post at the beginning of the row, double crochet "V"s alternating with double crochet shells across the row, and a double crochet for an end post to complete the row.

Materials:

- Approx. 1 ¼ 50 gr skeins (for each mat) of Jack Frost Comfort 12 yarn (100% DuPont Comfort 12), a Class C worsted-weight yarn.

Photo 44

• Susan Bates Quicksilver™ hook size F

Finished Size: Approx. 16″ × 11 ½″.

Gauge: One "V" and one shell = 1 ¾″.

Directions:

Loosely ch 80 to measure 19″ unstretched.

Row 1) In 5th ch from hk (dc, ch 1, dc), * sk 3 ch, [2 dc, ch 1, 2 dc = shell] in next st, sk 3 ch, [dc, ch 1, dc = "V"] in next st. Rep from * 8 times, end sk 2 ch, dc for end post, ch 3, turn. Stop, count and measure. You should have 9 shells across and piece should measure 16″ long.

Row 2) "V" in "V" and shell in shell across, end dc in top of t-ch, ch 3, turn.

Rep row 2 until piece measures 11 ½″ long. Fasten off. Hide in all tail ends of yarn. Enjoy!

TRIPLE CROCHET STRIPED AFGHAN

An Easy Beginner's Project
No experience necessary

On a cold rainy winter's night there is nothing nicer than cuddling up in a warm colorful afghan with a good book and a steaming mug of herb tea. I leave you to choose the book and the tea, but I choose this delightful and simple afghan pattern. (The colors of the afghan are your choice also. Select them to harmonize with the room in which it will be used.) For speed in making and warmth of finished afghan, this one is made with two strands of yarn worked together as one. The crocheted fabric is nothing more than triple crochet stitches that are worked in the back loop only, which causes an interesting raised texture. To avoid the weight of the whole afghan in your lap as you are making it, each different color is worked in separate strips. When all the strips are finished, the afghan is single crocheted together with a contrasting color.

(Photo 45 [Triple Crochet Striped Afghan] and instructions courtesy of Coats & Clark Red Heart®)

Photo 45

Materials:

● Coats & Clark Red Heart® 4-Ply (Class C) Worsted Handknitting Yarn (Article/E.267): 10 ½ ounces each of 6 different colors of your choice (for strips) and 8 ounces of a contrasting color (CC) for joining and fringe.

● Susan Bates Quicksilver™ crochet hook size K.

Gauge: The entire afghan is made with two strands held tog and worked as one throughout; 5 sts = 2 " and 2 rows = 2 ½".

Be sure to check your gauge before starting afghan. Use any size hook which will obtain the stitch gauge above.

Finished Size: Approx. 45" × 70" (not including fringe).

Directions:

Strip: (Make 1 ea of the 6 colors.) Starting at the narrow edge of afghan, with 2 strands held tog, ch 110, measuring to make sure you have 5 ch to 2".

Row 1) (Right Side) Tr in 5th ch from hk and in ea rem ch across (107 tr counting ch-4 as 1 tr). Ch 4, turn.

Rows 2 thru 9) Making sure not to work in the base of the t-ch, tr in back lp of ea tr across, tr in top of ch-4. Ch 4, turn. At end of last row, omit ch-4, fasten off.

Joining: Crochet strips tog as follows: With double strand of CC, hold Row 9 of first strip and foundation ch of second strip tog, with right sides out. Working thru both thicknesses, sc in ea st across. Fasten off. Join all strips in the same way.

Fringe: (See Chapter 27) Cut strands of CC ea 18" long. Fasten 4 strands in every other st along ea narrow edge and in end st of every row and bet rows along sides. Cuddle up and enjoy!

RAGLAN BABY SWEATER

A Creative Intermediate Project
Some experience necessary

The whole thrust of this book has been to give the art and creativity of crocheting back to the individual handworker, to put the hook-and-thread person in charge of what they make. This lit-

Photo 46

tle baby sweater is a case in point. (Whether or not you have or know of a baby doesn't matter. The object of this project is to teach you to improvise as you go along in a small, inexpensive, quick-to-finish item. If you don't happen to have a baby handy to give the completed sweater to, the Salvation Army, shelters for battered mothers and their children, and little girls with baby-size dolls love to receive them as gifts.)

Finished size: Infant 6 months. Sweater measures 21″ around chest and is 10 ½ inches long from the back of the neck.

Materials:

- Leewards® Craft Bazaar™ "Baby Civona" (100% Orlon®), a smooth classic worsted Class A fingering-weight yarn, two 2-oz balls.

- Susan Bates #3 Steel crochet hook.

I am a tactile/visual kind of a person. Often I will start a project and as I work along, as I feel and see the stitches take shape, I will allow the thread to tell me what *it* wants to do. That is one reason that I am so fond of made-from-the-neck-down raglan cardigan sweaters and jackets. I measure the back of the intended wearer's neck and go from there. As I work, the thread tells me when it needs a color change, a stitch variation, or a fancy pattern stitch addition. Another reason that I like top-down sweaters is that they *always* fit. At any time I can stop and try the partially finished

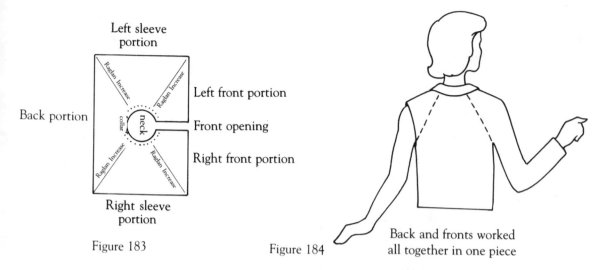

Figure 183

Figure 184

Back and fronts worked
all together in one piece

garment on the intended wearer and see how I'm doing. If I don't like what is happening, I can change it. I stop increasing when it is wide enough, and stop crocheting when it is long enough. When you have worked through this project and mastered the general idea behind the concept, you can take off on your own and make the same style of garment for any size person of any kind of yarn.

The theory behind made-from-the-top-down raglan garments is that if you start with a foundation chain that can be divided up into five segments, one for the left front, one for the left sleeve, one for the back, one for the right sleeve and the final one for the right front, and then make a right-angle increase at the imaginary seam between each segment on each row, you will end up with a yoke that grows wider as it grows longer and fits the human body to the underarm area. After the underarm area is reached, the sleeve stitches are passed over and the fronts and back are worked all in one piece to the desired length. Later the sleeves are worked separately, tapering them to the wrist if desired.

(For the sake of simplicity, I have restricted this discussion to cardigans without lowered front neck shaping. I have not included pullovers because often crocheted fabric does not have enough elasticity to allow the head to slip through the neck opening without special plackets or adjustments. I have not included lowered front neck shaping—which is easy to do starting with one stitch for each front, making front edge increases and then a chain stitch add-on for the center front neck—because I wanted to keep the instructions simple so that the student would first thoroughly understand the right-angle increases and the division of the sleeves from the body at the underarm.)

For the yoke section of this garment, I have chosen to use half-double crochet stitches. But that is just an arbitrary choice. See the section at the end of the directions for a discussion of other possible stitches. Regardless of what stitch you choose to use, you will first have to make an honest gauge swatch 4 inches wide and 2 inches long. My gauge swatch told me that I was getting 11 sc in every 2" or 5 ½ stitches per inch. I was also getting 13 rows in 2 inches or 6.5 rows per inch.

I like to begin my raglan cardigans with a fold-back collar. (1" deep for an infant, up to 4" for a large man.) Regardless of what size it is, the length of the outer edge of the collar is determined as follows (get out a pocket calculator and do it with me):

1) Back of neck width (3½" for a 6 months baby to 5" for a woman to 7" for a large man) = 3.5" wide × 5.5 sts per inch = 19.25 sts. Round the number off and call it 20 sts.

2) Top of each sleeve width (1" for baby to 2" for a woman to 3" for a large man) = 1" wide × 5.5 sts per inch = 5.5 sts. Round it off and call it 6 sts.

3) For each side of front, divide the chosen back neck measurement in half and then add an overlap allowance (½" for baby to 1" for a woman to 1½" for a large man). Take the number 20 from step #1 and divide it by 2. 20 sts ÷ 2 = 10 sts. Now add ½ inch of stitches (call it 3 sts) to the 10 front sts for the overlap, and you have 13 sts for each front.

4) Add them up.

2¼" × 5.5 or 13 sts (left front)
1" × 5.5 or 6 sts (left sleeve)
3½" × 5.5 or 20 sts (back)
1" × 5.5 or 6 sts (right sleeve)
2¼" × 5.5 or 13 sts (right front)
+ 2 sts (turning chain)
= 60 sts
− 1 (because the t-ch will always count as one st)
= 59 sts for foundation chain for collar (and neck)

59 sts divided by 5½ sts per inch = 10½" total length of collar.

Directions:

Beg at the outer edge of the collar, ch 59.

Row 1) Hdc in 3rd ch from hk and in ea ch across. Ch 2, turn. Counting beg t-ch as 1, 58 sts.

Row 2) Hdc in ea st across, ch 2, turn. Check yourself. Piece should measure 10 ½" across.

Rep row 2 until piece measures 1" long. Fold-back collar completed.

Row 3) (Beg raglan increases.) Stop and count 12 sts in from each edge (for right and left fronts). Put a knitter's slip-on ring marker in these sts. From those markers count in toward the center another 5 sts on each side (for right and left sleeves). Put markers in these sts. These 4 markers note the raglan inc points. You have subtracted one st from each front and sleeve because the raglan inc points use up one st. You should have 20 sts left for the back. If you are off a st or two, don't fret it; just keep on going. Now * hdc in ea st to marker, [hdc, ch 2, hdc = right-angle inc] in marked st, replace marker in ch-2 sp, rep from * across, end hdc in ea rem st to end, ch 2, turn. 4 sts have been inc, 1 at every raglan inc point.

Row 4) Count the sts in each section before you start & write the numbers down. Being careful to make a st in the last hdc before the ch-2 sp, and making sure to work a st on the left-hand side of the first hdc after the ch-2 sp, continue in the same manner, making right-angle inc's of [hdc, ch 2, hdc] in the center ch-2 sp of the inc of the previous row. Count your stitches again. You should have 1 more stitch on each front & 2 more stitches on each sleeve and the back.

After a few rows of incs, when you can easily see the raglan inc-points, you can throw out the markers and just go on without them.

Before long you will want to begin to make buttonholes. Which type you make, vertical or horizontal, will depend on what stitch you are using for the yoke. In sc or hdc you can make horizontal ones; in dc or tr they should be vertical ones. (See Chaper 10.) Buttonholes for females go on the right-front piece. For males they go on the left-front side. But at this point there is no right or wrong side to the crocheted fabric; it is all the same, so I usually make my buttonholes at the end of a row so that, as I begin the next row, I can quickly see if they look okay.

Keep on increasing on every row until *either* the back is the desired width (10" for our 6-month baby) *or* the underarm length is reached (4" for our baby to about 8" for a medium woman to 10" or 11" for a large man). Stop and lay the yoke over the shoulders of the intended wearer to make sure. If you get the desired width before you get the desired length, work a few rows without increases. If you get the desired length before you get the chosen width, you can make a chain to add additional width at the underarms when you join the back to the fronts.

Now then, you have a choice to make. Do you want the body of the sweater to be the same pattern stitch as the yoke? It doesn't have to be. You can choose to make any kind of pattern stitch that suits your fancy. For this baby sweater, I did not want the body the same as the yoke. I wanted a "shell in valley" stitch (see Chapter 21) for the bottom. To help you decide, pick up the gauge swatch you made at the beginning and experiment both for texture and for gauge. I found that to keep the same width in the body as in the yoke I needed to skip 2 sts before starting a shell and to skip another 2 sts before fastening it down with a sc. I also found that I needed a decorative row between the yoke and the "shell in valley" to set off the change of pattern stitches. I decided to make a row of open filet (see Chapter 21) before I started the shell body.

Please, for heaven's sake, don't worry and stew about having just exactly the right number of stitches to set up a change of pattern. Crocheting is so malleable and flexible that you can cheat and fudge to make things come out even.

(Of course, after you have made your choice and begun the body, if you don't like the way the sweater looks or feels, you can always change your mind. Just rip it out and start over with something else.)

Row 5) (Join fronts and body, and change to open filet pattern st.) Beg with a t-ch of 5, sk 2 sts, * dc in next st, ch 2, sk 2 sts *, rep bet *'s across front to sleeve, leapfrog over sleeve and dc into first st of back, sk 2, ch 2, rep bet *'s across to sleeve, leapfrog over sleeve and dc into first st of back, sk 2 sts, ch 2, rep bet *'s to end, fudging where necessary to end dc in last st, ch 1, turn.

If you need to add extra width to the body at the end of the yoke, chain one half the desired number of inches as you leapfrog between front and back and between back and front.

Row 6) (Set up shell in valley pattern.) * Sk 2 ch, [2 dc, ch 1, 2 dc = shell] in next dc, sk 2 ch, sc in next dc, rep from * across, fudging where necessary, ch 3, turn.

If the number of stitches doesn't happen to work out, you could always just end with a half shell instead of a whole one! I won't tell if you do.

Row 7) (2nd row of shell in valley pattern) 2 dc in last sc of previous row = beg ½ shell, * sc in next ch-1 sp, shell in next sc, rep from * across, ending [3 dc in top of t-ch = ending ½ shell], ch 1, turn.

Just keep on going making shells in valleys until the sweater is half as long as you desire. At this point, you can change to the next larger size hook to make the sweater imperceptibly flare a bit. Changing to a hook one size larger is an easy, almost invisible way to increase the width from chest to the hips, and let's face it, most of us gals have hips that are larger than our chests.

I made this little baby sweater 11½" long from the edge of the collar at the center back, but you don't have to finish the body before you start working on the sleeves. In fact, if you crochet a little first on the body, and then on the sleeves, you can judge the amount of yarn you have to work with and adjust body and sleeve length accordingly. If you are short on yarn, make the sleeves elbow length without a wrist band, and the body short like a sacque. If you have gobs of yarn to play with, you may want to make some increases at the underarm to give width for kicking legs, and make this a long baby coat instead of a sacque. Or perhaps you may choose to join the center fronts and go round and round to make this a baby bunting-bag instead of a sweater. The freedom, creativity and right to change your mind belongs to you.

In the shorter version pictured above, this baby sweater simply ends where it ends without a border, ribbing or a hem. However, some crocheters may choose to make a picot in the center of each shell on the final row, just for fun. Depending on the pattern stitch you have chosen for the body, on other garments, you may want to finish the bottom edge in some way. Some crocheters like to make a separate 2"-wide ribbing-like band of single crochet worked in the back loop only, and seam it to the lower edge. Others like to work a few rows of double crochet directly onto the bottom of the sweater alternating the kinds of stitches they make—first working in front of the post and on the next stitch working in back of the post. This too, gives a ribbing-like appearance.

Sleeves: (I made this example in the round, making straight tubes. For older children and adults you may wish to make them flat, back and forth, and decrease stitches at the underarm seam to taper the sleeves down to the wrist. If you made a chain-increase at the underarms on the body, you'll want to make a corresponding chain-increase at the underarms of the sleeves.) Work an open filet rnd and then shell in valley until sleeves measure 5" long, stopping directly below the underarm. I gathered the tube into a wrist band as follows: [Sc in ch-1 sp, ch 1, hdc in next sc, ch 1] around. Work hdc in ea st around for 1". Fasten off.

Other possible stitch choices for yoke with their increase formulas that will give a right-angle:
Single Crochet) (Firmer and stiffer.) In the raglan inc-point st make 1) open hole: sc, ch 1, sc; or 2) solid with no hole: 3 sc.

Double Crochet) (Also a good choice.) In the raglan inc-point st make 1) open hole: 2 dc, ch 1, 2 dc; or 2) solid with no hole, 5 dc.

Triple Crochet) (A bit too loose and wiggly.) In the raglan inc-point st make 1) open hole: 3 tr, ch 1, 3 tr; or 2) solid with no hole: 7 tr.

Of course, you can alternate or make a combination of rows of these stitches. For instance, you could stripe your yoke using sc or hdc of a dark-colored worsted yarn and then switching to dc of a light-colored mohair yarn. You can even skip the increases occasionally and throw in a row of crossed stitches or popcorns or violets or whatever. However, for good aesthetics it is usually not wise to continue the color and/or stitch variation beyond the point where the yoke moves under the arm. Make that area solid without variation.

BONNET

Now I leave you on your own to make a baby bonnet to match this sweater. Don't faint or run away in terror; just make a circle of hdc about 3" in diameter that cups up slightly and does not quite lie flat. Mark off one quarter of the circumference of that circle for the bottom back of the head. Around the remaining three quarters, work an open filet row, still making two chains between dc's, but skipping only one stitch instead of two. Add a row of shell in valley, but because we need a slight flare to the fabric to go around the sides and top of the head, space the shells somewhat closer than you did for the body at the yoke separation of the sweater. Now keep on with shell in valley to bring the sides up and around to cover the infant's ears. If you find that you need more width, use the changing-hook-size trick. Add ribbon to tie under the neck and, on your own, just as your foremother of crochet did, you have created a baby bonnet.

I hope that working through this learning lesson/project will have given you the courage and confidence to take off on your own and make raglan cardigan sweaters and jackets for yourself, friends and family—heavy, rugged tone-on-tone striped ones for men, dainty, lacy ones for lovely women, fluffy, fleecy mohair ones for young girls, and durable, colorful ones for growing children—each one uniquely different and delightful.

GLOSSARY

PLEASE NOTE that crocheting and knitting abbreviations do not have periods following them. In printed instructions, periods are used only at the ends of sentences.

afghan: A blanket or lap robe.

afghan stitch: A bad marriage of knitting and crocheting techniques that utilizes the worst characteristics of each. Also called "Tunisian Crochet." Made in a fashion similar to crochet with a single knitting needle which has a hook on the end of it.

approx: An abbreviation for "approximately."

asterisk(s): `*—*` Star-like punctuation marks that set off a definite set of instructions.

ball: A way in which manufacturers package or "put up" thread or yarn for sale. Often the thread or yarn is wound around a hollow paper tube.

batch number: The serial number of a "dye lot." A way of telling if all of the balls or skeins of thread or yarn were dyed at the same time and are the exact same color. (See Chapter 3.)

beg: An abbreviation for "begin," "beginner," or "beginning."

bk lp: An abbreviation for "back loop." (See Chapter 18.)

bl: An abbreviation for "block" or "square." Occasionally it is used as an abbreviation for "back loop."

bouclé: A type of yarn that has small nubs or loops in it spaced at regular intervals.

bp: An abbreviation for "back post." (See Chapter 18.)

brackets: [—] Brackets are used to set off a sequence of instructions. Sometimes the set is to be done in one location. If a number follows the brackets, the directions within the brackets are to be repeated over and over the number of times specified by the number that follows them.

ch: An abbreviation for the "chain stitch." (See Chapter 9.)

cl: An abbreviation for "cluster."

cluster: A group of stitches representing a distinct element of design, usually made in one location.

cm: An abbreviation for "centimeter(s)." A measure of length.

cone: A way in which manufacturers sometimes package yarn or thread for sale. Usually large amounts, weighing a pound or more, of thread are wound around inverted cardboard cones.

-cord: Preceded by a number such as 2- or 6-. It means the number of strands that were wound together to form the thread.

Crab st: Single crochet stitch worked from left to right instead of in the usual right-to-left direction. Sometimes also referred to as "reverse single crochet." (See Chapter 18.)

dc: An abbreviation for the "double crochet stitch." (See Chapter 12.)

dc next 2 sts tog: Abbreviated instructions for a "single double crochet decrease." (See Chapter 17.)

dec: An abbreviation for "decrease." To make less. (See Chapter 17.)

dir(s): An abbreviation for "directions."

dtr: An abbreviation for the "double treble crochet stitch." (See Chapter 13.)

dye lot and **dye lot number:** Used to denote a quantity of yarn or thread that was all dyed the same color at the same time. Because color may vary from one dye lot to another, it is imperative that all the thread or yarn for a project be purchased at one time from the same dye lot. (See Chapter 3.)

ea: An abbreviation for "each."

est: An abbreviation for "established."

even: Without increases or decreases. Straight. Also, any number divisible by 2.

fingering yarn: Class A yarn. A light-weight yarn. (See Chapter 3.)

foundation chain: A length of chain stitches made at the beginning of a piece. (See Chapter 9.)

fp: An abbreviation for "front post." (See Chapter 18.)

ft lp: An abbreviation for "front loop." (See Chapter 18.)

gauge: The number of stitches and rows in a square piece of crochet or knitting. The pattern may say, "3 sc and 5 rows = 1 inch," or "12 sts and 20 rows = 10 cm," or "2 pats = 3 ½."" (See Chapter 5.)

gm(s): An abbreviation for "gram(s)." A measure of weight.

gp(s): An abbreviation for "group(s)."

group(s): Groups can refer to such things as a shell [2 dc, ch 1, 2 dc] which is repeated over and over, or to a special formation of stitches such as a cluster.

hank: A way in which manufacturers package or "put up" yarn and thread for sale. Hanked yarns and threads must be wound into a ball before using.

hdc: Abbreviation for the "half-double crochet stitch." (See Chapter 11.)

hk: An abbreviation for "hook."

inc: An abbreviation for "increase." To make more. (See Chapter 16.)

incl: An abbreviation for "inclusive."

in(s): An old abbreviation for "inches." Contemporary instructions now use marks (").

ins: An abbreviation for "instructions."

inst: An abbreviation for "instructions."

k or K: A knitting abbreviation for the "knit stitch."

knitting worsted: Class C smooth classic worsted heavy-weight yarn. Commonly called "4-ply yarn." (See Chapter 3.)

lp(s): An abbreviation for "loop(s)."

lst: An old abbreviation for "first." It is very confusing and can easily be misread for "one stitch" or "last." Contemporary directions now always write out "first" and "last."

M: An abbreviation for "motif."

matte: Dull finish without gloss or shine.

medallion: A piece of crochet work, such as a circle or a square, many of which make up a completed project. (See also motif, below.)

Mercerized thread: Thread that has been treated by a chemical process to make it glossy and stronger.

motif: A repeated figure of recurrent design used as decoration. It can be synonymous with "medallion."

mtpl(s): An abbreviation of "multiple(s)."

multiple(s): The word has two meanings in crochet terms. It can mean the number of individual stitches that make up a sequence or set, as in "2 dc, ch 1, 2 dc." It can also mean the number of pattern stitch repeats, as in "6 leaf motifs."

nub: Blobs, slubs, or nebs of material in a thread or yarn that give it an interesting textured effect.

O: An old abbreviation for "yarn over the hook." It was a confusing symbol, often mistaken for zero. Contemporary instructions now use "yo" or "Y O" instead.

odd: A number not divisible by 2.

ombré: A term used to describe yarns which are dyed in multi-colored or multi-shaded hues and tones.

oz: An abbreviation for "ounce."

p or P: A knitting abbreviation for the "purl stitch."

parentheses: (—), often followed by a number. Sometimes the directions within the parentheses are to be done all in the same place, as in "(dc, ch 1, dc) in the next stitch." At other times they are to be repeated a number of times according to the number following them, as in "(tr, ch 1, tr, in the next st) 6 times."

pat(s): An abbreviation for "pattern" or "patterns."

pat st: An abbreviation for "pattern stitch."

patt: An abbreviation for "pattern" or "pattern stitch."

pattern stitch: Any sequence or combination of individual stitches that is repeated over and over again to create a uniform fabric.

pc: An abbreviation for "picot."

PC: An abbreviation for "popcorn stitch."

pearl cotton: A loosely twisted Mercerized cotton thread. It has a high gloss and good wearing characteristics.

perle: See pearl cotton.

ply: A verb meaning to twist strands together.

-ply: The number of threads that are twisted together to form a single strand of yarn. An example might be 4-ply knitting worsted or 8-ply cord. In today's world the term is meaningless in trying to figure out how thick a yarn is.

pop: An abbreviation for the "popcorn stitch."

popcorn stitch: Many stitches made in one spot and pulled together to form a bobble. (See Chapter 18.)

post: A synonym for "stitch" (especially the upright portion of it). At the end of a row the turning-chain counts as a post.

prev: An abbreviation for "previous."

PS: An abbreviation for "puff stitch."

puff stitch: Many stitches made in one spot and decreased together to form a bobble. (See Chapter 17.)

quality: The word has two meanings in crochet terms. It is synonymous with "name." A European term that is used to differentiate the various "names of the threads" that a manufacturer makes. The word also means "the characteristics of," as in bad or good wearing quality.

rem: An abbreviation for "remain(ing)."

rep: An abbreviation for "repeat."

repeat: The word has two meanings. It can mean "do over again," as in "repeat six times." It can also refer to a "pattern repeat" or "multiple of stitches" which make up a textured effect.

rib: An abbreviation for the noun "ribbing"; or the verb "to make ribbing."

rnd(s): An abbreviation for "round(s)."

rpt: An abbreviation for "repeat."

sc: An abbreviation for the "single crochet stitch." (See Chapter 10.)

sc next 2 sts tog: A type of decrease, i.e., a single single crochet decrease. (See Chapter 17.)

sk: An abbreviation for "skip."

skein: A way in which manufacturers package yarn for sale. Most skeins are intended to be used from the inside out.

skp: An abbreviation for "skip."

SKP: A knitting abbreviation for "slip, knit, pass the slipped stitch up and over the knitted stitch and off of the needle."

sl lp: An abbreviation for "slip loop." (See Chapter 8.)

sl st: Abbreviation for the "slip stitch." (See Chapter 14.)

sport-weight yarn: Class B yarn. A medium-weight yarn. (See Chapter 3.)

sp(s): An abbbreviation for "space(s)."

s s: An English abbreviation for the "slip stitch."

starting chain: Synonymous with "foundation chain." The length of chain stitches made at the starting of a piece. (See Chapter 9.)

st(s): An abbreviation for "stitch(es)."

t-ch: An abbreviation for "turning chain."

tension: A term that has two meanings. Tension is synonymous for "gauge" in many European instruction books, and may appear as "Tension: 14 sts = 10 cm." The word also means "flow" or finished appearance, as in, "It has an uneven and irregular tension."

tog: An abbreviation for "together."

tr: An abbreviation for the "triple crochet stitch." (See Chapter 13.)

treble: An alternate version of "triple."

triple: Synonymous with treble. (See Chapter 13.)

tr tr: An abbreviation for the "triple triple crochet stitch." (See Chapter 13.)

Tunisian crochet: The "afghan stitch."

work: A term that just means "do what you are supposed to be doing."

work even: A term that means to keep on going along in the same way without increasing or decreasing.

worsted: An adjective meaning "twisted" (or a noun denoting a certain kind of 4-ply yarn).

worsted-weight yarn: Class C yarn. Good old standard 4-ply knitting worsted. A heavy-weight yarn used for sweaters and novelty projects. (See Chapter 3.)

yo or Y O: Abbreviation for "yarn over the hook."

—: Asterisks, see above.

(—): Parentheses, see above.

[—]: Brackets, see above.

": A symbol for "inch" or "inches."

● Symbol for "slip loop" (sl lp).

○ Symbol for "chain stitch" (ch).

+ Symbol for "single crochet stitch" (sc).

✕ Symbol for "single crochet stitch" (sc).

⊤ Symbol for "half-double crochet stitch" (hdc).

Symbol for "double crochet stitch" (dc).

Symbol for "triple crochet stitch" (tr).

Symbol for "double triple crochet stitch" (dtr).

⌒ Symbol for "slip stitch" (sl st).

INDEX